# THE
# AFTER DEATH
# EXPERIENCE

# THE AFTER DEATH EXPERIENCE

## The Physics of the Non-Physical

Ian Wilson

William Morrow and Company, Inc.
New York

Library of Congress Cataloging-in-Publication Data

Wilson, Ian, 1941–
    The after death experience : the physics of the non-physical / Ian
Wilson.
        p.    cm.
    Bibliography: p.
    Includes index.

    1. Future life.    2. Spiritualism.    I. Title.
    BF1311.F8W55    1989
    133.9′01′3—dc19                                                    88-23474
                                                                         CIP

Printed in the United States of America

To the memory of the late Dr
Colin MacCallum of Nidderdale, Yorkshire
and to the patients and
staff of the 'Jospice' International,
Thornton, Lancashire,
who taught me that the living
have much to learn
from the dying . . .

# CONTENTS

# LIST OF PLATES

The Great Death Pit at Ur (*The Illustrated London News Picture Library*)

Mid-winter sunrise at Newgrange (*Commissioners of Public Works, Ireland*)

Opening the Mouth (*The British Library*)

Egyptian emerging from burial chamber (*The British Library*)

Dead Egyptian receiving offerings (*The British Library*)

Dalai Lama as two-year-old (*BBC Hulton Picture Library*)

Dalai Lama today (*Syndication International*)

The late Arnall Bloxham (*Al Campbell Photographer*)

Jacket of Louis de Wohl's novel (*Melvin Harris*)

'Katie King' (*Mary Evans/Psychic News*)

Fake stage props (*Mary Evans/Harry Price Collection, University of London*)

Ethel Beenham (*Mary Evans/Harry Price Collection, University of London*)

Doris Stokes (*Syndication International*)

Ghost of Brockley Court (*Cassell Publishers Limited*)

Death-bed scene (*Musée Carnavalet, Paris*)

Resuscitation of heart-attack victim (*Science Photo Library*)

Blake's *The Soul Hovering Above the Body* (*Bibliothèque des Arts Décoratifs, Paris*)

Dr Michael Sabom (*Kerr Studio*)

Hieronymus Bosch *Ascent into the Empyrean* (*Topham Picture Library*)

Margot Grey (*Photo Graphics*)

The Earl and Countess Spencer (*Central Press Photos*)

Dr Wilder Penfield (*Literary Executives of Dr Wilder Penfield*)

Exposed brain (*Director of the Montreal Neurological Institute*)

Dr Robert Thouless (*Mary Evans/Society for Psychical Research*)

Dr Robert Morris (*Ian Southern*)

Eleven-week-old foetus (*Hayes Publishing*)

'Jospice' (*Courtesy Jospice International*)

Dr Colin MacCallum (*Courtesy Mrs Marilyn MacCallum*)

# TEXT FIGURES

# AUTHOR'S PREFACE AND ACKNOWLEDGMENTS

Lest it be said of me that 'Wilson was much obsessed by death', any praise or blame for the basic idea for this book rightly belongs to London publishing executive Mark Booth, who quite unexpectedly telephoned one day to enquire if I might be interested in writing a book called *The After Death Experience*.

I have to admit that at the outset I failed to appreciate the full subtlety of the title Mark Booth had set me. Accepting the assignment as a broad review of the evidence for life after death, the most promising evidential area turned out to be that which its researchers have dubbed '*near*-death' experiences (or NDEs to the initiated), comprising the recollections of those who have been in a state of clinical death, yet returned to life to tell the tale. Arguably such individuals have never been fully dead, and therefore technically should be described only as 'near' dead; but the deeper question is whether they, along with other claimants through history, have glimpsed or experienced some real *after* death state. I have accordingly followed convention in accepting the 'near-death' label for such cases, while directing the thrust of this book towards the broader, deeper question.

Another semantic difficulty has been that of finding the right label for whatever element of us *might* survive physical death. Terms such as 'soul', 'spirit', 'mind', 'astral body', and 'etheric double' all raise such varieties of objections that wherever possible I have avoided them; likewise all jargon phrases and abbreviations, such as NDEs and OOBs (out-of-the-body experiences), which I believe do no service to making psychical research accessible to the general reader. One unexpected eventuality at the very time of the manuscript going for typesetting was the sudden death of the medium Doris Stokes, the subject of the investigation described in Chapter 6. It was easy enough to change references to her from the present to the past tense but inevitably somewhat blunted has been the original intention to check out (and in the event find wanting), Britain's best known *living* medium.

Overall the assignment has been both more demanding and in general more positive in its conclusions than I had initially ever

\

contemplated. The issue is so broad that inevitably I have drawn heavily on the writings of others, and in this connection I am particularly indebted to the pioneering 'near-death' researches of Doctors Raymond Moody, Elisabeth Kübler-Ross, Michael Sabom, Kenneth Ring, and, here in Britain, Margot Grey, all of whose work I have tried to synthesize, though with often liberal quotation from individual cases.

I have also tried wherever possible to seek out at first hand individuals whose stories corroborate or further illuminate the already published sources. Of these the most impressive, yet at the same time frustrating, feature is how many strange death-bed reminiscences, telepathic awarenesses of another person's dying, apparitions, and other apparent communications from deceased loved ones are confided by ordinary everyday individuals whose stories cannot be publicized because they are too personal, or because the informants are afraid of ridicule. Accordingly I am all the more deeply grateful to those individuals, such as Krystyna Koloziej, Beryl Statham, David Ayre, Ken Watson, and Captain Wilbourne, who have allowed themselves to be identified, and to others, such as Janet T., who have requested only the most modest constraints.

Among many to whom I am indebted for help, particularly deserving of mention are Eleanor O'Keeffe, the ever-efficient Secretary of the Society for Psychical Research, and Nicholas Clark-Lowes, the Society's Librarian, for numerous favours with book loans and photo-copied articles; the Revd Francis O'Leary and his helpers, for inviting me to spend a very memorable day visiting his hospices in Lancashire; the Revd Maurus Green and the Revd Stuart Burns, for introducing me to the very moving case of Dr Colin MacCallum; Melvin Harris, for his crucial discoveries of the literary sources of so-called 'past lives'; David Rolfe and television journalists Beth Miller and Siobhan Hockton, for their help in the investigations of Doris Stokes; my wife Judith, for setting the first draft of this book on to word processor; copy-editor Miles Litvinoff for his expert and judicious tidying of my text, and, not least, William Armstrong, Carey Smith, Anne Cohen, Kerry Hood, and others at Sidgwick & Jackson, for their enthusiastic support at every stage.

Bristol
April 1987

# INTRODUCTION:
## THE GREATEST MYSTERY

Some time about 2500 BC in the Sumerian city of Ur, several dozen colourfully dressed men and women descended into a reed-lined pit in which had been laid the dead body of their royal master. Copper-clad warriors of the former royal bodyguard took up positions near the entrance-way. Grooms and charioteers carefully backed their haulage oxen down the narrow passageway. Weapon-bearers stiffened to attention. Pretty, gold-head-dressed female attendants who had delighted the King in life sang their last songs to the accompaniment of harpists playing bull-headed lyres. Finally at some pre-arranged point in the ritual everyone dipped pottery cups into a central cauldron containing a lethal potion. Drinking deeply from these, they settled themselves for the oblivion by which they would join their former master in the realm of death.

Four and a half thousand years later, on Saturday, 18 November 1978 in a jungle clearing in steamy Guyana, South America, cult leader James Jones called over loudspeakers for his colony's near-thousand-strong followers to assemble before his throne. A few minutes earlier Jones's henchmen had gunned down an American Congressman Leo Ryan's fact-finding delegation, and Jones now exhorted his listeners that further living was useless. They must join him in a 'revolutionary act' by drinking from a potion his wife and the cult's medical officer had already prepared. Obediently, though not without tears and screams, 912 men, women, and children queued for the cardboad cups filled with cyanide-laced Flavor-Aid that would be their last earthly drink.

Separated as these incidents are by thousands of years of history, we know about both in some detail, thanks to archaeologist Sir Leonard Woolley's patient spadework on the one hand, and to a tape recorder left running beneath Jones's throne on the other. But what particularly links them is the remarkable intensity of belief on the part of all the participants, rightly or wrongly, that death in this world is not final, and that something of us continues to live on in some form of afterlife.

While these instances were extreme, none the less even the most sceptical among us has to face the fact that much of our civilization and awesome amounts of our ancestors' efforts have been founded on this same extraordinary idea that death is not the end. Without that idea we would have no pyramids, no Parthenon, no Westminster Abbey, none of the breathtaking churches and cathedrals that grace our skylines. In literature we would have no Bible, no *Iliad*, no *Hamlet*, and no *Christmas Carol*. We would be similarly bereft of much of our finest music and many of our greatest works of art.

Why this belief? On the face of it, it is totally irrational. On death a person whom we may have known as warm, lively, and quick-witted quite palpably becomes a cold, still, unresponsive, and quick-to-rot carcass. As Hamlet comments on the skull of the former jester Yorick: 'Here hung those lips that I have kissed I know not how oft. Where be your jibes now . . . your flashes of merriment that were wont to set the table on a roar?'

We know that even the art of an embalmer can only check the process of ultimate disintegration. Despite all the medical and scientific advances of the last hundred years, with spacecraft sent to distant planets and radio telescopes now probing into the furthest reaches of the universe, not only has no antidote for death been found, but there has not come to light the slightest reliable indication of the existence of any heaven, hell, or other abode of the non-living so picturesquely imagined by our ancestors. So far as our science is concerned, death is *the* end, after which our formerly animate bodies break down into inanimate compounds generative of new life only as meat or fertilizer. The 'us', with all the joys and sorrows, quirks and foibles it may have had in life, is no more.

Yet if this is the accepted wisdom of scientific orthodoxy, what also has to be faced is that at this very time there are vast sectors of the ordinary lay community among whom such ideas find little credence. Aside from the adherents of conventional religions, with their implicit acceptance of afterlife beliefs, recent yeas have seen even among those who never enter a church what amounts almost to a revolutionary backlash in the idea that 'we' cease to be after death. Currently in the United States, 'psychics' from New York to Los Angeles can command fees of more than $200 an hour for purporting to make contact with dead loved ones. Some 2,500 American bookshops specialize in books on life after death and similar 'occult' topics. Arch-priestess of this afterlife revival has been actress Shirley MacLaine, whose four zany 'biographies' extolling reincarnation and the 'channelling' of spirits have together sold five million copies. In Britain a similar euphoria has exuded from the sell-out stage shows and prime-time media appearances of grandmotherly medium Doris Stokes.

In essence, what has been pumped out by Shirley MacLaine, Doris Stokes, and their ilk is nothing new, but something deeply rooted in our past. Because of their ignorance of so much that we can now call scientific fact, people centuries ago could and did hold altogether more straightforward attitudes on matters such as life after death.

Thus, although they differed on the form it took, our ancestors were certain that on death they would go to some plane or place where they would spend eternity. The tradition of the existence of such a plane is found all over the world: in Greek, Egyptian, Celtic, Muslim, and Jewish thought, to name but a few. For the Greeks and Romans it was represented by the Garden of the Hesperides or the Elysian Fields. For the Vikings it was Valhalla. For Jews it was Sheol. For Christians it was, and continues to be, heaven and hell (and, according to some denominations, purgatory or limbo), even though many thinking Christians would shy from envisaging these with the traditional harps and pitchforks. Although for Hindus and Buddhists there is the modification that the death-surviving part of us is believed to pass into another body or incarnation, even these faiths require some intermediary plane where the death-surviving part lingers while awaiting a new body. As it is beautifully expressed in the Hindus' *Bhagavadgita*, 'Above this visible nature there exists another, unseen and eternal, which, when all things created perish, does not perish.'

Similarly our ancestors consistently believed that what survived death, and moved on to the eternal plane, was a disembodied something which, for want of a better word, we may best refer to as a soul. For hundreds of generations of ancient Egyptians it was axiomatic that when you died you went to your *ka*, their word for what the Christian would call the soul. For the Old Testament prophet Elijah, bringing back a widow's son from the dead meant pleading to God, 'May the soul of this child come into him again.' For Jesus' brother James, writing in his New Testament letter, it was self-evident that when 'a body dies . . . it is separated from its soul'. For the African, the Chinese, the South American Indian, in fact in whatever culture one looks to around the world, there were similar, virtually unquestioned concepts of this evanescent and near indefinable soul-element of us that is supposed to survive physical death.

So firm were our ancestors in such convictions that they scarcely even paused to consider whether there might or might not be something of them to survive physical death. For them the all-important question was not whether there was a soul but whether they had gone through all the right motions for this to reach its chosen resting place with the shortest possible delay. In the case of ancient Egyptians and Tibetans this meant chanting their respective Books of the Dead. In the case of medieval Christians, whose churches and cathedrals were picture story-books for the horrors that awaited the ungodly, contemporary authors provided best-selling manuals on 'the art of dying well'. A few medieval priests may have been prepared to provide for a fee any number of efficacious sacraments. In Britain it was not unusual for the medieval well-to-do to leave financial provision for ten thousand masses to be said for their souls after their demise.

Today we live in an age in which our understanding of matters metaphysical is substantially different. We know that, instead of our planet being linchpin of the universe, it is just an insignificant speck amidst the unimaginable vastness of space. We know that we are not immediate progeny of a human-faced Creator, but products of millions of years of evolutionary development from tree-climbing apes. We know that many of those elements that seem to denote 'us', or what we call our personalities, derive not from immortal souls but from the genes we have inherited from parents and grandparents, from the shaping effects of the environment in which we were brought up, even from the chemistry of our air intake, our diet, and our water supplies. To behavioural psychologists we are the products of so much genetics and conditioning. To chemists our mental well-being may be attributed in no small measure to the efficiency or otherwise of the workings of our endocrine system.

But is this really all there is to us? Clearly crucial to such a question is the nature of what, more than anything else, we subjectively imagine as truly 'ourselves', that element of us that we call our consciousness, which, to all outside observers, is what seems to disappear on physical death. While it is this that we fondly imagine as 'us' sitting up looking out on the world from some indefinable point in our brain-space, how much do we truly know about it? Is it all it seems?

For instance, in considering a death-surviving consciousness, just how conscious are you, dear reader, of reading this book? Oh, yes, you are now, because I have just asked you to think about it. But to what extent were you before? Were you consciously thinking: here am I, reading this book, how clever am I being able to identify these funny markings on the page as letters of the alphabet and the letters as parts of words and sentences? Hardly, for if you had been, you could scarcely have paid attention to anything I have been trying to communicate to you! In fact for many functions for which we think consciousness is most needed, whether playing the piano, driving a car, or giving a lecture, being fully conscious in the sense of self-aware can often only inhibit rather than aid our effectiveness. What then is our true operative 'self'?

The same problem arises if you ask a neurophysiologist where consciousness is in the brain. If he is honest he will probably mumble, with some embarrassment, that he really does not know. Yes, he can tell you that cutting into the part called the reticular formation causes permanent sleep and coma, and that electrically stimulating this same part will wake up a sleeping animal. But he will also give you good reasons for arguing that this can no more be considered the seat of consciousness than a record-player needle the source of Beethoven's Fifth Symphony.

The question that arises, if we know so little about where and what our consciousness is, is how can we be sure it does *not* survive our physical death? Since nothing in physical nature ceases to exist, but is simply changed into another form, either inanimate matter or pure energy, is it not possible, even reasonable, that the same principle may apply to our souls or consciousnesses?

We are therefore in the presence of a mystery, and one too long neglected for a variety of reasons. Our psychology, under the influence of behaviourism, has long tended to avoid exploring subjective, difficult-to-quantify concepts such as consciousness. Our medicine has devoted itself so single-mindedly to 'fighting' death – it is the very motif of some medical colleges – that any attempt to comprehend death itself scarcely comes into the curriculum. And not least our society, having overthrown other taboos, such as those relating to sex, has actually created one in respect of death. Whereas in many countries up to a century ago death was a social event, the tolling of the bell that signified the giving of the Last Rites being a call for even complete strangers to hurry to a dying person's bedside, today even close members of the family are encouraged to leave a dying person's last moments to 'the professionals'. Because death represents defeat in our success-motivated world, even the doctors are likely to be absent. Death has to be swept under the carpet, and left for the menials to tidy away.

Small wonder that if some form of soul or consciousness does survive after death, the hard evidence for this has yet to be found, because all too few serious resources and skills have so far been brought to bear. Yet is the question so insignificant that it deserves such neglect? If, just conceivably, it could be scientifically established that death is not the end, that something of us really does live on in some form, would we be totally unaffected by this, regarding it as of mere academic interest? Might it not be regarded as the biggest single life-changing scientific breakthrough this century? Certainly we might find it difficult to continue to pursue our present-day relentless materialism if we discovered, as was conceived of as early as the age of ancient Egypt, that accountability for our actions in life really does extend beyond the grave.

The purpose of this book is to explore the central question of whether death is quite unequivocally the end of our experience, or whether, just conceivably, something of us – consciousness, spirit, soul, call it what you will – carries on, to experience, and be experienced, after death. It is what some have called the 'big question', the greatest and most enduring mystery. Unlike popular gurus Shirley MacLaine and the late Doris Stokes, I cannot promise you slick, sure-fire answers. But neither will I necessarily scoff at what may seem at first sight incredible. We have a huge and conflicting mass of what at least purports to be evidence to try to evaluate. Let us begin at the beginning.

# 1

## THE OLDEST BELIEF

How far back in time can we trace belief that the dead continue to experience and to be experienced? All the evidence suggests that this was long before writing had been developed to record such belief. And if burial with ritual and offerings is to be interpreted as an indicator of belief in some form of survival after physical death, then we may need to look even before the evolution of man.

Although it is often supposed that man is the only creature to bury his dead, as diminutive creatures as ants of the genus *Atta* are known to tidy away their departed into deserted nest-chambers and galleries.[1] At the other end of the animal spectrum, both profound grief and unmistakable efforts to bury their dead have been reliably observed on the part of elephants. The well-known BBC naturalist Sir David Attenborough has filmed this procedure, which has also been very ably documented by consultant zoologist Sylvia Sikes in the course of her work among the Nigerian elephant herds:

> In a case where an animal is mortally wounded and cannot rise, the other members of the herd . . . circle it disconsolately several times, and if it is still motionless they come to an uncertain halt. They then face outward, their trunks hanging limply to the ground. . . . Eventually, if the fallen animal is dead, they move aside and just hang around . . . for several hours, or until nightfall, when they may tear out branches and grassclumps from the surrounding vegetation and drop these on and around the carcase, the younger elephants also taking part in this behaviour. They also scrape soil toward the carcase and then stand by, weaving restlessly from side to side.[2]

Among other naturalists, Iain and Oria Douglas-Hamilton have even reported elephant herds burying with their dead member not only foliage but large quantities of food, fruit, and even flowers.[3]

Whatever deduction we may care to make from such animal practices, in the case of man burial with yet more pronounced ritual was being carried out at least as early as the Neanderthal period 60,000 years ago, and may well have even earlier origins. This much is clear from some remarkable findings by University of Michigan archaeologist Professor Ralph Solecki, who in 1951, during an expedition to the Zagros mountains of Iraq, was taken by some local tribesmen to a huge cave called Shanidar. Here, as they told him, they had frequently come across very ancient stone implements. Needing little further encouragement, during the next nine years Solecki and his team dug their way through no less than 45 feet of successive layers of human habitation of the cave, finding a number of Neanderthal skeletons dating as far back as 60,000 BC.

One of these was of a man who had evidently been killed by a rockfall within the cave. As Solecki was able to deduce, his dead body had been visited by his friends and accorded a touching funeral ceremony. Some stones were heaped over the body, a fire lit above, and, as indicated by the presence of small broken animal bones, a funeral feast or 'wake' had been held.

Perhaps the most interesting of Solecki's finds was an unmistakably properly prepared burial, dubbed by him Shanidar IV, comprising the foetal-positioned skeleton of a well-built male adult, over whose corpse had been laid the additional bodies of two women and a child; these latter were perhaps deliberately sacrificed (or sacrificed themselves) to accompany him into an afterlife, just as we noted of the followers of the King of Ur and James Jones. Intrigued by this burial, Solecki carefully arranged for the taking of soil samples from the surrounds of the skeletons and the subjection of these to microanalysis. The report that followed was a model of the microscope's importance in bringing back life and meaning to even the most ancient of happenings. The soil was found to be rich in numerous pollens from no less than eight varieties of flowers: yarrow, thistle, grape hyacinth, yellow flowering groundsel, horse-tail, a variety of cornflower, and not least the hollyhock, long valued for its medicinal properties. There was no way in which so many diverse pollens could have found their way so deep into the cave by chance. As Solecki deduced:

> These flower pollens were not accidentally introduced into the grave, and hence must represent bouquets or clumps of flowers purposely laid down with the Shanidar IV burial. The hollyhock is especially indicative of this, since it grows in separate individual stands, and cannot be grasped in bunches like the others. Some person or persons once ranged the mountainside collecting these flowers one by one.[4]

So here, from a time before the last Ice Age, from even before our evolution into *Homo sapiens sapiens*, we find unequivocal evidence of a practice still performed to this day at funerals the world over, the strewing on to the deceased of wreaths and bouquets of pretty flowers with all their symbolism that new life will return. The deep-rootedness of this custom in our psyche is readily corroborated by the fact that when, in 1926, Egyptologist Howard Carter lifted the lid of the sarcophagus of Pharaoh Tutankhamun, there on the forehead of the first inner coffin lay the remains of a tiny wreath of flowers, almost certainly a last touching farewell from the King's youthful widow, Ankhes-en-Amun. As Carter commented:

> Among all that regal splendour, that royal magnificence –
> everywhere the glint of gold – there was nothing so beautiful
> as those few withered flowers, still retaining their tinge of
> colour. They told us what a short period three thousand three
> hundred years really was – but Yesterday and the Morrow.[5]

Can we be sure that these are true indications that peoples of so long ago really believed that something of them survived death, despite all physical signs of life seeming to have long expired? In the case of the ancient Egyptians, at least, there can be no question. Their pyramids and tombs were designed for the deceased to use as their home into perpetuity. The Egyptians' elaborate attempts to preserve the bodies as mummies, and the encasing of these in anthropomorphic sarcophagi, bespeak that something living of the dead person was believed to continue to inhabit these. Because of the Egyptians' development of writing, and the ability of modern Egyptologists to translate this with reasonable accuracy, we can, far more than in the case of most other ancient peoples, genuinely know something about what they thought about life after death. For an explicit statement of their views on this we need look no further than the inscription associated with every pyramid: 'No, not as a dead king did you depart; as a *living* king you did depart.'

In other words, elaborate burial was considered not just a mark of respect to commemorate someone believed to be finished, as might be the interpretation of the more sceptically minded of today. It was a thoroughly functional exercise carried out by a social machine as elaborate as the British National Health Service, and intended for the continued well-being of the death-surviving element of the individual, from his or her last breath through to as many future generations as political and other circumstances might permit.

To the Egyptians, the prime component believed to live on after

Fig. 1. The Egyptian good Khnum forms a king and his *ka* double on his potter's wheel. From a relief of the Eighteenth Dynasty

physical death was, as in so many other religions, nothing solid or tangible, but instead what they called the *ka*; they represented this in their hieroglyphs by two uplifted hands on a stand reserved for divinity. As evident from some Eighteenth Dynasty reliefs which show the god Khnum moulding a man and his *ka* on a potter's wheel (Figure 1), the *ka* was believed to be a sort of spirit-double of the earthly individual, distinguished only by the *ka* holding a hand up to its mouth, as if it were some form of inner voice. Despite some minor disagreements of interpretation, Egyptian texts essentially make clear that in death the deceased went to his *ka*, that his tomb was the house of his *ka*, and that any offerings provided for the dead individual by his grieving relatives were received by his *ka*. In other words, although in Egyptian thought it was supplemented by an additional fluttery, bird-like entity called a *ba*, the *ka* was as near to what we would understand by soul, spirit, or consciousness as makes little difference.

The more it is studied, everything of Egyptian funerary practice can be seen to have been geared to providing the newly passed-over *ka* with the maximum possible help for its entrée into the life beyond death. As everyone knows, there was the process of mummification during which, over a period of up to seventy days, the corpse was disembowelled and dehydrated to the substantiality of a blown egg. Despite popular belief, this was done not so much for the total preservation of the physical body;

for although they kept certain organs, elements such as the brains that we would regard as among the most vital they simply threw away.

The usefulness of the mummy was as a short of shell or home-base for the *ka*. Should the mummy be destroyed, this need not be a total disaster, for depending on the deceased's wealth the *ka* would have been provided with other earthly bases, such as sarcophagus moulded or painted in the deceased's likeness, a statue or spare head in the tomb, and perhaps another statue or relief set in the exterior tomb chapel where the deceased's relatives brought offerings. The *ka* was thus envisaged as not in any way trapped within its coffin or coffins, but free to 'go forth by day and penetrate the nether world' (in other words, to move at will between the realms of the living and the dead), limited only by whether or not the necessary spells for this had been inscribed on the sarcophagus.

With the right magic, anything was possible for the *ka*. Special rituals such as 'opening the mouth' were performed so that it might have all the senses and faculties the deceased had enjoyed in life. Little statuettes, or *ushabti* figures, were imparted with the necessary powers to be able to carry out any onerous afterlife duties the *ka* might be called upon to do, thus avoiding the necessity (which we have seen was felt in the case of Sumer) for real-life servants to die for this purpose. Not least, on the coffin, on the tomb walls, and sometimes on accompanying papyri, the *ka* and its owner were provided with a *Book of the Dead*, a sort of 'How to Survive in the Hereafter', with all the expected questions, stock answers, and salutary spells needed for that dread moment when, as fate decreed, the deceased would find his heart weighed in the balance and his earthly actions subjected to divine scrutiny before the throne of the mighty white-clad Osiris, god of the dead.

Because we know so much about what the Egyptians believed on these subjects, it is all too easy to assume that they were exceptional among ancient peoples in being, to all appearances, so obsessed by this urge to make elaborate provision for their hereafter. Yet nothing could be further from the truth. First, as is evident from the vibrancy of their tomb decorations, the Egyptians were a sunny, life-loving people whose funerary actions were largely motivated by their strong desire to continue to enjoy their earthly pleasures into perpetuity, when they hoped to be freed from the dental and intestinal ailments which we know plagued so many of them during life. Second, and much more importantly, virtually everyone in antiquity, perhaps because of a life expectancy less than half that of today, had the strongest belief in an afterlife, and the strongest interest in their soul's welfare in this state. Because of the absence or non-survival of written records, and the poorer preservation of funerary remains outside Egypt's exceptional climatic conditions, we often know considerably less about other peoples' afterlife thinking; but it is none the less certain that all had their own, albeit modified, versions of the same beliefs and practices.

Five hundred years before any ancient Egyptian had even thought of building the first pyramid, at Newgrange near Ireland's river Boyne what was probably little more than a handful of early Irishmen shifted 200,000 tons of stone to construct their own monumental 'house of eternity' for their royal dead. They did this with such careful planning and technical skill that they contrived that just once a year – at dawn on the year's 'deadest' day, the winter solstice – the sun's light would shine through the structure's special roof-box, dart along its 701 foot tunnel-like passageway, and illuminate for just a few minutes the chamber that once housed the dead, a happening they knew would continue into perpetuity (Figure 2). Dating as it does from Ireland's late Stone Age, this alone provides an extraordinary evocation of the intensity of our ancestors' belief in a life beyond the grave. And this was merely one of many such megalithic edifices to be dotted around Europe, today sadly all long stripped of the no doubt impressive internal fitments they once contained.

In country after country during the pre-Christian period, we find with mere variations of decoration and scale the same idea of the dead being provided with home-from-home furnished dwellings for eternity, and with much the same spells to help them in the after death world. Vandalized and looted though so many of their tombs have been, in Italy the pre-Roman Etruscans, like the Egyptians, are known to have been buried with all their armour and other accoutrements in tombs

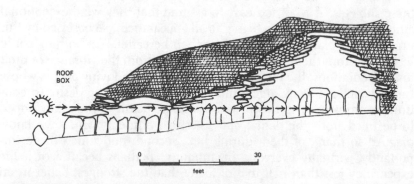

Fig. 2. Cross-section of the Newgrange passage grave, showing how the roof box was carefully aligned to the winter solstice's sunrise

gaily painted with frescoes, some of which show winged figures transporting the deceased on their journey into the afterlife. Despite the Etruscan language being one that remains to be deciphered, bandages from a mummy of what would appear to have been an Etruscan girl buried in Egypt have been found inscribed with Etruscan writing from what was most likely their equivalent of the Egyptians' *Book of the Dead*.[6] Burials with jewellery, furnishings, food, weapons, even whole chariots, have been either found or deduced to have been the norm among the Celts of western Europe, the Bronze Age peoples of Turkey, the Sumerians of Mesopotamia, the Scythians of the Steppes, the Shang, Han, and other dynasties of China, the Inca and other Indian peoples of South America, and many more.

Similarly, mummification, far from being, as often supposed, a rite exclusive to the Egyptians, was practised among peoples widely scattered across the world. As the Greek historian and travel writer Herodotus recorded of the Scythians:

> When a king dies . . . they take up the corpse, which has been previously prepared the following way: the belly is slit open, cleaned out, and filled with various aromatic substances, crushed galingale, parsley-seed and anise; it is then sewn up again and the whole body coated over with wax.[7]

In ancient China varying methods were tried of artificially preserving the dead. One technique was to encase the deceased from head to toe in suits made up of tiny pieces of jade, as in a magnificent example made for the second-century BC Princess Teou-Wan of Tchong-Shan. Although in this instance the intended preservation process failed, spectacularly more successful was the hermetic sealing and mercury treatment accorded to another redoubtable Chinese woman of the same period, the Lady of Dai, perhaps the best preserved of any corpse from antiquity.

As for the New World, throughout many centuries the Incas of the Andes mummified their dead using evisceration and dehydration methods strikingly akin to those of the Egyptians. According to the Spanish *conquistador* Garcilaso de la Vega's description of the Inca royal mummies he saw collected together in Cuzco in 1559: 'The bodies were so intact that they lacked neither hair, eyebrows, nor eyelashes. They were in clothes just as they had worn when alive.'[8]

Even when as in some cultures destructive practices such as cremation and exposure to the elements were used, the thinking behind them was still that of the dead person having become a disembodied spirit.

Fig. 3. Mummified bodies of Inca ruler, his queen and a retainer being carried on a litter. These were treated as if still alive. From a post-Conquest Spanish woodcut

The difference was that in these instances it was the destruction rather than preservation of the physical body which was supposed to be efficacious in releasing the dead person's soul from earthly ties, thus freeing him for the world beyond the grave. Inevitably the process was accompanied by appropriate ritual rites. In Tibet, for example, before the deceased's corpse was taken to a deserted spot to be hacked to pieces and carried away by birds and beasts of prey, a lama or holy man would take up position at the deceased's head and intone chants and spells from the Tibetans' *Book of the Dead*, the *Bardo Thodol*. Among Tibetans the soul's eventual destiny was thought to be a rebirth, or reincarnation, into some new body.

In ancient Greece, where a funeral pyre accompanied by offerings and celebratory games was the lot of the deceased, the intended purpose of these proceedings was very similar. In the twenty-third book of Homer's *Iliad* the spirit of the dead hero Patroclus is described as appearing in a dream to his friend Achilles, pleading:

> Bury me instantly and let me pass the gate of Hades. I am kept out by the disembodied spirits of the dead, who have not let me cross the river and join them, but have left me to pace up and down forlorn on this side of the gaping gates [of Hades]. And give me that hand I beseech you, for once you have passed me through the flame, I shall never come back again from Hades.[9]

In other words, Patroclus' speedy admission to Hades could be achieved only by cremation and the other appropriate ritual. And so the Greeks are described as dutifully burning Patroclus' body on a huge pyre heaped with offerings (including twelve specially sacrificed Trojan youths), gathering up his bones into a special golden urn, raising a commemorative mound over this, and holding celebratory games. All this to free his soul or spirit. Yet even having been given such rites, the soul of a dead man might still be accorded a tomb heaped with his armour and other furnishings, as in the case of Alexander the Great's father, Philip of Macedon, whose impressive last resting place was recently rediscovered at Vergina in northern Greece.

The root of all these procedures can only have been a powerful belief that something of us survived physical death. This belief seemed to involve the dead person's soul journeying to some celestial sphere, yet paradoxically also demanded the soul having an equipped tomb to use as its earthly base. Furthermore, this belief had for people of antiquity an importance – in terms of the time, effort, and thought accorded to it –

altogether disproportionate to anything we would consider reasonable, particularly given the resources these races and civilizations had available to them. Even the most unspiritual of Egyptian pharaohs and Chinese emperors were punctilious in initiating preparations for their tombs as one of their very first priorities on assuming power. So prevalent was belief in life after death among people of antiquity that it is no coincidence that so much of what we know about them derives from the work they put into making their houses for the hereafter.

The question that immediately arises is *why*? Why were intelligent people such as the ancient Egyptians prepared to expend huge efforts on the construction of such ostentatious burial chambers as their pyramids? Why were seemingly down-to-earth Sumerian men and women apparently so meekly willing to give up their lives for what is to us the all-too-uncertain privilege of joining their dead masters in a life beyond the grave? Should we suppose that life, earthly life, was any less precious to Sumerians, and other nations who adopted such practices, than it is to us? Should we just dismiss them as mere ignorant and deluded primitives? Or, bearing in mind their undoubted greater familiarity with death and dying than most of us are used to in modern life, could they have known something we don't know? Could this be the clue to why they were so apparently sure in their beliefs?

# 2

# IN TOUCH WITH THE DEPARTED

There is a story of an Englishman and a Chinese visiting a cemetery to pay their appropriate respects to deceased loved ones. The Englishman has brought a bunch of flowers. The Chinese has brought food. Appalled at the apparent waste, the Englishman asks of the Chinese:

'When do your dead come to eat all this food?'

'When your dead come to smell your flowers,' replies the Chinese.

The story highlights one of the most widespread yet seemingly most baffling features of early (and still practised) obsequies: the offering of food not only in the form of provisions included with the initial burial, but also as regular gifts made thereafter, whenever the bereaved visited the deceased's tomb or memorial. So standard was this rite in ancient Egypt that one of the commonest scenes of Egyptian art, particularly on funerary stelae, the equivalent of our gravestones, was that of the dead man seated, as if alive, at a table heaped with the offerings his living relatives have brought him. The popularity of this scene was due partly to the belief that in the event of the cessation of supply of real provisions, the dead person's *ka* could be nourished magically by this stela depiction alone. The pharaohs, wanting nothing but the best, arranged for their statues in their mortuary temples (the most convenient outside-world vehicles for their *kas* to inhabit), to be regularly 'fed' with real food by priests employed for this sole purpose; in return for these favours, the priests were free subsequently to take their fill. Not wanting to be outdone, the families of lesser mortals would wherever possible similarly bring real food to place before the statues of their deceased, usually set in chapels, with false doors for the coming and going of the *ka*, built above the tomb in which the dead person had been laid.

As in so much else, it would be wrong to suppose that such practices were in any way peculiar to ancient Egypt. The provision of offerings of food was almost universal. As has been revealed by some brilliant recent archaeological work, the prehistoric inhabitants of Britain's far northern Orkney Islands, who had a hard job just finding enough sustenance for their living bodies, regularly took choice joints of meat, and carcasses of their totem-bird, the white-tailed sea eagle, as offerings to the bones of their ancestors, whom they enshrined in a special 'house of the dead' at Isbister on the southern Orkney island of South Ronaldsay.[1] In Mesopotamia some of the oldest examples of writing are ration-lists of the monthly quantities of bread and beer to be provided for the souls of ordinary citizens who had died. In the more archaic Greek graves, besides the normal funeral provisions, there have been found feeding tubes through which the bereaved would seem to have poured liquid foods for the benefit of the corpse.[2] In Tibet, despite a belief that the deceased would go on to inhabit another body, the corpse was provided with dishes of food during the waiting period before it was hacked to pieces. Most bizarre of all, in Inca Peru (Figure 3), where the mummified royal dead were accorded special palaces with their own living staffs, the mummies − besides being provided with food and drink − had their clothing washed, flies whisked from their brow, and audiences with visitors arranged for them; they were even lifted when their minders 'sensed' that they wanted to urinate![3]

Precisely like the Englishman's reaction to the Chinese, our instinctive response to such practices must be one of astonishment and revulsion. It all seems such absurd, superstitious nonsense. Yet why should people, who had far more struggles to obtain food than we do, have been so willing to give so much to their dead − even if afterwards some of them did eat what their dead left over? What can have compelled them to behave in a manner that seems to us so alien?

Clearly whatever the answer this has to be something very ancient and deep within human consciousness. It is not unreasonable therefore to commence our enquiries with some of the more primitive societies which continue to make offerings to their dead relatives, among these some of the remoter tribes of Africa. In this context few more remarkable insights into the thinking of such tribes have been obtained than by an unconventional anthropologist, Adrian Boshier, a director of Johannesburg's Museum of Man. Back in the 1960s, as a result of unusual, seemingly magical help he had given to the Makgabeng tribe of South Africa's north-west Transvaal, Boshier was invited to receive initiation as one of the tribe's witch-doctors. To Boshier's astonishment he was given two separate courses of instruction, seven years apart, the second reserved for tribal elders, in which he was freely told much information about tribal thinking that previously, as an outsider, had been denied him. He has described the key element to this:

> From both the tribal and witch-doctor schools my tutors'
> instructions continually emphasized the remarkably close

ties the living have with their departed relatives. Virtually all their waking life they contend with the whims and fancies of these very real entities. More likely than not their sleep will also be influenced by them, for dreams are considered direct communications from the spirits. Their discussions about these ever-present beings are absolutely matter-of-fact and completely free of embarrassment. . . . On very rare occasions they even indulge in humorous songs like bemoaning the vain nature of a long deceased great-aunt whose continual demands for ornate bangles and colourful beadwork leave no money for food.[4]

In other words, offerings were accorded to deceased relatives because the living continued to experience them, while awake and asleep, and to hear demands from them.

Virtually the same has been said of African Negroes by another anthropologist, Geoffrey Gorer:

It may be taken as axiomatic that if we are sane, all primitive negroes are raving mad. They are not childlike, or simple, or ignorant: they are just mad, far madder than most of the inhabitants of our asylums . . . . Primitive Negroes *know* that the world is entirely spiritual; what we treat as the physical universe . . . is to them nothing but clods of matter . . . only taking on the qualities of the spirit, whether human or inhuman, which inhabits them.[5]

Such thinking has been held by other peoples besides Africans, as has been made clear by, among others, M. S. Seale, for more than forty years a teacher and missionary in Syria and the Lebanon. As Seale has noted of pagan, pre-Islamic Arabs:

In Arab society, friends and relatives kept in touch with the deceased, lingered at the burial place, and even pitched a tent at the graveside; they could not tear themselves away. Coming upon the grave of an acquaintance, they would call his name and greet him: the deceased was believed to return the greeting. Owls fluttering around were thought to be the spirits of the departed . . . Besides food [the pagan Arab] . . . would also provide the deceased with a riding camel which was tethered at the graveside and left there to die without food or water.[6]

Extraordinary as this may seem, once one begins to look for them, surviving traces of very similar ways of thinking can be found associated with feasts of the dead held to this day all over the world. Such feasts may be those nominally celebrated as the Christian Feast of All Souls, yet in reality have altogether more ancient, pagan origins. In Mexico, for instance, on 2 November Nahuatl-speaking Indians (descendants of the Aztecs) gather in their droves at cemeteries, bringing with them specially baked raisin-filled bread, baskets of fruit, bottles of wine and beer, *jalapeño* peppers, and armfuls of flowers.[7] According to the Nahuatl, once they have set the food before the graves they believe that the souls or spirits of the dead emerge to partake of the savours and flavours, after which the living families can proceed picnic-style to consume the food themselves. Just as in the case of the Makgabeng tribespeople investigated by Boshier, these Central American Indians speak of their dead with total familiarity and without any form of dread or fear; they affectionately refer to them as their 'little dead ones' and unselfconsciously describe themselves as able to *feel* these beings around them. As might be expected, the locations for these encounters tend to be cemeteries, precisely where Boshier's Makgabeng instructors told him that the deceased can be felt most strongly:

> Although the ancestors can travel at will, the strongest spot for making contact with them is on the site where their bodies are buried. Thus, individuals are continually making pilgrimages all over the subcontinent to family graves for the purpose of delivering prayers or making offerings.[8]

What may at first seem surprising in this passage from Boshier is his mention of prayers. Why pray to departed relatives? Although this concept often gives rise to assertions that Africans, Chinese, and others worship their ancestors, this is a serious misunderstanding of the whole way of thinking. For the real point of prayers to departed relatives seems consistently to be based on the dead person's role as an intermediary between the living and the unseen world of the spirit – assuming that one believes in a world of the spirit. Historically, although its true origins are most likely far older, we can trace this intercession role at least as far back as the ancient Egyptians. The following supplicatory lines are part of a letter written by a grieving and ailing Egyptian widower, Merertifi, to his deceased wife, Nebeyotef, about the year 1850 BC:

> I am your beloved upon earth. Fight on my behalf and intercede on behalf of my name. . . . Remove the infirmity

of my body. Please become a spirit before my eyes, so that I may see you fighting for me in a dream. Then I will deposit offerings for you when the sun has risen.[9]

However, such prayers can be seen to be genuinely closer to ones of the full-blown worshipful variety when they are directed to the graves of more important individuals – kings, chiefs, or others who in their lifetimes were individuals of great power or wisdom. According to what Boshier was told by his Makgabeng informants, 'parties of tribesmen frequently travel to the site of a past chief's grave, as the chief's spirit is the most powerful in the tribe and certain requests must be channelled his way'.[10] The chief's spirit is the most powerful.

Suddenly a keystone to what is to us such an alien way of thought begins to fall into place. The experience of the dead was not just a one-way traffic of departed souls relentlessly and seemingly senselessly making demands for offerings upon the living. The dead were expected to provide something in return for the offerings bestowed upon them. The more powerful the dead (and the proportionately more generous offerings put their way), the greater might be the help they would be expected to provide. A classic instance of this is the dramatic scene in Homer's *Odyssey* in which Odysseus, seeking help on how he might get his ship and his men safely back to Ithaca, takes offerings of sheep, and the mortgaged promise of a heifer, to the Abode of the Dead, in order to consult the dead sage Tiresias, who dutifully expounds his wisdom.[11]

Suddenly the underlying justification for the scale and studied permanence of places such as the pyramids and Newgrange comes into focus. These were not just profligate repositories for the corpses of vain rulers who lashed their peoples into submission to build them, as often popularly supposed. They were places in which the really important dead, in return for all the comfort, the security, and the offerings provided, could not only continue to be experienced by the living, but also continue to provide the properly informed wisdom and judgement, plus perhaps a few extra powers, for which they had been famed in their lifetime. It suddenly makes sense when we learn, for instance, in Irish legend that it was to Newgrange, alias the Brú na Boyne, that Oengus brought the body of the dead hero Diarmaid to 'put an aeriel life into him so that he will talk to me every day'.[12] We see here the touch-point of the idea of gods.

However much it might make sense of their offering rituals that primitives and ancients experienced their deceased chiefs and relatives in this way, at another level it raises the obvious question: how? Few of us who live in the present-day world would claim any faculty of being able to communicate with the dead. So might those who professed, or continue to profess, such experiences have some different kind of consciousness or receptivity to ourselves? Or alternatively, could it all just be ascribed to their imagination, perhaps in some instances aided by drugs?

It is interesting that, quite independently of any of the anthropological insights of Boshier and others, a strikingly original yet soundly rational case for a shift of consciousness has recently been put forward by a somewhat maverick psychology lecturer from Princeton University: Julian Jaynes, author of *The Origin of Consciousness in the Breakdown of the Bicameral Mind.* Happily, Jaynes's arguments are by no means as indigestible as his book's title. His main thesis is that what we today talk of as our consciousness, in the sense of self-awareness, is not something that humanity has always had; instead we have developed it only comparatively recently, largely during the last three thousand years, and to differing degrees among different peoples. According to Jaynes, previously people did not introspect, in the way we do now. This left them open to the hearing of voices, in the place of our 'thoughts', which they rightly or wrongly interpreted as those of their deceased leaders and departed relatives.

Crucial to Jaynes's argument are his observations of Homer's *Iliad*, the composition of which he ascribes to just before the change to self-aware consciousness. In this he notes not only that there is no usage of any word for 'mind' or 'consciousness' as such, but that the characters show no capacity for conscious thinking as we do. All this is done for them by 'gods':

> When Agamemnon, king of men, robs Achilles of his mistress, it is a god that grasps Achilles by his yellow hair and warns him not to strike Agamemnon.[13] It is a god who then rises out of the gray sea and consoles him . . . a god who whispers low to Helen to sweep her heart with homesick longing. . . . It is the gods who start quarrels among men,[14] that really cause the war,[15] and then plan its strategy.[16] It is one god who makes Achilles promise not to go into battle, another who urges him to go. . . . In fact, the gods take the place of consciousness.[17]

Nor, as Jaynes points out, do we have to look far for who the 'gods' are. In many cultures the words for 'god' and the dead are one and the same; and from a study of an 11,000-year-old burial of a king or chief found in 1959 at Eynan in Galilee, Jaynes argues for the ease by which such an individual could become revered as a 'god' once the premiss is accepted that his voice and admonitions continued to be experienced by those living after his death. As noted by Jaynes, this chief, whose slightly disarticulated bones were laid with those of his wife in what may have been the house they inhabited in life, was deliberately half propped up by those who buried him, as if to facilitate his ability to listen to petitions made to him and to be able to give commands. Reinforcing this idea is the special attention his grave was subsequently accorded. First a red-ochred wall or parapet was built around this. Then the whole structure was roofed over and topped with a hearth that must have been for the cooking of the offerings brought to the chief in return for his services. There were later further embellishments, presumably marking a phase when this individual's 'power' had achieved yet wider fame and recognition.[18] To Jaynes, this dead chief could be interpreted as one of the first living 'gods', and his burial place a prototype for all the 'god house' pyramids and ziggurats that would follow.

From such thinking, and given, as discussed in Chapter 1, the idea of a dead man's *ka* inhabiting his statue as well as his corpse, it becomes much easier to understand the shortness of the step to the practice that seems to us the very epitome of pagan 'idolatry': the offering up of gifts, prayers, and supplications, and the putting of questions, to 'inanimate' statues. Present-day Egyptologist John Romer has described how in ancient Egypt just such practices were carried out with statues of Amenhotep I, the patron god-pharaoh of Egypt's tomb-builders:

> As Amenhotep I [i.e. his statue, carried about in a sort of sedan-chair] went about his peregrinations, he often arbi-trated in village disputes, as did other statues of the King kept in various shrines throughout Western Thebes. As he was carried through the village, questions were asked of him and the statue would answer by 'nodding its head' or moving backwards and forwards.[19]

Interestingly, Romer specifically likens the statue's apparent responses to instances of 'felt' communications from the dead he had come across on the part of present-day Egyptians:

> It is quite wrong to put these movements down to simple connivance on the part of those carrying the god. Still in Luxor today, during funerals, where corpses are similarly carried upon wooden coffin boards, bearers often feel the dead person's spirit pressing down upon them or hurrying the

procession to the graveyard. Occasionally the spirit will slow the bearers down, rarely it will fix to a spot outside the graveyard and then a special tomb must be built to accommodate the demanding corpse. Just as it would be callous to suggest that these modern mourners deliberately play games, so it would be pointless to attribute modern tricks to the movements of King Amenhotep's statue. The god simply moved or nodded, and his bearers felt the pressure.[20]

Despite Romer's commendable open-mindedness, however, we can scarcely expect otherwise than for our natural, materialist-minded reaction to be to dismiss such experiences as hallucinations. Even Julian Jaynes, for all his arguments that early peoples had a different type of consciousness to our own, makes no attempt to argue that ancient peoples *genuinely* experienced their dead – only that they *thought* they did.

A further complication arises from the fact that many present-day primitive peoples, among these tribes of Africa and South America, use hallucinogenic drugs such as peyote and coca to induce in themselves what is arguably an entirely illusory sensation of experiencing their dead ancestors. Compounding this is good reason to believe that such chemical means, whatever their relevance to experiencings of the dead, were well enough known to people of Jaynes's pre-conscious antiquity. A late second-millennium BC Cretan statuette of a goddess represents her with a head-dress made up of poppies, incisions to the pods of which suggest knowledge of how to extract the poppy's opium (Figure 4). Archaeologists have been familiar for a long while with certain Cypriot juglets from the same period, the so-called base-ring juglets, the shapes of which, when turned upside down, similarly resemble incised poppies. From gas and high-performance liquid chromatography tests on these, capable of identifying one part in a billion, it is certain that some were used as containers for opium.[21] In fact, opium is known to have been used in ancient Egypt both for scalp disorders and as a sedative for wounded warriors.

Are all ancient and primitive peoples' claimed experiencings of their dead, then, to be attributed just to drug 'trips', or merely some of them? Separated as we are by wide distances of time, space, and culture, no categoric answer can be given. But we may perhaps suggest that in the case of the ancients the use of drugs may have been specifically to try to bolster the faculty that Jaynes argues civilized humanity has mostly lost. One of the most impressive indicators that not all such experiences were imagination and hallucination derives from instances in which the

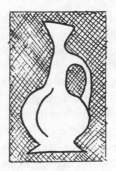

Fig. 4. *Left*: Late Minoan goddess found at Gazi, Crete, showing head-dress of poppies with incisions for the extraction of the opium. *Above*: Late Bronze Age base ring juglet, featuring poppy shape when reversed

experiences were in no way sought by the experiencers, but were actually unwelcome.

That such instances could occur and were of serious concern for people in antiquity is, for instance, evident from the Tibetan *Book of the Dead*, in which the deceased was given specific instructions not to haunt. It is also apparent from Viking practice, in which if the deceased became a malignant spirit it was the duty of his relatives to break open his grave and 'kill' him again – a course which, according to Viking specialist A. W. Brøgger,[22] may well account for some of the intrusions into Viking graves discovered by archaeologists.

Perhaps the most striking instance of unwelcome 'haunting' comes from comparatively recent times. The case was reported by an Oxford University folklore specialist, the late Dr W. Y. Evans-Wentz:

A European planter . . . having died in the jungles of the Malabar country of south-west India, was buried there by the people. Some years after, a friend of the planter found the grave carefully fenced in and covered with empty beer and whisky bottles. At a loss to understand such an unusual sight, he asked for an explanation, and was told that the dead *sahib*'s ghost had caused much trouble and that no way had been discovered to lay the ghost until an old witch-doctor declared that the ghost craved whisky and beer, to which it had long been habituated when in the flesh and which were the real cause for its separation from the fleshly body. The people, although religiously opposed to intoxicants, began purchasing bottled whisky and beer of the same brands which the *sahib* was well known to have used, and with a regular ritual for the dead, began sacrificing them to the ghost by pouring them out upon the grave. Finding that this kept the ghost quiet, they kept up the practice in self-defence. [23]

The first intriguing feature of this story is that in the case of the planter these people clearly had an after death experience they would certainly not have taken hallucinogens to bring upon themselves. But African peoples, along with many Asians, suggest that after a time in the world of spirit our souls reincarnate back on earth into new bodies, a phenomenon for which an impressive array of after death experiences, in the form of 'past-life' memories, has been assembled. So, in order to be totally comprehensive in our approach, it is to these after death experiences of the 'past-life' type that we will now turn.

# 3

# HAVE WE LIVED BEFORE?

The usual stereotyped Christian idea of an afterlife with winged angels and harps has become an obviously outmoded one in our scientific age. So it is perhaps hardly surprising that recent years have seen a dramatic increase, here in the West, in the traditionally eastern belief in rein-carnation. This is the belief that on death the deceased's consciousness or soul becomes reborn into a new body, and that by implication we have all lived before in earlier bodies, even though we do not normally remember these.

Although at first sight the reincarnation concept might appear to be incompatible with the ideas of the living continuing to experience the dead discussed in the previous chapters, in reality this presents little difficulty. Most schools of reincarnationist thought suppose an interval of what may be several years between one life and the next, thus readily allowing for some discarnate, limbo-like state in which, arguably, the deceased might still be experienced by the living. Only certain isolated groups, such as Jains, argue for no interval. Furthermore, a central feature of at least modern forms of the belief is that the living can and do experience the dead, sometimes as snatches of memories of their previous lives floating to the surface during childhood, sometimes in more complete form via consciousness-altering processes such as hypnosis.

In line with the increased interest in eastern culture in recent years, adding to reincarnation's popularity for western minds, and giving it a distinct edge over ideas of heaven and hell, has seemed to be the system's apparent greater fairness. After all, what is the justice of a wicked man being condemned to hell if much of his evil has been the result of a bad upbringing which circumstances gave him no opportunity to repent? And what about souls dying in infancy? And the insane? Many fully committed Christians have preferred not to go into the rationalities or otherwise of heaven and hell, because they are too deeply aware both of the outdatedness of these concepts as traditionally understood, and of the lack of any viable replacement.

Not surprisingly, therefore, aided by media attention to stories of individuals purportedly experiencing their past lives, interest and belief in reincarnation have leapt in popularity in recent years among people of many countries and all walks of life. In Britain, according to Gallup polls, belief in reincarnation rose from 18 per cent to 28 per cent between 1969 and 1979, with some third of all adult women having become believers in reincarnation.[1] There has been a similar dramatic upsurge in the USA, with one in four of the population claiming the belief, a proportion that rises to nearly 30 per cent among the under-25s.[2] This gets even stronger the closer one gets to California, where Shirley MacLaine has made herself a sort of reincarnation apostle, proclaiming the idea to all humanity.

New and exciting though the reincarnation fad might be in the West, it is also an idea which has been around a long time, and is surprisingly well spread around the world. Among the lesser known groups who have traditionally held it as part of their beliefs are the Tlingit and Haida Indians of Alaska, several tribes of West Africa, and the Druses of Lebanon. The peoples with whom the idea is most closely associated are the adherents of the great Hindu, Jain, and Buddhist religions of India and South-East Asia. Of particular interest, because of the apparently demonstrable incidence of reincarnation among their high lamas, are the Buddhists of Tibet.

Until 1951, when the Chinese took over the country, Tibet's rulers had been a succession of Dalai Lamas. Each one, from certain peculiar clues best known to the initiated, was believed to be the reincarnation of the one before. How this has been thought to happen is best illustrated by the story of the choosing of the present, fourteenth Dalai Lama, whom the Chinese ousted, and who for many years has been living in exile in India. As is well known, the Tibetan equivalent of Roman Catholicism's Vatican is the towering and breathtaking Potala Palace that dominates Tibet's capital, Lhasa. It was here in 1933 that the thirteenth Dalai Lama died, leaving certain special clues as to how his successor, the fourteenth incarnation – who would be born somewhere without even his mother being aware of the baby's identity – could be recognized. To Tibet's Regent, the man principally responsible for the quest for the new Dalai Lama, there appeared a vision of a monastery with roofs of jade, green, and gold, and a house with turquoise tiles. Other clues suggested that the child would be born in the north-east.

Equipped with no more than a few cryptic hints such as these, groups of Tibetan high lamas set out on a nation-wide search to find this mystery child. After three years, one search-party, arriving at the north-eastern monastery of Kumbum, immediately noted this to have a roof of green and gold. A little later at the nearby village of Takster they came across a house with turquoise tiles. To their astonishment, out of the house a two-year-old boy came running who seemed to recognize them, despite the fact that they were disguised as servants. Although the child was of peasant parentage, and one of sixteen children, when the lamas began to test him for signs that he might be the Dalai Lama they found a variety of responses that seemed to indicate this. Offered a selection of walking-sticks, some obviously expensive and showy, the little boy correctly chose the humble one that had formerly been used by the thirteenth Dalai Lama. On the boy's body the lamas reportedly found birthmarks which they knew to be peculiar to those reborn as the Dalai Lama.

So the child was taken back to Lhasa with his family to commence the long training by which he would become fourteenth Dalai Lama, 'Ocean of Wisdom', and god-king to Tibet's six million Buddhists. Although he has lived in exile for much of his life, all those who meet him attest to his profound personality, a testimony either of his finders' percipience, or of the subsequent rigours of the training they gave him.

The problem with this intriguing story of how the Dalai Lama's new incarnation was identified is that so much has to be taken on trust from sources culturally and linguistically a long way removed from us. Rather more encouragingly, however, throughout those countries whose populations traditionally believe in reincarnation – among them India, Sri Lanka, and Thailand – there occur similar instances of individuals appearing to remember past existences, particularly when such memories surface during early childhood. Such cases, as potential prime evidence for a form of after death experiencing, should be checkable for what validity they may have. Fortunately, one particularly well-qualified western investigator has made this his chosen speciality; the investigator in question is Dr Ian Stevenson, a psychiatry professor at the University of Virginia, Charlottesville, since 1957.

Who is Stevenson, and what light do his researches throw on reincarnation cases as a form of after death experience? Born in Montreal in 1918, Stevenson had a full, formal training in medicine at McGill University, before subsequently specializing in psychiatry. For reasons he has never made entirely clear, his first foray into the field of reincarnation was in 1958, just a year after joining the University of Virginia, with an essay on 'The Evidence for Survival from Claimed Memories of Former Incarnations',[3] submitted for a competition set by the American Society of Psychical Research. Although this essay was largely a gathering of second-hand reports of cases suggestive of reincarnation, none of which he had personally investigated, Stevenson brought a fresh, professional approach to the subject, and won the prize.

With the money from this and other support grants, from 1961 Stevenson began the first of what he calls 'field trips' to the reincarnationist countries of the East, trying to meet up directly with subjects claiming past life memories. As his case-files began to increase, Stevenson began to recognize that they conformed to a pattern, a pattern persuasive in itself of the validity of each example. In Stevenson's own words:

> A typical case . . . begins when a small child, usually between the ages of two and four, starts to tell his parents and anyone else who will listen that he remembers living another life before his birth. His statements about the previous life which he claims to remember are nearly always accompanied by behaviour which is unusual in the child's family, but which harmonises with the statements about the deceased person he claims to be. For example, if the child claims to remember a previous life as a wealthy man with many servants, he is likely to refuse to do any household chores or other menial work, no matter how poor his family is.
>
> A child claiming to remember a previous life usually asks to be taken to the place where he says he lived during that life, and for this reason, or to satisfy their own curiosity, his parents nearly always try to find the family to which he has been referring. If the child has furnished enough details, especially identifying proper names, and if the distances involved are not too great, the search for the family of the person he has been talking about is nearly always successful . . . the child is then usually found to have been accurate in about 90% of the statements he has been making about the deceased person whose life he claims to remember. Reports about that person's behaviour made by surviving members of his family usually indicate also close correspondences between that behaviour and the unusual conduct which the child has been showing in his family.
>
> In the usual case of this type, the child's utterances concerning the previous life reach a peak of volume and detail between the ages of three and five. After this, the imaged memories of the previous life appear to fade in most cases . . . about the same age, but often some time later, his unusual behaviour also recedes.[4]

Dr Stevenson's reports on such cases, many of which have been published by the University of Virginia's publishing house, are prodigiously detailed and as such undeniably represent the most authoritative and scientific approach supportive of belief in reincarnation available in any language.[5] In detailing the experiences claimed by each child indicative of these having lived a previous life, Stevenson is punctilious in trying to obtain witnesses to check and cross-check each statement, and looks wherever he can for further clues.

A typical Stevenson case is that of Ravi Shankar, an Indian boy born in 1951 in one of the crowded outer suburbs of the city of Kanauj, in Uttar Pradesh state.[6] Ravi Shankar's father was called Ram Gupta, but from the age of two the child began saying that he was really the son of a barber called Jageshwar. According to Ravi Shankar, in his past life as Jageshwar's son he had had his throat cut by a washerman called Chaturi and a barber called Jawahar. As apparent proof of his story the young Ravi Shankar pointed to a birthmark at his throat which strongly resembled a knife wound. He also kept asking for the toys that he had owned in his previous existence.

Upon local investigation it emerged that only half a mile away there indeed was a barber called Jageshwar whose son Munna had been murdered at the age of six just as Ravi Shankar had described. Furthermore, although a washerman named Chaturi and a barber named Jawahar had been strongly suspected of having committed this crime, the case against them had been dropped on the grounds of insufficient evidence. Munna's murder had been just six months before Ravi Shankar was born.

By the time Ian Stevenson managed to investigate the case some nine years had elapsed, and so all he could do was try to piece together what relatives and neighbours could remember, and check out some notes taken by a schoolmaster at the time. None the less, Stevenson managed to assemble a list of some twenty-six items of factual information which seemed to suggest that Ravi Shankar really could be a reincarnation of the dead Munna; particularly compelling was the scar on Ravi Shankar's neck, still discernible at the age of thirteen. As Stevenson described this from his examination of it:

> Under the ridge of the chin, somewhat more on the right side than on the left, I observed a linear mark crossing the neck in a transverse direction. It ran about two inches long and was about ⅛ to ¼ inch wide. It was darker in pigment than the surrounding tissue, and had the stippled quality of a scar. It looked much like an old scar of a healed knife wound. This, I

was told, was what remained of a considerably longer mark which, during early childhood, had also lain low in the neck about one third the distance between the sternal notch and the chin.[7]

Stevenson has published case after case of this kind, all set down in considerable detail, everyone interviewed carefully listed, and the satisfactory as well as the unsatisfactory features thoughtfully appraised. Anyone's first impression on reading these has to be admiration for such assiduous scholarship. Stevenson commendably never claims his cases as 'proof' of reincarnation. He simply describes them in their entirety as strongly suggestive of reincarnation, while accepting that in almost every case unsatisfactory features can crop up which fall short of what the scientist would accept as 'proof'. Yet certainly, if reincarnation memories are a genuine form of after death experience, nobody has done more than Stevenson to try to set these on a proper scientific footing. As one of his colleagues has said of him, 'Either he is making a colossal mistake, or he will be known (I have said as much to him) as the Galileo of the twentieth century.'[8]

It is still a big 'if'. For far too many ostensibly shrewd enquirers into evidence for an afterlife have simply skimmed through Stevenson's rarely sparkling prose, eyed the impressive outward detail, acknowledged the impracticality of any form of cross-check (what is the point of battling one's way to some dusty Indian village if the child has already long forgotten his past-life memories?), and taken the view that nobody can have put in the amount of research Stevenson has without there being *something* to it.

However, with the right approach, checking-out methods can be applied to Stevenson's work, with results that can hardly be said to be encouraging. For instance, if reincarnation genuinely is what happens to all of us after death, then we might expect the process to exhibit certain recurring patterns or rules among those claiming to remember their past lives. In particular we might expect indications of the length of time between one life and the next, also the sort of distances the soul or consciousness may travel in order to become reincarnated into a new body. Of course, there need not necessarily be any hard-and-fast rules to this, and we should therefore not necessarily be sceptical if in Stevenson's cases the between-life intervals vary, as they do, from months to decades, and the between-life journeyings from yards to hundreds of miles. But where credulity begins to become strained is when Stevenson reports different apparent rules pertaining between one culture and the next, as among the Jains, for instance, who contend, virtually uniquely, that on death the soul immediately reincarnates into another body. The Tlingit Indian of Alaska believe that they will reincarnate within the same family; again, near uniquely among other cases, theirs conform to this pattern.

Perhaps the most telling indicator of something seriously amiss comes from one simple exercise which anyone can do using Stevenson's case reports, but which Stevenson himself has not done, despite his prodigious efforts in so many other ways. This is to set down in a single column the social circumstances – that is, the status, rich or poor, high caste or low caste – of each child for whom reincarnation memories are claimed, then to set down in a second column the social circumstances of the dead person whose reincarnation the child purports to be. A sample from Stevenson's most fully published Indian and Sri Lankan cases is shown below:

| Child | Parentage | Alleged past life |
|---|---|---|
| Prakash | Living in mud hut | Family of wealthy shopkeepers living in brick house |
| Jasbir | Low-caste peasants | High-caste brahmin |
| Sukla | Railway worker | Family wealthy and well known |
| Gopal Gupta | Kept petrol filling-station | Millionaire's son |
| Sunil | Poor and often unemployed shopkeeper | Very wealthy factory-owner |
| Bishen Chand | Railway clerk | Wealthy landowner |
| Dolon Mitra | Humble poultry supervisor | Extremely wealthy family |
| Ruby Kusuma | Poor vegetable seller | Wealthy landowner |
| Indika | Poor cultivator | Wealthy building contractor[9] |

As is obvious, while the middle column, that of the child's parentage, conveys a typical cross-section of India's breadline and below-breadline poor, the right-hand column, that of the deceased being remembered, features individuals or families of outstanding wealth within their communities. The list has been excerpted to highlight this contrast, and there are some minor exceptions, but the trend is so marked across so many of Stevenson's cases that it surely indicates only one thing: a motive. And in reincarnationist countries teeming with so many poor it is not too difficult to guess that motive. Thus in India or Sri Lanka a poor family can have much to gain, and very little to lose, by representing their child as the reincarnation of a recently deceased member of a rich family. If the rich family can be persuaded to believe the claim, then they are unlikely to let their unfortunate dead relative continue to suffer in his new incarnation. They will try to do something to improve the child's, and thereby the whole poor family's, lot.

Once we take such a motive into account, it begins to show through in all too many of Stevenson's cases for comfort, particularly those in India and Sri Lanka, to which he has devoted the highest proportion of his effort. An example is the case of Sunil Dutt Saxena.[10] Here we find Sunil, the son of a poor and often unemployed shopkeeper of the northern Indian city of Bareilly, to the east of Delhi; at the age of three he purportedly began announcing that he had come from Budaun, some thirty-five miles away, having travelled, as a person of some importance, in a horse-drawn carriage. If he was asked to help with any housework, Sunil would disdainfully decline, telling his mother, 'I used to sit only on the *gaddi* [a cushion on which an Indian employer traditionally sits to conduct business].'

Without too much difficulty the individual whom all Sunil's statements were found to fit turned out to be one Seth Sri Krishna, the wealthiest and also one of the most philanthropic men in Budaun up until the time of his death, eight years before Sunil's birth. How did Sunil fare when subjected to the acid test of being presented to Seth Sri Krishna's family? Apparently not too well, for he failed to recognize certain key individuals, and exhibited a liking for meat and fish, whereas Seth Sri Krishna had been a staunch vegetarian. With commendable percipience Seth Sri Krishna's family failed to be convinced, but not so Ian Stevenson. Despite being told directly by a doctor that Sunil had been coached by one Sheveti Prasad to pretend he was Seth Sri Krishna reborn, Stevenson preferred to dismiss the doctor as unreliable, concluding, against all the odds: 'the case was genuine, although I am not prepared to say that all the items denied by the dissenting witnesses happened exactly as the affirming ones stated'.[11]

In fairness to Stevenson, it has been acknowledged that there are some instances, such as that of Ravi Shankar, in which there are no glaring inequalities of wealth between the two families. But in all these, special circumstances can be found. Thus in the case of Ravi Shankar no less than three of the family's neighbours intimated that the child had been taken by his father to be coached by barber Jageshwar before making the reincarnation claims, contradicting Ravi Shankar's father's contention that he and Jageshwar had not previously been known to each other. If these allegations are accepted, we are merely witnessing a different motive. Given barber Jageshwar's burning urge to bring his son's murderers to justice, it is all too easy to see Ravi Shankar's story as a ploy between Jageshwar and Ravi Shankar's father to try to get suspects Jawahar and Chaturi re-arrested. The scar 'birthmark', which Stevenson describes as most resembling a healed wound, may well have been created deliberately as additional evidence.

How can a serious and competent investigator such as Stevenson have been so readily deceived in this way? The clue appears to lie in his stance on a rare case of a reincarnation claim much closer to home. Edward Ryall, a retired English pay-clerk and estate agent from Benfleet in Essex, began claiming in the 1970s to have clear and orderly memories of a past life as a West Country farmer called John Fletcher, living in Weston Zoyland, Somerset, at the time of the Monmouth Rebellion of 1685.

According to Ryall, as John Fletcher he had led a prosperous and rather idyllic rustic existence, married to one Cecily Fuller, and the proud father of two sons; then, one night, at the behest of a friend, he had rashly agreed to act as a guide to the Duke of Monmouth's army. This turned out to be for Monmouth's abortive attempt to surprise the royalist forces of King James II under cover of darkness. In the ensuing action, which became known as the battle of Sedgemoor, Fletcher was apparently killed. Ryall peppered his story with period speech and various authentic allusions, such as to Weston Zoyland's two contemporary vicars, the Revd Thomas Holt and the Revd Thomas Perrott, and wrote it all up in a book, *Second Time Around*.[12] Stevenson provided an appropriate introduction to the book, describing some of his own apparently supportive researches on the subject.

Unfortunately, as subsequent professional investigation has shown, Stevenson's judgement was again sorely wanting. Vicars Holt and Perrott happened to keep very careful records of all the births, marriages, and deaths in their parish, records which survive to this day in the Somerset County Record Office in Taunton, and which I have personally examined. While according to Ryall the Revd Holt buried Fletcher's father in 1660, performed Fletcher's marriage ceremony to Cecily Fuller in 1674, and should almost inevitably have baptized Fletcher's sons, John and Jeremy, on their purported births in 1675 and 1677, no entries for these events occur anywhere in the parish records; nor is there the slightest evidence for the existence of any Fletcher family answering Ryall's description.

According to Ryall, the family house in which these Fletchers lived was one of 'a fair size', with a variety of rooms on two floors, built in 1530; a well-established residence, therefore, of some substance. Yet when Michael Green, a government Inspector of Ancient Monuments and Historic Buildings, contacted Ryall to ask whether he might be able to provide the exact location of this place, Ryall proved evasive, despite having previously claimed his memories to be 'remarkably easy and free from effort' and 'present in my waking consciousness'. When Green provided a specially prepared map setting out all the seventeenth-century landmarks that any genuine John Fletcher would have known, Ryall reluctantly pin-pointed the house and its lands on this, only to choose what Michael Green has subsequently shown was open moor, entirely without permanent dwelling, until the late eighteenth century.

These findings, along with a variety of anachronisms and inaccuracies – plus the fact that the real individual to guide Monmouth's troops was a peasant called Godfrey – leave no reasonable doubt that Ryall's 'John Fletcher' was nothing more than an old man's pipe-dream, a figment of his imagination. Indeed, an interviewer of Edward Ryall's widow who called on her a year or so after her husband's death in 1978, obtained the admission from her that 'she thought him somewhat living in a make-believe world' and in later years often found him looking at his own painting of his 'earlier wife' and talking to himself.[13]

Stevenson's reaction to all this has been of considerable interest. Even before any of these revelations, a historian whom he had directly asked to look at the case tried to persuade him that it was a hoax; Stevenson refused to believe him.[14] Presented with the more recent and yet more damning evidence, he has turned a similar Nelson's eye. In other words, he will believe only what he wants to believe. The regrettable deduction has to be that however much Stevenson may appear on paper to be the diligent, impartial, no-nonsense investigator, he is nothing of the kind. Despite affecting, towards most if not all who meet him (including myself), such scientific reticence and aloofness that he will neither talk to journalists nor allow himself to be photographed, he uses as his so-called fieldworkers individuals who are often committed, even obsessive, reincarnationists. An Englishman called Francis Story whom Stevenson has acknowledged accompanied him on several of his field trips 'and added greatly to the gathering of data and their analysis' was a committed Buddhist from the age of sixteen up to his death in 1971, and, as is evident from his writings, had the most simplistic and uncritical attitude towards reincarnation. Another helper and interpreter, Dr Jamuna Prasad, who runs a centre for the development of psychical powers in Allahabad, is an ardent Hindu. To use such individuals for a genuine scientific investigation into reincarnation seems about as inept as asking Dr Ian Paisley to rewrite the constitution of Northern Ireland.

Detailed and exhaustive attention to Stevenson has been necessary because to so many researchers into life after death his has represented *the* scientific approach to the question, and the Asian concept of successions of lives the most convincing mode of after death experience. None the less, all is not lost. Even if, as now seems evident, so much of Stevenson's material is hopelessly flawed, there remain the apparent experiences of past lives produced via hypnosis. The literature on these is yet more prodigious than Dr Stevenson's voluminous output. So might these offer a genuine form of after death experience?

# 4

# 'YOU'RE GOING BACK THROUGH TIME . . .'

Few moments can have seemed more promising for a breakthrough in the search for hard evidence of continued experience after death than the events of the evening of 29 November 1952 at an ordinary American household in Pueblo, Colorado. In a deep hypnotic trance lay 29-year-old Virginia Tighe, wife of an insurance salesman. Over her, intoning the hypnotic commands he had long practised, leaned business man and amateur hypnotist Morey Bernstein. For Bernstein, Virginia had proved an extraordinarily good subject for his party-trick demonstrations of hypnosis; in particular, when told she was 'going back through time' to the days of her childhood she uncannily talked in a convincingly childish voice.

Thus encouraged, this particular evening Bernstein resolved to try something he had never attempted before; to suggest to Virginia that she was going back in time to before she was born, to memories of a previous existence. With a tape recorder documenting every word, Bernstein whispered:

> I want you to keep on going back and back in your mind. And surprising as it may seem, strange as it may seem, you will find there are other scenes in your memory. There are other scenes from far lands and distant places in your memory. . . . Now you are going to tell me what scenes come into your mind. What did you see? What did you see?[1]

Suddenly Virginia's eyelids fluttered, as if responding to images far in the back of her memory. Then, to the utter astonishment of all present, including Hugh, her husband, she began speaking in what was unmistakably a soft Irish brogue: 'Uh . . . scratched the paint off all my bed. Jus' painted it, 'n made it pretty. It was a metal bed and I scratched the paint off it; dug my nails in every post and just ruined it. Was jus' terrible.'

In the course of the following minutes, under Bernstein's gentle questioning, everyone present heard Virginia, who had never been outside the USA, describe herself as Bridey Murphy, a young girl living in Cork, Ireland, during the early years of the nineteenth century. In what subsequently became a series of 'regressions' or hypnotic trips back into a purportedly pre-birth past, she told how she had been born Bridget Kathleen Murphy on 20 December 1798, how her father was a Protestant barrister called Duncan Murphy, how she lived just outside Cork in an area called The Meadows, and how at the age of twenty she married Sean Brian Joseph MacCarthy, a teacher at Belfast's Queens University around the year 1847. She spoke as if with total familiarity of kissing the famous Blarney Stone, of Irish jigs, of the Irish Uillean pipes, and of other minutiae of traditional Irish life.

There and then, for those present knowing Virginia as an ordinary, outgoing American housewife, with no special interest in either Ireland or the paranormal, it all seemed extraordinarily convincing. Surely here was the proof everyone had been seeking that some form of experience really does continue beyond the grave, and that all of us may have similar 'past lives' locked away within ourselves? Although Bernstein had not been the first to conduct an experiment of this kind, his was the first to hit the headlines, and with all the razzmatazz the American media could muster. The inevitable book he was commissioned to write on the story, with Virginia's identity protected by the pseudonym 'Ruth Simmons', was launched in a blaze of publicity, topping the best-seller list for weeks. Although checks were made in Ireland which failed to reveal documentary evidence for the existence of any Bridey or the other members of her family, this could be readily explained by the fact that Ireland had no compulsory registration of births, marriages, and deaths during the period of the 'Bridey' memories. Even when the *Chicago American*,[2] which had lost out on the battle for serialization rights in Chicago, managed to track down Virginia's true identity, and reveal that she had spent part of her girlhood in Chicago with an Irish aunt from whose stories she might well have imbibed the background material for her 'Bridey' life, this did little to stem the idea that hypnotic regression back into past lives was *the* key to proving that experience continues beyond death.

Bernstein's experiment had opened flood-gates that extended well beyond the shores of the United States. Anyone and everyone who fancied their hypnotic prowess tried replicating what he had done, with encouragingly similar results. There can be no doubt that in any public gathering there will be some who, when hypnotized, will turn out, like Virginia Tighe, to be good 'deep trance' subjects and therefore suitable for regression. In this regard the phenomenon has the satisfaction of something genuinely scientific, in the sense that if certain guide-lines are followed it can be repeated and demonstrated by people who have never tried it before.

On suggestion that they are back in earlier times in their present lives, for instance, suitable subjects may vividly 'relive' childhood parties, perhaps to the extent of appearing to list all their friends who attended one of these events decades ago. They may talk in a childish manner, and if asked to write their names may scrawl these in handwriting which appears to correspond to the particular phase of childhood to which they have been taken back.

Far more remarkably, when told that they are back in times before they were born, they can and do exhibit such striking changes of voice and mannerisms (even to alterations of the set of their facial features) that to all appearances it looks as if something of a person they once were has taken over, and someone long dead is speaking through them. I have personally witnessed dozens of regressions conducted by British hypno-therapists Joe Keeton, Derek Crüssell, Leonard Wilder, and others, and have studied tape recordings and transcripts of hundreds more. Of one thing I am entirely sure: there is not the slightest evidence for deliberate, conscious fraud on the part of either the hypnotist or the subject hypnotized.

Is a genuine 'past life' coming through? Or is the hypnotized subject going through an act, just like he will if told he is a typewriter or a chimpanzee, because he has effectively allowed himself to become a puppet for whatever strings the hypnotist may pull? One first point which needs to be made clear is that the apparent 'past-life' cases which make magazine headlines, or are featured in television programmes – some of these undeniably dramatic and full of apparently convincing detail – are not the general rule. At an average regression the hypnotized person may produce only garbled and very laboured information, punctuated by long silences, and many signs of desperately trying to dredge up something to satisfy the hypnotist's demands.

Furthermore, many of these run-of-the-mill regressions can often show signs of the subject fantasizing, or drawing on present, twentieth-century knowledge rather than knowledge of the period appropriate to his or her 'past life'. A typical instance is when a subject, professing, for example, to be recalling a life lived in ancient Egypt (and typically using twentieth-century English for this), perhaps describes himself as living in Thebes in the reign of Pharaoh Rameses III. The first problem with this is that no ancient Egyptian from the time of Rameses III would ever have known Thebes by that name, since the name was given to it much later, when it came under Greek rule; the Egyptians had previously known it as Waset. The second is that no ancient Egyptian would have known Rameses III as Rameses III, for the simple reason that it was modern Egyptologists of only a century or so ago who first allotted the pharaohs numbers, in order to be able to refer to them more easily. The Egyptians knew them by much longer and more cumbersome names and titles. Thus even if one accepts some long-dead ancient Egyptian being able to speak through the language of his present, English body, it is difficult to understand him adopting such modern terms of reference.

An additional difficulty, as in the Ian Stevenson cases, is that hypnotic regressions to past lives reveal no consistent rules for the theoretical reincarnation process. No regular pattern emerges as to whether or not a person's soul goes immediately on death into another body, or stays temporarily removed from the earth-bound state, in some form of limbo; or as to whether a soul is likely to travel widely between one incarnation and the next. The reincarnation 'rules' seem in fact to vary from one hypnotist to another according to the hypnotist's own ideas on the way rebirth is supposed to operate.

Thus Britain's Joe Keeton, who like most hypnotists gives his subjects a 'warm-up' of what he expects of them beforehand, tells them, 'There is no limbo, no rest between one life and another. From death to conception is instantaneous.' Sure enough, the subjects exhibit what appear to be mere nine-month intervals between one life and the next, and are rarely 'reborn' more than a hundred miles from where they previously 'died'. Conversely, subjects of the rather esoteric Welsh hypnotist, the late Arnall Bloxham, implanted with no such restraints, exhibited 'past lives' that hopped cheerfully from the Stone Age to ancient Egypt, to ancient China, to Inca Peru, to medieval Bavaria, and ultimately to South Wales, with often centuries-long intervals between. There has to be the strongest implication that at least some of the subjects are producing fantasy lives, perhaps hypnotically dredged up from long-forgotten memories of historical scenes in books and films, in order to conform to what the hypnotist is expecting of them.

Can all claims of hypnotic 'past-life' memories be dismissed in this way? What has to faced in this field is that, every now and again, a subject under regression, often without any special education, can produce a 'past life' of such vividness, emotional intensity, and depth of detail, that it seems impossible to dismiss it so easily.

In this regard for people in Britain perhaps the most remarkable and memorable instances of hypnotically retrieved 'past lives' have been certain cases of the late Arnall Bloxham, a Cardiff hypnotherapist featured in 1976 on a BBC television programme, *The Bloxham Tapes*, and subsequently set out more fully in a book, *More Lives than One?*, by the programme's producer, Jeffrey Iverson.[3] Bloxham was a lifelong believer in reincarnation who practised as a hypnotherapist. In 1969 his help was sought by a thirty-year-old housewife, pseudonymously known as Jane Evans, who had been suffering great discomfort from rheumatism. On treating her, Bloxham recognized that Jane, like Virginia Tighe, was a natural 'deep trance' subject. Accordingly, as he had done with several similar patients, he invited her to be a subject for the 'Bridey Murphy' type of regression experiment.

In the event Jane proved outstanding, producing apparent memories of no less than six previous existences. Regressed back to Roman times, she recalled a life as 'Livonia', wife of a tutor to the family of a Roman legate, Constantius, resident in Eboracum, the Roman name for York, early in the fourth century AD. Progressed eight centuries forward, she found herself still in York as 'Rebecca', a Jewish financier's wife caught up in the city's Christians' bloody persecution of the Jewish community in AD 1190. Moved in time a little over three centuries forward, she assumed the personality of 'Alison', Egyptian-born housekeeper to the wealthy fifteenth-century financier Jacques Coeur at his magnificent mansion in Bourges in France. A mere generation or so forward and she became Anna, a handmaiden among the Spanish entourage of Katherine of Aragon, arriving in England in 1501 for Katherine's marriage to the short-lived Arthur, eldest son of the Tudor King Henry VII. Two centuries further on she was 'Ann Tasker', a bored teenager working as a sewing-girl in disease-ridden early eighteenth-century London. In a final 'life' before her present one, she assumed the personality of 'Sister Grace', an arthritic Roman Catholic nun, apparently living in Maryland, USA, some time between 1850 and 1920.

Astonished at the range, vividness, and detail of Jane Evans's apparent recollections, Jeffrey Iverson recognized that they needed to be checked for their historical content. Bloxham simply assumed they must be genuine, but Iverson rightly sought out the advice of specialists in the period of each phase of Jane's lives. Compellingly, this advice, and all other accompanying researches, proved remarkably positive.

Of considerable interest, for instance, were Jane's memories as the Roman matron Livonia. The opening regression featured Livonia in the garden of her employers' house, watching a young man called Constantine being trained in the use of Roman weapons by his military tutor, Marcus Favonius Facilis:

> *Bloxham*: Is this your garden?
> *Livonia*: No, it is the garden of the house of the Legate
>      Constantius. His wife . . .

*Bloxham (interrupting)*: What is her name?

*Livonia*: The Lady Helena.

*Bloxham*: Is the Lady Helena with you now?

*Livonia*: We are all in the garden. We are watching the legate's son with his military tutor. They are fighting in the garden. He is teaching him tactics and how to use his sword, his armour and his shield.[4]

Using this set of names, and further details later in the regression, Iverson deduced from his own researches that Livonia seemed to be watching a scene from the youth of the mighty Constantine the Great, son of Constantius and Helena, who became the first Christian Roman Emperor. Although there was no direct historical information that Constantine's father Constantius had spent his early career in Britain, this part of his life had gone unrecorded, and so it was perfectly possible, indeed plausible. Particularly impressive, and with undeniable historical accuracy, was Jane Evans's fluency in describing *domina* Helena's shocked reception of the news of her husband's rejection of her as a result of a complex marital arrangement into which he had entered for political reasons while away in Rome:

> *Livonia*: Oh, poor *domina*. Oh! She is waiting for Constantius, but she does not know that Curio is going to tell her that Constantius has rejected her and has married the daughter of Maximianus – Theodora – and he is bringing her here. He is bringing the Princess Theodora here and yet the *domina* is waiting for him here – what can we do?
>
> *Bloxham*: I thought they were happy together?
>
> *Livonia*: Yes. There must be a reason. Curio told Titus that they have made Constantius – Caesar Constantius. And they have made a man called Galerius – Caesar Galerius. And Constantius married Theodora, the daughter of Maximianus, and Galerius married the daughter of Diocletian. (*Pause.*) And Titus tells me that he [Constantius] had to renounce his first wife in the Temple of Jupiter and take the Princess Theodora as his wife. He already has a child – two children – by her.[5]

Historically it is known that, as part of a political deal with former emperors Maximian and Diocletian, Constantius and Galerius did marry these respective emperors' daughters. But what is breathtaking is Livonia/Jane Evans's fluency in describing these arrangements – as if she were really living at the time of these events. Even Brian Hartley, the Roman specialist whom Iverson consulted, was obliged to acknowledge: 'On the whole it is fairly convincing and checks out, as far as one can check, against known historical facts.'[6]

Similar astonishing historical detail, emerging quite naturally in her accounts of the often violent events in which she became caught up, is the keynote of Jane Evans's other two most vivid regressions, as the Jewess Rebecca and the French housekeeper Alison. The massacre of York's Jews in 1190 is not one of the best-known events in English history (despite taking an Oxford degree in history, I had not previously come across it), yet Jane seemed to know a great deal about it. Furthermore, while the main historically known episode is of the Jews, desperate to escape Christian mobs, committing a Masada-style mass suicide inside York Castle, Jane as Rebecca described herself as hiding, separated from the others, inside the crypt of a York church, where she was ultimately discovered and murdered by English soldiers. One historical problem regarding this regression seemed to be that, with the exception of the Minster (which could be discounted), none of York's forty-odd churches dating from 1190 was known to have a crypt, including the one that seemed most to fit Rebecca's description, St Mary's Castlegate. But then, six months after having conducted his researches in York, Iverson received a letter from Professor Barrie Dobson, the medieval specialist whom he had consulted on the York massacre:

> In September, during the renovation of the church [St Mary's], a workman certainly found something that seems to have been a crypt . . . under the chancel of that church. It was blocked up immediately and before the York archaeologists could investigate it properly. But the workman who looked inside said he had seen round stone arches and vaults. Not much to go on, but if he was right this would point to a Norman or Romanesque period of building, i.e. before 1190 rather than after it.[7]

Similar verifications had come from Iverson's visit to Jacques Coeur's house in Bourges. There he noted in the main banqueting hall a fireplace decorated with precisely the 'animals and a shield' which Jane had described in her regression as a fifteenth-century housekeeper.

The question that plagued Iverson was how, unless it really had come from previous lives, could an ordinary South Wales housewife have been able to produce so much astonishing detail, some of it, as in the case of the crypt, unknown even to the historians until they had made further enquiries? As Jane Evans stated emphatically in the closing moments of Iverson's television programme:

> My only visit to France was two days in 1958 – not leaving, I suppose, the boundaries of Paris. I have never read about Jacques Coeur, I have never heard the name. I have been to Yorkshire but have never been to York itself. I knew that Jews had been persecuted, not only in this country, but everywhere, but I did not know there was a specific incident in York. My Roman history is the same as any school-girl Roman history. We know about Julius Caesar, probably Caligula. I could name a few others, but not the people named on one of the tapes. I know I have not read these things. I have a fairly good memory and I cannot recall having read them. The only explanation I can give is that I must have had a previous life.[8]

Although open-mindedly considering alternative explanations, Iverson discounted these. On his book's publication the Bloxham tapes, and Jane Evans's regressions in particular, were hailed by the publishers' blurb as 'the most staggering evidence for reincarnation ever recorded . . . accounts so authentic that they can only be explained by the certainty of reincarnation'.[9] Further endorsement was provided by the television personality Magnus Magnusson.

However, the very detail of Jane Evans's memories, and in particular those of Roman 'Livonia', provide the vital clue that their real explanation, and by implication that of the gamut of other hypnotic 'past lives', has nothing to do with reincarnation. First it needs to be explained that it is well known by psychologists that in our unconscious memories – the pool which is tapped by hypnosis – we can and do store a great deal more of books we have read, films we have seen, etc., perhaps from many years ago, than anything we have conscious access to. The phenomenon even has its own label: cryptomnesia, or hidden memory. A Finnish psychiatrist, Dr Reima Kampman, has shown that subjects of regression can sometimes be rehypnotized and persuaded to reveal the particular cryptomnesic source upon which they have unconsciously moulded their 'past life',[10] as in the case of one subject whose apparent medieval English 'summer song' was eventually traced to her having, as a teenager, one day glanced at the ballad 'Summer is Icumen in', reproduced in simplified medieval English in Benjamin Britten and Imogen Holt's *History of Music*. The cryptomnesia possibility was one that Iverson had considered but rejected on the grounds that, if the material of Jane Evans's memories was not even in history books, where could she have got it from in the first place?

Nobody has done more to provide the answer to this than the broadcaster, writer, and compulsive scourer of second-hand bookshops Melvin Harris. From a variety of clues Melvin Harris deduced that Jane Evans's true sources, despite her television denial, were most likely to be historical novels, magazine short stories, and/or radio and television plays. He was faced with the needle-in-a-haystack problem of trying to track down which among the thousands of these produced over the last several decades might have been set around the early life of Constantine the Great, or the York massacre, or the career of Jacques Coeur. Here his enthusiasm for browsing among second-hand books proved its worth. For by a lucky breakthrough Harris stumbled upon a particular historical novel, Louis de Wohl's *The Living Wood*, published in 1947, which happened to be specifically devoted to the lives of Constantine, Constantius, and Helena.[11] As Harris leafed through the book, he came, on page 37, to the Livonia regression's very scene of the young Constantine being taught how to use Roman weapons by his 'military tutor', Marcus Favonius Facilis. Here was the same terminology, 'military tutor', being used, and even the same tutor's name, despite the fact, as author de Wohl acknowledged elsewhere, that Marcus Favonius Facilis was a character he had completely invented for his story, the name merely inspired by a first-century Roman centurion's tombstone at Colchester.

As Harris read further, more and more of the Livonia regression's familiar elements tumbled before his eyes. Referring to Helena, Livonia had spoken of her as the *domina*, Latin for 'mistress'. So did de Wohl. In correctly giving towns their Roman names – Eboracum, Londinium, Gessoriacum, etc. – Livonia had oddly abbreviated Verulamium (St Albans), to 'Verulam'. So did de Wohl. No longer was there any mystery about how Jane Evans might 'know' the historically unrecorded British phase of Constantius's early career. The whole crux of de Wohl's novel was a brilliant fictionalization on this very theme. Livonia's dramatic scene of Curio arriving at Eboracum to tell Helena that Constantius had forsaken her in favour of Theodora could be read detail for detail from pages 116 to 118 of *The Living Wood*. Dispelling the slightest doubt that *The Living Wood* might be other than Jane Evans's source is the fact that, besides the historically known characters Constantine, Helena, and Constantius, Livonia speaks of historically *un*known characters such Curio, Valerius, Hilary, and Marcus Favonius Facilis, all of whom were specially invented by de Wohl to suit his story and feature in

The servants of a Sumerian king assemble to join their master in death. Reconstruction based on Sir Leonard Woolley's excavations at Ur

The mid-winter sunrise seen through the roofbox at Newgrange. The structure was designed so that this illumination would happen for a few fleeting minutes solely on the deadest day of the year

Opening the mouth: the ancient Egyptian ceremony whereby the dead man's speech and other faculties were believed to be restored to him. From *The Book of the Dead of Hunefer*, *c.* 1310 BC

Egyptian deceased emerging through the false door of his burial chamber in order to receive his food offerings. From tomb of *c.* 2400 BC

A dead ancient Egyptian receives the offerings to sustain him in the afterlife. One of the commonest motifs in ancient Egyptian art, from tomb of Rahotpe, Maidum, c. 2550 BC

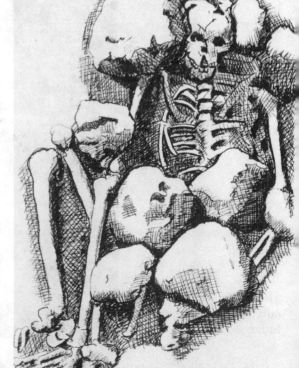

Still communicating with the living? Dead king of Eynan propped up on a pillow of stones, c. 9000 BC, as discovered during excavations in Israel, in 1959

The Dalai Lama as a t[wo]
year-old boy. Via bir[th]
marks and other signs, [he]
was purportedly recogni[zed]
as the reincarnation of [the]
13th Dalai Lama so[me]
three or four years after [the]
latter's death

The Dalai Lama today,
now resident mainly in
India

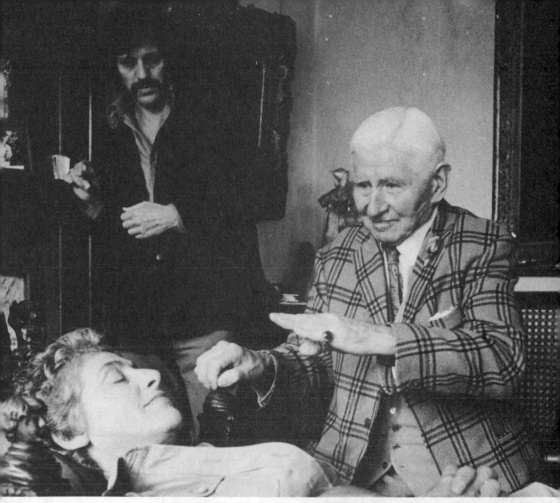

The late Arnall Bloxham, of Cardiff, south Wales, 'regressing' a woman subject back into a 'past life', watched by author and T.V producer, Jeffrey Iverson

BESTSELLER LIBRARY 3/6

*Helena*

LOUIS DE WOHL

A stirring story of a British girl to whom Ancient Rome brought triumph — and disaster.

THE EMPRESS HELENA · Louis de Wohl

Key to Bloxham subject Jane Evans' 'past life' as the Roman 'Livonia': the paperback version of the Louis de Wohl novel, *The Living Wood,* whose historical *and* fictional characters she recalled in her regression

'Materialization' of purported spirit 'Katie King' during a seance conducted by spiritualist medium Florence Cook. 'Katie' would appear to have been none other than Florence herself

Exposed: the crude stage-props of another turn-of-the-century spiritualist medium. In the darkness of the seance room these would be used to represent spirits of the dead

How the alleged 'spirit' substance, ectoplasm, can be faked: a demonstration by Ethel Beenham, secretary to psychical researcher, Harry Price, using cheesecloth rolled up inside her mouth

Spiritualist medium, the late Doris Stokes, mobbed by admirers during one of her stage shows. Unknown to her audiences, her most impressive subjects were specially invited to her shows, and were known to her beforehand

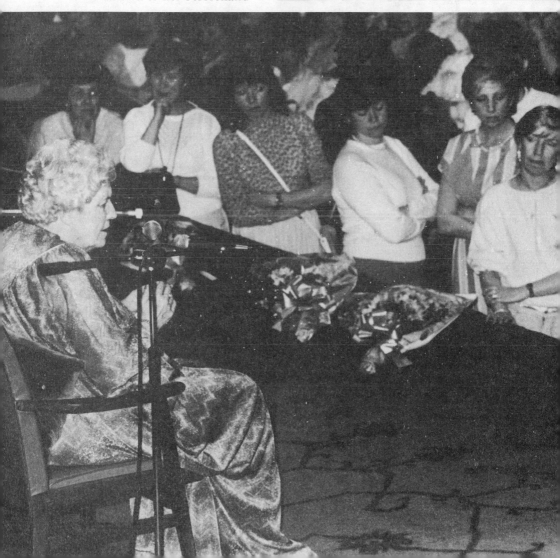

The so-called 'ghost' of Brockley Court, south of Bristol. A simple double exposure, the photograph was created as a Bristol University student prank in 1909, yet even Sir Arthur Conan Doyle was fooled by it

If there is life after death, some death-bed experiences seem to offer particularly compelling evidence for this. The dying moments of an eighteenth-century Frenchman

his book under the same names and in the same roles. De Wohl published in 1947, twenty-two years before Jane Evans first consulted Bloxham, so there can be no question of whose was the priority.

Given this breakthrough by Melvin Harris, the credibility of the rest of Jane Evans's regressions as being real evidence for the survival of the soul from one incarnation to another rapidly begins to fall apart. Although the exact source of the 'memories' of Jewess 'Rebecca' still has not been positively traced, three independent individuals with whom I have been in correspondence recall having heard a radio play on the subject of the York massacre some time during the 1950s. Since nobody has come forward with the title and author, the play has so far proved impossible to trace in the BBC archives; none the less, for quite separate reasons, this regression, like that of 'Livonia', no longer carries its original claim to credibility. In the original, full transcript, unpublished by Iverson, Rebecca spoke of herself and her wealthy husband Joseph as living in the 'ghetto' to the north of York, a quarter apparently without street names in which only the rich Jews lived. She also mentioned a poor Jew who was obliged to live in 'the middle of York in a street called Coney Street'. But in fact there never was a Jewish 'ghetto' in York in 1190, the Jews living scattered among the rest of the community. The very concept of a ghetto did not come into being until 1516, when the first real *ghetto* – the word is Italian for 'foundry' – was set up on a foundry site in Venice.[12] As for the idea of a poor Jew being obliged to live in Coney Street, historically this very street happened to be the address of Josce, the head of York's Jewish community. If such gaffes derived from the writer of the elusive radio play, clearly he or she had not done their background research as meticulously as Louis de Wohl.

Similarly, the seemingly convincing detail about the crypt of St Mary's Castlegate no longer carries the conviction it once held. As confirmed by the authorities who worked on the church's restoration, in reality there never was any crypt. This has been made clear from a recent report on York by the Royal Commission on Historical Monuments, specifically referring to the feature mentioned by Professor Dobson: 'Beneath the East end of the chancel [of St Mary's Castlegate] is a charnel vault with a barrel-vault of stone rubble, probably a later insertion and now inaccessible.'[13] According to my own enquiries of those who worked on the restoration of St Mary's, the date of this vault is likely to have been seventeenth century, five centuries after 'Rebecca' is supposed to have hidden in it. This assessment, and the spuriousness of the 'Rebecca' regression, has now been fully endorsed by Professor Dobson.

As for Jacques Coeur's fireplace, there is a very good photograph of this in Dame Joan Evans's book *Life in Mediaeval France*.[14] Most if not all of Jane Evans's 'Alison' memories could have been obtained from a reading of T. B. Costain's historical novel on the life of Jacques Coeur, *The Moneyman*, which was published in 1947, the very same year as *The Living Wood*.[15] Interestingly, the one detail that 'Alison' did not seem to know was that Jacques Coeur had been married.[16] This is very explicable from Costain. As he explained in his Introduction:

> I have made no mention of Jacques Coeur's family for the reason that they played no real part in the events which brought his career to its climax . . . When I attempted to introduce them into the story they got so much in the way that I decided finally it would be better to do without them.[17]

Yet even if Jane Evans must now be regarded as totally discredited (I have personally pleaded with her to discuss all these findings, accompanied by unconditional promises of preserving her anonymity, but she has adamantly refused, and will not even look at *The Living Wood*), what of claims that people have sometimes spoken unlearned languages when regressed? Well-documented instances of this are nearly as rare as hen's teeth, and in fact even these evaporate when subjected to searching scrutiny. In 1974 Dr Ian Stevenson published in his usual impressive detail the case of an American doctor's wife who, when regressed by her husband, purportedly recalled a male personality called 'Jensen Jacoby', speaking in a seventeenth-century form of Swedish.[18] Although concealing the identity of the doctor and his wife by pseudonymous initials, Stevenson affirmed that he had made five separate checks on the doctor's integrity without revealing anything untoward. Yet by a single fortuitous enquiry I traced not only the doctor's identity but also such disquieting accompanying information that I challenged Dr Stevenson to explain himself. Stevenson replied that if I disclosed what I knew on this case I would cause untold psychological distress to the now widowed doctor's wife. The widow's lawyers swiftly followed up with a letter informing me that Dr Stevenson had published the case entirely without her knowledge or consent, and that he had a legal sword of Damocles hanging over him. In deference to a widow, most anxious to preserve her privacy, I can say no more except that the case is not worth a candle.

Given the collapse of so much of the apparently most convincing evidence for the soul experiencing successions of lives, there seems little justification for taking any more seriously the vaguer and more bizarre reincarnation claims of Shirley MacLaine, despite the huge popular success these have enjoyed. Miss MacLaine has admitted deliberately fictionalizing, for identity-concealment purposes, some of the information about the British politician featured in her book *Out on a Limb*.[19] One can only wonder, fine actress though she is, whether she has not detached herself, perhaps as a result of taking too many sulphur baths in the Andes, from knowing where fiction ends and fact begins.

Shirley MacLaine has swallowed, from her bath-companion David, guru Kevin Ryerson, and others, some totally erroneous ideas about reincarnation that are all too regularly repeated elsewhere. In her best-selling *Out on a Limb* she has described how David told her that Jesus Christ travelled to India during the unknown years before he began his public ministry, and that when he returned he 'taught what he had learned from the Indian masters, that is the theory of reincarnation'. Independently Shirley herself had learned of this same idea from a book by Janet and Richard Brock, who had 'compiled stacks of evidence researched by respected archaeologists, theologians, students of Sanskrit and Hebrew writings, etc.'. When Shirley asked David why such teachings were not recorded in the Bible, he told her:

> They are . . . the theory of reincarnation *is* recorded in the Bible. But the proper interpretations were struck from it during an Ecumenical Council meeting of the Catholic Church in Constantinople sometime around 553 AD, called the Council of Nicaea. The Council members voted to strike those teachings from the Bible in order to solidify Church control.[20]

In David's opinion, 'when the Church destroyed those teachings, it screwed up mankind from there on'.

The true facts are different. All Jesus' surviving teachings can be demonstrated to be firmly rooted in the Jewish tradition and way of life,[21] and there is not a shred of evidence, nor a single scholar of genuine repute, to support the idea that Jesus spent time in India or anywhere else in the Far East. Since scraps of the Gospels survive from as early as a century after the time of Jesus, and full texts from the fourth century on, it is difficult to understand how any doctrine of reincarnation (which is not in these texts) could have been struck out by a council meeting as late as AD 553. As in everything else which Shirley MacLaine quotes of him, David has hopelessly muddled his facts. The real Council of Nicaea took place in AD 325 and had nothing to do with the subject of reincarnation. In AD 553 there was a Council of

Constantinople which did have on its agenda a motion condemning a doctrine of the pre-existence of souls, which had been taught by Origen. But nothing was 'struck from the Bible', and the pre-existence doctrine is quite different from the succession of lives by which reincarnation is generally understood. However, if you will believe from Shirley MacLaine that David had a girl-friend called Mayan who came from the constellation of stars known as the Pleiades, then you will believe anything.

While all this might seem totally destructive of the idea that anything of us survives into successions of lives, the real message is that even the most apparently compelling evidence for reincarnation has to be taken with more than a large grain of salt. Conceivably reincarnation might still happen, and we simply have not isolated the right evidence for this yet. What should additionally not be overlooked is that, despite the fact that 'past life' regressions are not what they seem, the cryptomnesia revelations in respect of Jane Evans have in fact highlighted something positively indicative of some form of continuance of life after death. Given the premiss that Jane Evans did read *The Living Wood* and listen to the radio play about the Jews of York, it is genuinely extraordinary (and I would dearly have loved to question her on this) that she should have unconsciously retained such detailed memory of material she most likely read decades before being regressed by Arnall Bloxham. In fact, given her fluency in the trance state, it would have been little less extraordinary even if she had read *The Living Wood* only minutes before.[22]

The profound question raised, then, is *why* we retain in our minds material that we cannot even get access to without the aid of a hypnotist? Does not this in itself suggest that 'we', whatever 'we' might be, are something of rather more permanence than our physical bodies? With this thought kept in mind we will now turn to that other broad branch of belief, that after death we move into some form of eternal world of the spirit.

# 5

# RAISING SPIRITS

Earlier we noted how certain ancient and primitive peoples seem to have had a faculty for communication with their dead. This real or imagined faculty was, according to psychologist Julian Jaynes and his theory of the growth of what we call consciousness, already markedly disappearing among Mediterranean peoples around the year 1000 BC.

In this context, of considerable interest from around this early period (there are scholarly disagreements over the exact date of composition) are two contrasting descriptions of attempts to contact the dead. The first is in Homer's *Odyssey* – Odysseus' already mentioned visit to the Land of the Dead to consult with the dead sage Tiresias. The second comes from the biblical Book of Samuel – the attempt by Saul, King of Israel, to consult with the dead prophet Samuel, via the witch of Endor.

What is described as taking place in the case of Odysseus is a scene totally foreign and unmistakably 'pagan' for us today, even though it would have been familiar enough in culture after culture prior to the end of the first millennium BC. In book XI of *The Odyssey*, we are told of Odysseus arriving at a place noted for contact with the dead, 'the deep-flowing River of Ocean and the Frontiers of the World'; there he digs a trench for the blood of his offerings, cuts the throats of several sheep, then waits for spirits of the dead to flood before his gaze, among whom he espies Tiresias, whose help he is seeking, and his mother, whom because of his absence from home he does not know to be dead.

The overriding feature here is that no 'medium' is involved, nor priest, nor any other form of intermediary. The offering of the blood sacrifice appears to be the means of making contact with the dead; allowing this to be received by chosen 'spirits' is the key to enabling these particular dead to be heard as well as seen. Tiresias is represented as specifically explaining this to Odysseus when the latter, who wants to talk to his mother, asks how he can persuade her to speak to him: '*Tiresias*: There is a simple rule . . . any ghost to whom you give access to the blood will hold rational speech with you, while those whom you reject will leave you and retire.'[1]

At Ephyra in north-west Greece there are to this day by the river Acheron, traditionally the River of the Dead, the ruins of an ancient cult centre called the Nekromanteion, or 'Place for the Oracle of the Dead'. Here in antiquity pilgrims are known to have come to talk to their dead relatives, using rites that may well have been similar to those described of Odysseus, the offerings being given, then the dead apparently being directly experienced, just as conjectured by Julian Jaynes.

A fascinating contrast is provided by the situation described of King Saul in the biblical Book of Samuel. Saul, it will be recalled, was the first king of Israel, faced with the unenviable task of trying to bring order to a country riven from within by conflicts between the Israelites' Law of Moses and indigenous Canaanite paganism, and seriously threatened from without by the all-too-successful incursions of the warlike Philistines. As part of Saul's attempt to impose the Law of Moses, he had banned some of the Canaanite witchcraft-type practices traditionally supposed to facilitate communication with the dead – invoking the Book of Deuteronomy's 'there must never be anyone among you who . . . consults ghosts or spirits or calls up the dead. For the man who does these things is detestable to the Lord your God.'[2] As a result of Saul's legislation, those who had been responsible for such practices – which had clearly been rife earlier – were either driven out of Israelite domains or obliged to continue in secret.[3]

Despite this, even within Saul himself, although repressed, the old beliefs still exerted a strong superstitious hold, just as to this day many professed Christians still feel urged to consult their 'stars', or astrological horoscopes even though these things form no part of their faith. Heavily beleaguered by a declaration of war by the Philistines, and finding no automatic source of advice coming by the old way into his mind ('the Lord gave him no answer, either by dream or oracle or prophet'),[4] Saul felt he had to go even against his own laws in order to find out what fate had in store for him. His only recourse seemed to be to seek communication with the one man sure to be able to give him the right advice: the recently deceased Samuel, by whom he had been anointed as first king of the Israelite people.

There follows one of the most intriguing and dramatic episodes in the Book of Samuel: Saul's seeking out, with the help of aides, of the sinister and necromantic witch of Endor. After a 24-hour fast, Saul goes to this woman under cover of darkness and in disguise, commanding her: 'Disclose the future to me by means of a ghost (*'obh*). Conjure up the one I shall name to you. . . . Conjure up Samuel.'[5]

The witch protests about the illegality of what she has been asked to do, but being assured by Saul of her safety, she answers him: 'I see a ghost [the word in the original was *elohim*, Hebrew for a 'god'] rising up from the earth.'

Saul asks: 'What is it like?'

The witch replies: 'It is an old man coming up; he is wrapped in a cloak.'

We are told: 'Then Saul knew it was Samuel.'

To Saul's chagrin the emergent Samuel grumbles at him in no uncertain terms for his temerity in calling him up. But he tells Saul what he has come to hear, except that this prognostication turns out to be what Saul most definitely does not want to hear: that he will fail.

The intriguing feature is that here we have from three thousand years ago (Saul is thought to have flourished between *c.* 1030 and 1010 BC) an example of a purported communication with a dead person that not only significantly differs from Odysseus' offerings method, but also essentially embodies all the elements we would today associate with spiritualism. There is the intermediacy of a 'medium', in the form of the witch. There are surroundings of darkness and secrecy. And there is the need for this medium to tell Saul what she is purportedly seeing and hearing on his behalf – perhaps, although we are not told this directly, by appearing to allow the dead Samuel to speak through her.

Inevitably, in a manner quite different to what had gone on before, we are immediately presented with the opportunity for fraud, and the problem of one person having to accept another on trust. Such considerations would appear to have been already familiar even to those as early as the fifth century BC, as evident from the remarks about the so-called 'seers' or *manteis* of the time put into the mouth of the Messenger in Euripides' play *Helen*:

> I perceived how seers' craft is rotten and full of false-
> hood. . . . Why . . . do we have seers at all? We should ask
> good things directly from the gods with sacrifices, and leave
> seers alone. For this invention was a snare and a delusion.[6]

With the majority of the population no longer experiencing the dead for themselves, those isolated individuals who retained or appeared to retain this faculty were highly prized. The gift was recognized as such by no less a person than St Paul in his first letter to the Corinthians: 'The particular way in which the Spirit is given to each person is for a good purpose. One may have the gift of preaching . . . another prophecy, another the gift of recognising spirits.'[7]

Yet when St Paul's Christianity spread around the known world, oddly it did not bring with it any greater certainty about the nature of the after death state, but rather a greater uncertainty. For although shrines were built upon the graves of the revered dead, as if there was a certain power to these (as in the case of the Vatican, built upon the grave of St Peter), no one seems to have been sure whether the dead remained effectively unconscious in their graves, waiting for a final Day of Judgement, or whether they passed with full consciousness either into some intermediate state or directly to heaven or hell. To this day Roman Catholics include in their mass prayers for the dead, as if these can be helped by some intercessions even beyond the grave. But Protestants have traditionally rejected such ideas and only recently have relaxed in these views.

Despite these differences, Christians of all denominations have agreed on one thing: just as in Saul's day, all attempts to raise the spirits of the dead are totally unacceptable. In line with such views, most particularly from the end of the Middle Ages to the end of the Reformation, anyone who even mildly exhibited some of the 'old' faculties was likely to be burnt as a witch – thus further reducing the incidence of 'throw-backs' to the old forms of consciousness except in more remote areas such as the Scottish Highlands.

It was perhaps fortuitous, therefore, that, just at the time when the burning of witches was beginning to wane, there was born in Sweden one man who, because of his apparent natural faculty for communication with the dead, might well have had his career abruptly checked had he come on the scene earlier. This was Emanuel Swedenborg, born in Stockholm in 1688. The son of a rather tendentious Lutheran bishop and professor of theology, Swedenborg had, by all contemporary accounts, inherited more of his mother's more desirable characteristics, 'smiling blue eyes', and a 'reasonable, polite and open-hearted' disposition.[8] One of Swedenborg's particularly interesting features is that initially everything in his career suggests that he had a firmly practical rather than a 'head-in-the-clouds' frame of mind. At the University of Upsala he learned mathematics and science, subsequently journeying to London and Oxford to talk about these subjects with, among others, the astronomer Edmund Halley. He worked for the king of Sweden as royal engineer, became a specialist in mining and metallurgy, founded Sweden's first Scientific Society, recommended decimal coinage, and conducted some original researches in a variety of other fields, including geology, algebra, and crystallography.

Alongside such interests Swedenborg developed a fascination for questions concerning the nature of what we call the mind or soul. Puzzling about the 'inner voice' he could hear within himself, he kept notes on the dreams he experienced – including, to the shock of subsequent generations, those of a sexual nature. From 1743 he began receiving some extraordinary night-time experiences that included visions of angels and saints ascending heavenly staircases. However much Swedenborg tried to rationalize these away, for him they seemed unmistakably to be insights into the 'Kingdom of God', and culminated in what might be described as the core experience of his life, the night of 6 April 1744 in Amsterdam, during which he seemed to have a direct vision of Jesus:

> I . . . saw him face to face. It was a face of such holy mien and everything indescribable and smiling so that I believe this was how he looked when he was alive. . . . I woke, trembling, and came again into the state where I was neither asleep nor awake but in thought as to what this might mean, was it Christ, the son of God, whom I saw?[9]

Whatever the nature of this experience, it changed Swedenborg's life and marked the jumping-off point for some extraordinary claims by him of virtually spontaneous communications with the dead and other insights of a supernormal order. By direct experience, for instance, Swedenborg contended he now knew what happened to the soul after death; it certainly did not lie unconscious in the grave waiting for some Last Judgement. When Swedenborg's former teacher, the engineer Christopher Polhem, died, Swedenborg noted in his diary:

> Polhem died on Monday. He spoke with me on Thursday; and when I was invited to his funeral he saw his coffin, and those who were there, and the whole procession, and also when his body was laid in the grave; and in the meantime he spoke with me, asking why he was buried when he was still alive: and he heard also when the priest said that he would be resuscitated at the Last Judgement and yet he had been resuscitated for some time; and he marvelled that such a belief should exist, as that men should be resuscitated at the Last Judgement, when he was still alive; and that the body should rise again when yet he himself was sensible of being in a body.[10]

The idea of an individual's lifelong sinfulness being swept aside by a last-minute show of penitence was, according to Swedenborg, discredited by his experiencing of the after death state of another individual he had known in life, executed nobleman Eric Brahe. Swedenborg wrote: 'after two days [following his death] he began to return to his former state of life, which was to love worldy things, and after three days he became just as he previously was in the world'.[11]

From apparent experiences such as these, Swedenborg talked with increasing confidence about what the after death state was like. Among many features he said were too incredible to relate, he remarked on the dead person's customary meeting up with friends and relatives who had gone before:

> A spirit of a man recently departed from the world is . . . recognised by his friends, and by those whom he had known in the world . . . wherefore they are instructed by their friends concerning the state of eternal life.[12]

What most impressed Swedenborg's contemporaries were the instances in which he appeared to be able to demonstrate proof that he was in touch with the dead. In 1761, for example, he was approached by the Countess de Marteville, widow of the late Dutch ambassador, a woman in great distress on account of being pressed for payment of a very large sum of money by a goldsmith called Croon. Croon said he was owed this money for a silver service which, before his death, the Count had ordered from him for a gift to the Countess. Although the Countess was convinced her husband had paid for the service, she could find no receipt or any other form of proof among his papers.

Three days after the Countess had come to him Swedenborg arrived at her house when she was entertaining guests to coffee. He told her that he had managed to contact the dead Count – according to some sources in one of his 'dreams' – and that the money had been paid to Croon seven months before the Count's death, the receipt being apparently in the Count's bureau. On the Countess's insistence that she had already searched this bureau, Swedenborg explained that

> after pulling out the left-hand drawer a board would appear which required to be drawn out, when a secret compartment would be disclosed containing his [the Count's] private Dutch correspondence as well as the receipt.[13]

Sure enough, when the Countess's guests accompanied her to the bureau, there was found the secret compartment; inside was the receipt, just as Swedenborg had described. By the most unexpected of means Croon's attempt at extortion was seemingly exposed.

Another such story involved no less a personage than Queen Louisa

Ulrica of Sweden, sister of Frederick the Great of Prussia, a woman described by the rationalist Immanuel Kant as 'a princess whose great understanding and penetration ought to have made an attempt at imposition almost impossible'. Here is the contemporary courtier Count von Höpken's account of the incident:

> Swedenborg was one day at a Court reception. Her Majesty asked him about different things in the other life, and lastly whether he had seen or had talked with her brother, the Prince Royal of Prussia [with whom, prior to his death, Queen Ulrica had been secretly corresponding while Sweden and Prussia were at war] He [Swedenborg] answered No. Her Majesty then requested him to ask for him and to give him her greeting, which Swedenborg promised to do. I doubt whether the Queen meant anything serious by it. At the next reception, Swedenborg again appeared at Court . . . and approached her Majesty, who no longer remembered the commission she had given him a week before. Swedenborg not only greeted her from her brother, but also gave her his apologies for not answering her last letter; he also wished to do so now through Swedenborg, which he accordingly did. The Queen was greatly overcome, and said, 'No one except God knows this secret.'[14]

One of the impressive features of many of these stories is that, rather than being merely completely anecdotal, they were often noted at the time in the diaries of individuals who either were direct witnesses of what took place, or had personally interviewed those who were direct witnesses. Queen Ulrica, for instance, when questioned on her particular encounter with Swedenborg, preferred not to go into the details; but she described herself as 'hard to fool', and confirmed the incident's essential truth.[15]

Such stories were buttressed by others, equally well attested, of Swedenborg's apparent powers of viewing events at a distance. In July 1759, when he was reportedly one of fifteen guests at the Gothenburg house of a wealthy merchant, William Castel, he suddenly became very agitated at about six in the evening, and announced that three hundred miles away in Stockholm where he had his home a very big fire had broken out. He described where it was burning and where and when it had started, and began to calm down only when, via whatever was the source of these insights, he satisfied himself that the fire had stopped before reaching his house. He reported the fire to Gothenburg's governor the next day, and it took a further day before news of the fire reached the city via normal channels, the details apparently corresponding exactly with what Swedenborg had described. In another instance, while attending a dinner in Amsterdam in July 1762, he 'saw' the murder, hundreds of miles to the east, of Tsar Peter III of Russia, asking those who were with him to note down the date and details of what he told them, so that these could be checked when news of this event reached them several days later. Apparently everything he told them turned out to be correct.

For the rationalists who came across Swedenborg in such circumstances one of his most disarming qualities was his matter-of-factness and lack of signs of mental derangement. In the words of one contemporary, 'all this he reports without a screw seeming to be loose in the clockwork in other respects'.[16] Without the slightest bitterness Swedenborg accepted that many would receive his claims with considerable scepticism:

> I am well aware that many will say that no one can possibly speak with spirits and angels so long as he lives in the body; and many will say that it is all fancy, others that I relate such things in order to gain credence, and others will make other objections. But by all this I am not deterred, for I have seen, I have heard, I have felt.[17]

Perhaps because of these qualities, plus the fact that he seemed so thoroughly pleasant, polite, and inoffensive, Swedenborg lived until a ripe old age. He died in London on 29 March 1772, having created sufficient impact that a new church grew up in his name, which continues to this day. Of course he did not convince or impress everyone; Immanuel Kant levelled a stringent attack on him. And however warmly we from two centuries on might feel disposed towards him, some of his claims, such as to have conversed with creatures from the Moon, Venus, and Mars, take a little swallowing. But whatever we are to make of him, if Swedenborg had any validity this was as a one-off, gadgetless, natural communicator-with-the-dead of the old type, and therefore a far cry from what would follow within a century of his death: the birth of the so-called spiritualist movement.

In December 1847, across the Atlantic in the small community of Hydesville, near Rochester, New York State, Methodist farmer James D. Fox moved into a clapboard cottage, to be shortly joined by his wife and family (Figure 5). The cottage was one in which a previous tenant, Mr Weekman, had been disturbed by inexplicable loud knocks, and

Fig. 5. The Fox family's Hydesville cottage, and the Fox sisters. The cottage, of which a replica stands on the present-day site, is claimed as the birthplace of modern Spiritualism

these continued with the Foxes. Daughters fifteen-year-old Margaretta and eleven-year-old Kate became so used to their 'ghost' that they gave him a pet-name, 'Mr Splitfoot', although they also professed to be sufficiently frightened of his disturbances to insist on sleeping in the same bedroom as their parents, but in separate beds.

Then, on Friday, 31 March 1848, Kate, the younger daughter, appears to have had an idea. Deciding to try to strike up some direct form of communication with the intruder via a code, she called out, 'Mr Splitfoot, do as I do', and began to snap her fingers. To everyone's astonishment, the noises were repeated as if by an echo.

Intrigued, Mrs Margaret Fox, the girls' mother, tried her turn at the experiment. 'Do as I do,' she called out, starting to clap her hands very deliberately. Again what seemed to be exactly imitative sounds were heard in response. As Mrs Fox subsequently set down in her account of the event:

> I then thought I could put a test that no one in the place could answer. I asked the noise to rap my different children's ages, successively. Instantly, each one of my children's ages was given correctly, pausing between them sufficiently long to individualise them until the seventh, at which a longer pause was made and then three more emphatic little raps were given, corresponding to the age of the little one that died.[18]

Deciding to use the rapping method to enter into a fuller means of communication, Mrs Fox now asked the unseen entity if it was a human being. Receiving no reply, she then asked:

'Is it a spirit? If it is, make two raps.'

Promptly the cottage appeared to resound to two very loud bangs. By further questions of this kind Mrs Fox established that this 'spirit' seemed to be that of a man who had been murdered in the house. He had been thirty-one years of age at the time of his death, and had a wife and five children.

The Foxes then called in their neighbours. It was one of these, William Duesler, who by patiently continuing with Mrs Fox's rapping codes elicited from the purported spirit the information that his name was Charles B. Rosma, a pedlar apparently murdered five years previously by the cottage's tenant at that time, a Mr Bell. Enquiries subsequently made of a maid who had worked at the cottage, Lucretia Pulver, revealed that there had indeed been a pedlar who had briefly stayed at the cottage during Mr Bell's tenancy. Lucretia had been sent back to her home on one particular night; and on her return the next day, the pedlar had disappeared.

On the Sunday further contacts were made with the purported spirit, who indicated that his body had been buried in the cottage's cellar. Although everyone immediately began digging in the cellar, their efforts were foiled by flooding of the underlying subsoil, and it was only four months later, when this had dried out, that beneath a plank at a depth of five feet there came to light some human hair and a few bones in quicklime. This discovery was sufficient to cause some questions to be asked of Mr Bell on his being traced to Lyon, New York, but it was insufficient for any charge to be brought, not least because no one at any time found evidence of the one-time existence of any Charles B. Rosma.

Accordingly, to this day the saga of the Fox sisters remains enigmatic. A case can be made out for it all having begun as a slightly premature April Fool's Day joke which went too far, for perhaps more than suspiciously the night of the rappings was that of 31 March. Similarly suspicious is the fact that when Kate and Margaretta were moved away from Hydesville they continued to be able to engender 'spirit' rappings wherever they went. Their elder sister Leah swiftly claimed the same 'powers', losing little time putting them to commercial use. Most pointedly, forty years after the original events, by which time Margaretta and Kate were in their fifties and had become alcoholics, Margaretta came to an arrangement with a journalist whereby for a fee of $1,500 she appeared on the stage of New York's Academy of Music to confess to having faked all the 'spirit' communications by cracking a double joint in her big toe, even giving a demonstration of how she did this.

It might all therefore seem open and shut, were it not for the fact that *in extremis* alcoholics can and will say almost anything for money, and Margaretta did subsequently retract her confession. Oddly enough, when in November 1904 a wall of the Foxes' Hydesville cottage collapsed, behind this, apparently having been deliberately walled in, was found a male skeleton and a pedlar's tin box. Although one would like to know more about this particular find, the possibility remains that these really were the bones of Charles B. Rosma and might account for his mysterious rappings.

Whatever their credibility, the events in that Hydesville cottage sparked off a revolution of enthusiasm for 'spiritualist' phenomena that swept not only the United States but also most of Europe. Within a few months of the Fox sisters' first-ever public demonstration of modern spiritualism at their local Corinthian Hall in Rochester in November 1849, they were at the Barnum Hotel, New York, giving their first professional seances. Not far away, in Buffalo, New York State, three other young people, Ira, William, and Elisabeth Davenport, began producing more 'spirit' messages via raps, table turning, and automatic writing. In Dover, Ohio, farmer Jonathan Koons built a log cabin where his eight purportedly psychic children could hold seances, and in which invisible 'spirits' played on thoughtfully provided musical instruments.

In England there appeared an extraordinary medium in the person of Daniel Douglas Home, whom some people occasionally thought they saw rise in the air of his own accord. Like the Koonses, Douglas Home seemed to be able to cause instruments such as accordions to play in the air.

During the ensuing decades Home was followed by all manner of other practitioners of the art of communicating with 'spirits', all attempting to provide yet more elaborate 'proof' of their powers. For some this was 'materializations', both of 'spirits' and of physical objects. The enormously proportioned medium Mrs Agnes Guppy, for instance, 'materialized' whole showers of fresh flowers, a large block of ice, and even, according to one story, herself, having on one occasion 'tele-ported' herself over a distance of four miles to arrive with a great crash in the midst of a hushed and darkened seance.

To Mrs Guppy's chagrin, however, in terms of popularity such feats were no match for the less spectacular but altogether more sexy performances of her attractive young rival Florence Cook. At the latter's seances – conducted, in the prevailing fashion, in near total darkness – Florence would take up position inside a carefully curtained cabinet, from which in due course a white-clad female 'spirit' would emerge and mingle with those present, even allowing herself to be felt. No less an individual than the physicist William Crookes, later to become Sir William Crookes, heard of Florence's powers and devised a series of apparently foolproof tests, carried out in his own home and at the medium's seance rooms, which seemed to confirm her genuineness.

Such was the inter-medium rivalry that Mrs Guppy, convinced that Florence Cook's 'spirits' had to be Florence herself in disguise, planned for vitriol to be thrown during one of Florence's 'materializations'. Her ruse backfired when those whom she tried to persuade to carry out this deed threatened to expose her instead. None the less that Agnes Guppy was right would seem to have been demonstrated by no less an individual than Sir George Sitwell, father of Edith, Osbert, and Sacheverell. On attending a Florence Cook seance in 1880, Sir George broke all the rules by seizing the materialization of the moment, a spirit called 'Marie', and holding her struggling and all too-solid-body fast until a light had been brought. As might be expected, 'Marie' turned out to be none other than Florence Cook herself, clad in just her Victorian-style underwear, with her outer clothes back in the cabinet. To explain it all Florence insisted that she had been in a trance, and did not know what she was doing – an explanation which Sir William Crookes, for reasons best known to himself, accepted. For the sceptic the only sensible interpretation has been that Sir William, probably along with many other Victorian gentlemen, used his apparent scientific investigations into Florence's 'materializations' as a cover for a clandestine affair with her, not surprising given the intimacies which darkened seance rooms made possible. In her later life Florence became a Battersea prostitute, and is said ultimately to have confessed that Sir William was in collusion with her all along, [19] although some still hold Crookes in too high regard to believe this.

It was a mad, mad world, a far cry from the unsophisticated experiences which Swedenborg had claimed, and all too needing of a spirit not of the 'materialization' kind but of sound sense. Not before time, therefore, was there born of the inspiration of two Fellows of Trinity College, Cambridge, Edmund Gurney and Frederick Myers, the idea for an organization properly to investigate after death and similar experiences, an organization which in 1882 took formal shape as Britain's Society for Psychical Research. In the course of subsequent years this would attract, besides its inevitable share of those who would continue to be gullible, individuals of genuine critical calibre; its membership would include two Nobel prizewinners, eight Fellows of the Royal Society, a variety of philosophers, physicists, psychologists, psychiatrists, medical specialists, electrical and electronics experts, and even a future Prime Minister, A. J. Balfour. Not to be outdone, within three years, across the other side of the Atlantic, William James and others founded the American Society for Psychical Research, which dedicated itself to similar aims.

As the subsequent years showed, the need for proper scrutiny of all those who claimed to be able to raise spirits and the like had been long overdue. On proper investigation the performances of one medium after another proved to have nothing to do with real communications from the dead. There were, for instances, those seances in which so-called 'physical' mediums produced materializations of physical objects of the kind pioneered by Mrs Guppy and her contemporaries. For one of these Society for Psychical Research investigator Everard Feilding equipped himself with a pair of scissors and pink baby ribbon, and deliberately arrived early. Shown into the seance room and asked to wait, he looked behind the curtains where he noted some attached prawns. What happened next has been described by Society for Psychical Research editor Renée Haynes:

He instantly provided each with an elegant pink sash; and so adorned they later appeared as 'psychic apports from the seaside'. History does not relate either whether they had been boiled or what the medium, or the other sitters, thought.[20]

In other seances, without full physical materializations of the Florence Cook kind, there were shadowy human 'spirit' – forms glimpsed in the semi-darkness. When investigators smuggled in flash-light cameras, the 'spirits' were revealed as nothing more than crude stage-props. There were mediums who appeared to produce from their mouths a psychic substance they called 'ectoplasm'. When these were photographed, and clandestine means found for obtaining physical samples of the 'ectoplasm', this was found to be nothing more than butter-muslin, of which a considerable quantity could be popped into the mouth to be dribbled out at appropriate moments.

There were those like William Eglinton, who professed to be able to receive 'spirit' messages on a special slate – until sharp-eyed Mrs Sidgwick, wife of one of the founders of the Society for Psychical Research, spotted him to be indulging in nothing more than a conjuring trick. Others purported to levitate tables – until smuggled-in photography revealed them to be using hidden rods and other contrivances. There were those such as G. H. Moss, who made as his speciality 'spirit' photographs of those who had died, seen wraith-like alongside the real photograph of the bereaved – until investigator F. Barlow spotted the signs of how Moss had doctored his photographic plates. Not least were those who produced 'spirit voices' of the dead, as in the case of one William Roy, highly successful until 1955, when it was found that he had an accomplice who would search his audiences' belongings for informational data while they were seated in the seance room. The accomplice would then relay this to Roy, along with some of the appropriate 'voices', via a tiny radio receiver hidden in Roy's ear.

The early psychical researchers were often accused of being too hyper-critical. As the Irish poet W. B. Yeats once told a woman researcher: 'It's my belief that if you psychical researchers had been around when God Almighty was creating the world, He couldn't have done the job.'[21] But in view of the long, consistent, and depressing history of exposures there can be not the slightest doubt that the vast majority of supposed communications with 'spirits' of the dead produced during the last hundred years can be explained away as fraud, leaving the serious question of whether anything of such material can be considered genuine. On this the American Society for Psychical Research's William James uttered some still apposite words of wisdom nearly a century ago: 'If you wish to upset the law that all crows are black, you must not seek to show that no crows are, it is enough if you prove the single crow to be white.'[22]

In other words, even if there could be found only one truly verifiable mediumistic demonstration of an after death experience this could compensate for all the hundreds of frauds. Has there ever been such a 'white crow'? Could there be one practising today?

# 6

# IN SEARCH OF WHITE CROWS

For William James, back in 1885, if there was a 'white crow' it was a stout and matronly Bostonian lady by the name of Mrs Leonora Piper, who had begun her career in mediumship merely a year before the formation of the American Society for Psychical Research. James happened to be told about Mrs Piper by his mother-in-law, and when he inquisitively visited her for a trial seance he carefully concealed his identity. But, in the trance state she assumed, Mrs Piper told him such astonishingly accurate details about his family background, including the death the previous year of his son Herman (whom she called Herrn), that James felt impelled to investigate her further.

In fact, pressure of work prevented James from doing this for the next five years. But during this time another investigator, Richard Hodgson, who had had his own equally revelatory sitting with Mrs Piper, set private detectives following the medium's every move in order to try to find some way in which she might have been cheating. Nothing untoward came to light.

The difficult-to-take feature of Mrs Piper's seances – as in those of other mediums – was her use of various bizarrely named 'spirit guides' or 'controls'. One of her favourites was French-accented 'Dr Phinuit', purportedly a French doctor, yet one who appeared to exhibit little knowledge either of medicine or of the French language. Others included 'Julius Caesar', 'Moses of Old', 'Longfellow', 'Sir Walter Scott', 'George Eliot', and 'Imperator'. Some talked arrant nonsense; yet, whether imaginary or otherwise, they seemed to be needed as mediators between Mrs Piper and the world of the dead. So far as most studies on Mrs Piper and others have determined, these 'controls' appear to be nothing more than splinterings of the medium's personality, akin to the sort of multiple personalities – all of them illusory – assumed by individuals such as 'Eve' of the famous 'Three Faces of Eve' case.

As William James was aware, however bizarre the means, what mattered was the results, and it was difficult not to be impressed by the detail and fluency (although we have met these very features before in the case of Jane Evans) of the material which 'come through' to Mrs

Piper via her intermediaries. The following is a transcript of a sitting which Mrs Piper held on 8 December 1893 for a Revd and Mrs S. W. Sutton of Athol Center, Massachusetts. The Suttons had recently lost their daughter Katherine, and had been pseudonymously booked in for their appointment, via the investigator Hodgson, as a Mr and Mrs Smith; so theoretically there was no way in which Mrs Piper should have known anything about them. The details in italics are Mrs Sutton's notes and observations on what Mrs Piper, via 'Phinuit', told her:

> Phinuit said . . . A little child is coming to you. . . . He reaches out his hands as to a child, and says coaxingly: Come here, dear. Don't be afraid. Come, darling, here is your mother. He describes the child and her 'lovely curls'. Where is Papa? Want Papa. [*He (Phinuit) takes from the table a silver medal.*] I want this – want to bite it [*she used to bite it*]. [*Reaches for a string of buttons.*] Quick! I want to put them in my mouth. [*The buttons also. To bite the buttons was forbidden. He exactly imitated her arch manner.*] . . . Who is Dodo? [*Her name for her brother George.*] . . . I want you to call Dodo. Tell Dodo I am happy. Cry for me no more. [*Puts hands to throat.*] No sore throat any more. [*She had pain and distress of the throat and tongue.*] Papa, speak to me. Can you not see me? I am not dead, I am living. I am happy with Grandma [*My mother had been dead many years.*] Phinuit says: Here are two more. One, two, three here – one older and one younger than Kakie. [*Correct.*] . . . Was this little one's tongue very dry? She keeps showing me her tongue. [*Her tongue was paralysed, and she suffered much with it to the end.*] Her name is Katherine. [*Correct.*] She calls herself Kakie. She passed out last . . . [*Correct.*] Kakie sings: Bye, bye, ba bye bye, O baby bye. Sing that with me, Papa. [*Papa and Kakie sing. These two were the songs she used to sing.*] Where is Dinah? I want Dinah. [*Dinah was an old black rag-doll, not with us.*] I want Bagie. [*Her name for her sister Margaret.*] I want Bagie to bring me my Dinah. . . . Tell Dodo when you see him that I love him. Dear Dodo. He used to march with me, he put me way up. [*Correct.*][1]

The problem that arises is how 'Phinuit' alias Mrs Piper could possibly have known so many genuinely intimate personal details, such as Katherine's pet-name for her brother and the names she gave her dolls, unless he/she was somehow in communication with the dead child. If it might be thought that Mrs Piper had an efficient spy network, or gathered her material from local gossip, this tends to be discounted by the fact that four years prior to her sitting with the Suttons she had been invited to England, where she performed with equal fluency and apparent 'inside' knowledge from the very first night of her arrival. Even with officers of the Society for Psychical Research monitoring her every move, and controlling her post, nothing suspicious was noted.

Another possibility that William James considered early on in his study of Mrs Piper was that of telepathy – that perhaps she was just tuning into or tapping into information in the living minds of her subjects. Accordingly, with the medium's ready agreement, he tried hypnotizing her while she was in the ordinary waking state, then subjecting her, while she was in hypnotic trance, to various tests for telepathy. But she showed not the slightest aptitude for these.

One of the only jarring notes in all that is known of Mrs Piper came in 1909 when a· sitter called Dr Hall asked her if she could help him communicate with his dead niece, Bessie Beales. The 'control' of the time duly obliged with various reminiscences, only to be told by Dr Hall that 'Bessie' was a person he had completely invented to test out Mrs Piper's mediumship. The 'control' brushed this aside by explaining that 'he' had genuinely been in touch with a real person called Jessie whom he now realized was related to another sitter. And despite this incidental aberration, James never wavered from the conclusion 'My own white crow is Mrs Piper. In the trances of this medium I cannot resist the conviction that knowledge appears which she has never gained by the ordinary waking use of her eyes and ears and wits.'[2]

In England very much an equivalent to Mrs Piper, though younger, was Mrs Gladys Osborne Leonard, who began her career on the stage, in minor acting roles, and married into the same profession. Gladys's youthful dabbling in 'spirit communication' by table-tilting and other means was severely frowned on by her conventionally minded parents, but it was in fact a 'death experience' of her mother which seems to have impelled Gladys into her mediumship. One morning she woke up at two o'clock to be confronted by a vivid image of her mother looking much younger and healthy, seemingly bathed in light. Later that day there arrived a telegram: 'Mother passed away at two o'clock this morning.' After this she became increasingly more interested in spiritualism, soon developing her own equivalent of Mrs Piper's 'Dr Phinuit' in the form of a 'control' called 'Feda', purportedly the spirit of an Indian girl who had died in childbirth, after a marriage to one of Mrs Leonard's ancestors, about the year 1800.

At face value 'Feda' is as difficult to take seriously as Mrs Piper's 'Phinuit' and companions. Characteristically she spoke in the third person in a very squeaky, high-pitched, almost baby-talk manner. Yet through 'Feda' Gladys Osborne Leonard's mediumship rapidly became as convincing as Leonora Piper's. She turned professional on the outbreak of the First World War, thus taking advantage of the large number of bereaved at this time who would come flocking for her services.

To those who came to her, Mrs Leonard would sometimes produce insights very similar to those of Swedenborg. For example, in 1921 a certain Mrs Dawson Smith sought the medium's services in an attempt to communicate with her son, who had died just a year before. During this sitting, 'Feda' seemed to try to convey from the son some importance attached to 'an old purse with a receipt in it, a counterfoil'. Initially this meant little to Mrs Dawson Smith, until she found herself pressed for payment, via the Enemy Debt Clearing Office, of a bill for a large sum of money that her son apparently owed to a firm in Hamburg. Like Swedenborg's Countess, Mrs Dawson Smith felt sure that the money had been paid, but was at a loss for any means of proof; then she recalled the medium's message about the purse and the receipt. After a search, her son's 'old purse' came to light, and inside, sure enough, was a money order counterfoil made payable in Hamburg for the amount in question.[3]

Cases like these, in which even the sitter had no direct knowledge of the message being imparted, seemed to rule out telepathy between medium and sitter. None the less, as in the case of Mrs Piper, the Society for Psychical Research's investigators tried to devise every means of eliminating this as a possibility. The Revd Drayton Thomas, who made an exhaustive study of Mrs Leonard, made a particular practice of attending sittings with her on behalf of other individuals who might be hundreds of miles away. Yet still in these so-called 'proxy sittings' remarkably impressive details 'came through'. One example was a sitting Thomas attended on behalf of a Mrs Lewis, who wanted to communicate with her dead father, former hydraulics engineer Frederick William Macaulay. As in Mrs Piper's seance with the Suttons, particularly interesting were Mrs Lewis's comments on the transcript of 'Feda's' utterances that Thomas provided for her:

*Feda*: There is a John and Harry, both with him. And Race . . . Rice . . . Riss . . . It might be Reece but sounds like Riss, and Francis. These are all names of people who are connected with him, or linked up with him in the past,

connected with happy times. I get the feeling of an active
and busy home in which he was rather happy.

*[Mrs Lewis: This is a curious passage. . . . Probably the
happiest time of my father's life was in the four or five years
before the war, when we, his five children, were all at
school, and the home was packed with our friends during
the holidays. John, Harry and Francis could be three of
these. . . . But the most interesting passage is 'It might be
Reece but it sounds like Riss'. . . . My elder brother was at
school at Shrewsbury and there conceived a kind of hero-
worship for one of the 'Tweaks' (sixth-form boys) whose
name was Rees. He wrote home about him several times
and always drew attention to the fact that the name was
spelt 'Rees' and not 'Reece'. In the holiday my sister and I
used to tease him by singing 'Not Reece but Riss' until my
father stopped us. . . .]*

Feda: I get a funny word now . . . could he be interested
in . . . baths of some kind? Ah, he says I have got the right
word, baths. He spells it, BATHS. His daughter will
understand, he says. It is not something quite ordinary,
but feels something special.

*[Mrs Lewis: This is, to me, the most interesting thing that has
yet emerged. Baths were always a matter of joke in our
family – my father being very emphatic that water must not
be wasted by our having too big baths or by leaving taps
dripping. It is difficult to explain how intimate a detail this
seems. . . . The mention of baths here also seems to me an
indication of my father's quaint humour, a characteristic
which has hitherto been missing.]*[4]

According to Drayton Thomas's overall evaluation of this at-a-
distance sitting with Mrs Leonard, out of 124 different factual elements
which 'Feda' provided, only 22 were doubtful and 5 definitely wrong,
while 51 were positively right and a further 12 classifiable as 'good'.
Independently, a three-mouth-long monitoring experiment conducted
on Mrs Leonard by the Society for Psychical Research in 1918, during
which Society officers handled all her appointments and made comprehensive stenographic notes, produced a considerable amount that
was accurate, and only occasional though none the less serious
gaffes. One client, a Mr L. P. Jacks, was told that his son had been
killed in the war, whereas, as subsequently emerged, he was very
definitely alive. In another instance the reverse was the case: 'Feda'

reported a missing soldier alive when, as it transpired, he was already dead.

Thus, while Mrs Piper and Mrs Leonard have both seemed astonishingly convincing, and neither was ever proved to be fraudulent, they were not totally unimpeachable, and frustrating question marks hover over each. Since Leonora Piper died in 1950 at the ripe old age of ninety-three, and Mrs Leonard died in 1968 at the age of eighty, neither is available today – at least on the physical plane! – for any fresh attempt at determining once and for all whether one or the other might really have been a 'white crow'.

So might there be a Spiritualist medium of the present-day who could be considered something of the Piper and Leonard calibre? Although she died just at the time this book was being prepared for press few both inside and outside of Spiritualist circles, would deny that there has been one person who, because of her remarkable public performances, on stage, on television, and on the radio, became virtually a household word for her mediumship: Doris Stokes. She was the subject of adulatory television shows in Britain, the United States, and Australia. Many show-business personalities became convinced by her. And she seemed doubly plausible because of her apparent tuning into the dead without any of the normal mediumistic paraphernalia of trances, darkened rooms, and quaverings of 'Are you there . . . ?' Like Piper and Leonard before her, Doris Stokes professed yet another improbable-sounding guide, a Tibetan lama called 'Ramonov'. But if he existed he had none of the intrusiveness of a 'Phinuit' or 'Feda'. To all appearances Doris Stokes seemed a totally 'natural' medium, with a pleasant smile and down-to-earth manner that seemed to reduce the business of talking to the dead almost to the ordinariness of a transatlantic telephone call.

From her writings, which include the best-selling autobiography *Voices in my Ear*,[5] it can be gleaned that Doris Stokes was born just after the end of the First World War. She was the daughter of blacksmith Sam Sutton and his washerwoman wife Jen, who lived in the small Lincolnshire town of Grantham, the same town where British Prime Minister Margaret Thatcher's father ran his grocery business. The Suttons were poor. To make matters worse, father Sam died when Doris was only thirteen, almost certainly the delayed result of the gassing he had sustained during the war. Even at this time Doris appeared to have had occasional 'after death' experiences, as when an elderly Grantham resident called Tom died when his house burned down. According to Doris, as Tom's blackened corpse was being carried away on a stretcher, she saw him 'real and solid, not a hair singed'.

Such occasional flashes of intuition reportedly continued into Doris's adult life. When war broke out she joined the WRAF to find herself uncannily 'knowing' which aircrafts would be the ones that would fail to return from a particular night's mission, In 1943 she married a paratroop sergeant, John; and her baby by him, John Michael, was born at a time when John was reported missing, believed killed, during the raid on Arnheim. Doris said that at this point her dead father appeared to her to tell her two items of news, one good, one bad. The good news was that husband John was still alive and would in due course be returned to her. The bad news was that baby John Michael would shortly die. Both these items of information proved correct, John Michael living for only six weeks, and paratrooper John, though a prisoner of war and with head injuries that would impair him throughout his working life, eventually gaining his release. Unable to have any further children, in due course Doris and John adopted Terry, an orphan, to bring up as their own son.

It was about the time of Terry joining the Stokeses' modest home that Doris, her fascination for after death matters continuing to grow, attended a seance conducted by Spiritualist medium Helen Duncan. Helen, a medium of the Florence Cook school of 'materialization', was warmly referred to by Doris as 'one of the greatest materialization mediums who ever lived', and seems to have been the direct inspiration for Doris to try the practice of mediumship herself, to supplement John's meagre earnings as a hospital porter. Not long afterwards Doris underwent and passed her first Spiritualist 'test seance' at Nottingham. Although she subsequently trained and qualified as a State Enrolled Nurse in Lancaster, she continued to practise her mediumship in her spare time, producing material as impressive-sounding as that of Piper and Leonard before her, as is evident from the following transcript made by one of her sitters:

> *Doris Stokes*: Does anybody know of someone that has died recently?
> *Sitter*: How recently?
> *Doris Stokes*: During this year.
> *Sitter*: Yes, I do.
> *Doris Stokes*: Does the name David mean anything to you?
> *Sitter*: Oh yes.
> *Doris Stokes*: This man has a young voice. It comes and goes, which means he hasn't been over very long and can't hold it. David is doing well but he finds it difficult. Did he die suddenly?
> *Sitter*: Yes.

*Doris Stokes*: My chest hurts and now my heart; did he have a heart condition?

*Sitter*: I don't know.

*Doris Stokes*: He asks if his car is at home all right.

*Sitter*: I don't know.

*Doris Stokes*: He mentions an inquest.

*Sitter*: Yes, that's right.

*Doris Stokes*: David says he remembers going out, coming back, going to the bathroom and nothing more until he found himself here. He came up with you today. He is trying to say your name, it begins with an 'M' (*She tried and tried and kept murmuring Majorie, Maisie, etc. but couldn't get it.*) Do you know of a relation on this side called Peter?

*Sitter*: Yes.

*Doris Stokes*: Now you are tired, David, rest a few moments and I will get someone else's vibrations. (*She mentioned names, illnesses and various happenings to everyone there. She paused and then said:*) I hear the word 'antiques'.

*Sitter*: David collected antiques, and so do I.

*Doris Stokes (holding up four fingers)*: Does this mean anything to you?

*Sitter*: Yes, David's four children.

*Doris Stokes*: David has three girls and a boy. Does the name Christopher mean anything?

*Sitter*: Oh yes, his son.

*Doris Stokes*: David says Christopher is not to be blamed in any way. He says he is sorry for what he did, he was doing so well for his children and wanted to do more. I have the name Jane.

*Sitter*: Yes, David's daughter.

*Doris Stokes*: Does anyone know the name Caroline?

*Sitter*: Yes, David's youngest daughter.

*Doris Stokes*: How long has David been over?

*Sitter*: Sunday evening.[6]

Such a string of correct names and other details was by no means unusual for a Doris Stokes seance, and was not only for the observation of those who attend formal Spiritualist meetings. As is now well known, Doris Stokes demonstrated her apparent powers to capacity audiences at some of the world's largest auditoriums, including the London Palladium and the Sydney Opera House. Wherever she went she seemed to be able to pick out apparently at random individuals for whom she volunteered messages from their dead loved ones, peppered with the same sort of homely detail that made the Piper and Leonard mediumships so convincing.

Just such a demonstration, which I personally attended, was one she held at the London Palladium on the evening of Sunday 16 November 1986. Typically, it was a complete sell-out, and four out of five of the audience were women. During the waiting beforehand the air seemed almost electric with expectations of Doris producing messages from dead loved ones. Indeed a straw poll of the evening revealed that one in two had previously attended a medium.

When Doris emerged on stage, taking her seat on a gilded and red velvet 'throne' facing the audience, it all seemed so disarmingly natural. She immediately relaxed the tension with a few jokes, explaining how she is not infallible and can sometimes get her wires crossed between 'this side' (that of the living) and the 'other side' (that of the dead). Since even telephone exchanges do the same, this was reasonable enough. Then, with a mere momentary stroking of her left ear-lobe as her only affectation of the onset of a 'trance', she was suddenly away. Almost immediately she reported hearing from the 'other side' someone whose name seemed to be Kelly or Kerry, with a surname sounding like Stennett. It was enough for a gasp to come from a smartly dressed mid-thirtyish woman in the front row. Ushered to the nearby microphone, this woman emotionally explained that her name was actually Stenning, and that Kerry was her daughter who had been critically injured in a road accident, and had recently died from her injuries.

Then the detail seemed to come thick and fast. Doris Stokes said she was getting the name 'Marilyn'. Mrs Stenning tremblingly identified this as her own Christian name. There was something about 'Kingston Road', which Mrs Stenning said was where she lived. Had Kerry died from a blood clot? Mrs Stenning confirmed this was correct. There were some names – 'Damian or Daniel . . . Peter . . . Peggy . . . Paul' – which did not seem to mean much to Mrs Stenning. But then Doris settled on 'Robert', whom Mrs Stenning identified as Kerry's boy-friend. The number '209' seemed to be important. Mrs Stenning said she thought this must be '239', the number of her address in Kingston Road. Doris described a 'Bill' as being on the 'other side' with Kerry. Mrs Stenning identified Bill as Kerry's dead grandfather, Bill's widow being actually with her in the Palladium audience, though in the upper circle. Doris Stokes said that Kerry was telling her that either her mother or her sister (sitting next to Mrs Stenning) was wearing something that had belonged to her. It transpired that Mrs Stenning was wearing Kerry's watch.

After the revelation of further incidental details, Doris Stokes seemed to tune into other apparent communicators on the 'other side'. There was a 'Bill' and an 'Irene', who were claimed by a silvery-haired widow, Mrs Elsie Scott, as her dead husband and daughter. Although to most in the audience these messages were somewhat confusing and difficult to follow, they seemed to satisfy Mrs Scott.

Then the atmosphere became electric again with Doris's announcement that she was getting messages from a young man called 'Graham'. He had only recently died, seemingly from a fall. The response was immediate from a smartly dressed and again emotional young woman, seated in the front row directly next to the microphone. As she was led forward, Doris Stokes said she was getting the name 'Dawn', which the young woman confirmed as her own name. According to Dawn, Graham had been her husband and had died a few weeks before. Doris told her she was actually 'seeing' Graham on the other side. He was auburn-haired – modified to fair-haired by Dawn – and was muscular and fond of exercise, which Dawn confirmed was correct. Doris imparted that Graham wanted to know whether Dawn had been to a solicitor; Dawn confirmed she had. Doris said that Graham was telling her 'the scaffold should have been safe'. Dawn explained that the cause of Graham's fall had been a scaffolding accident. There seemed to be private conversation between Doris and the unseen Graham, Doris then disclosing that Graham was telling her Dawn had been quite right to give the decision to switch off his 'ventilator'. This was apparently the life-support machine to which Graham had been attached on his admission to hospital. She said that as someone who had been 'always doing things' Graham would not have wanted to spend the rest of his life as a 'cabbage'.

Continuing in her communication with the unseen 'Graham', Doris imparted that he and Dawn had 'just had a baby'. This was a little girl called Tara, which Dawn confirmed was correct. Doris said she was getting the names 'Pat' and 'John'. Dawn identified these as her parents. There was also 'Margaret'. This was Graham's mother. She then appeared to go into another private conversation with 'Graham', in the course of this asking whether, with so many people listening, she could tell Dawn directly. Apparently told that she could, she gently conveyed to Dawn that, because she was still so young, Graham wanted her to know that she should not feel guilty about remarrying. As a final touch, she told Dawn that Graham had been with her while she had been looking at the photographs of him in their bedroom before leaving for the theatre.

After one other, more minor communication for a widow called Mrs

Crawforth, there was the show's interval, and then a question-time jumbling into a free-for-all of further much less specific names of individuals purportedly trying to communicate from the 'other side'. To anyone in the audience Doris's performance appeared totally, compulsively convincing. The grief of Marilyn Stenning for her daughter and of Dawn for her husband was all too obviously genuine, as was their gratitude to Doris Stokes for having been able to put them in touch with their dead loved ones. How could anyone as warm-hearted and down-to-earth as Doris be anything but what she seemed?

Should we therefore accept that Doris Stokes was a 'white crow' of our own time? Was she really in touch with those dead people that November night at the London Palladium? With me on that occasion, in a theatre box from which the whole show could be carefully observed, were television journalists Beth Miller and Siobhan Hockton, deputed, as originally intended, merely to the task of collecting the names and addresses of those audience members for whom Doris Stokes produced her communications, the intention being for these to be interviewed afterwards in proper depth.

But within a matter of a mere fifteen minutes Beth and Siobhan learned far more than they had expected, and on their return their reactions were of shock, disbelief, and downright anger. For as they had questioned one after another of those for whom Doris Stokes had produced messages, it emerged that there was nothing either psychic or coincidental in the fact that these were mostly seated close to, if not actually in, the theatre's front row. Not only had the key individuals been known to Doris beforehand; each been specially invited to the show by none other than Doris herself.

As Mrs Stenning disclosed, a friend had written to Doris Stokes on her behalf, telling her about Mrs Stenning's loss of her daughter Kerry. As a result, Doris Stokes had personally telephoned her at her home just the week before, offering her two complimentary tickets for the Palladium show. For Mrs Stenning this seemed nothing but an act of kindness to console her in her grief. As she told the researcher, 'All Doris knew about me was by name and phone number.' But she said this almost as if it was what Doris had told her was all she knew of her. And to my personal knowledge Doris Stokes's performance at the Palladium had been completely sold out several weeks beforehand – so why should Doris make Mrs Stenning the munificent gesture of such specially reserved front-of-house seats unless she knew sufficient about her to use her? At the very least the fact that Doris undeniably knew beforehand Mrs Stenning's surname, Christian name, and deceased daughter's name makes a charade of her professed hearing of these names as 'other side' voices. And with Doris's similarly undeniable prior knowledge of Mrs Stenning's telephone number, there is scarcely anything other-worldly about how she could have known Mrs Stenning's 239 Kingston Road address. She had only to look in the London telephone directory. It is in the list immediately below the entries for Stennett.

What of the elderly Mrs Elsie Scott? As if to allay suspicion, her seat happened to be some way back from the front row, and this had not been a complimentary one. But as she freely told the researchers, she came to see Doris as many times as she could. She always tried to get a seat near to the front so that she could get to the microphone easily, and 'Bill' and 'Irene' had come through on no less than three previous occasions. Two audience members, a Mrs Joan Oxlade and a Mrs Gladys Sellers, remembered Doris having produced similar messages for Elsie on previous occasions. So Elsie was a camp-follower, a doting and totally supportive regular whom Doris undoubtedly already knew of – just like Mrs Stenning – and could virtually count on to make a communication for if she so chose.

If all this already seemed more than mildly suspicious to Beth and Siobhan, what they learned relating to the tragic Dawn and her husband was even more so. As in the case of the other bereaved, they discovered that Doris Stokes again knew all about Dawn and Graham before she had ever set foot on that Palladium stage. When, after his fall, Graham lay in London's University College Hospital effectively brain-dead, the medical staff had gently advised Dawn that they might need her permission to switch off the life-support machine, and asked if there might be anyone she would like to talk to about this, perhaps a surgeon or a psychiatrist. Because she had read about Doris in a women's magazine, Dawn asked for Doris Stokes.

Accordingly as Dawn herself subsequently disclosed, someone whom she thought to be a hospital social worker telephoned Doris Stokes's agent, Laurie O'Leary, to ask if Doris Stokes might be persuaded to talk to Dawn. Shortly after, the medium was on the line to the hospital, speaking comfortingly to Dawn, and requesting her to telephone the next day with the news of the final, decisive tests that were to be carried out on Graham. She also spoke at some length to Dawn's mother, the 'Pat' referred to in her stage performance. When all was over, there was yet another call to Dawn; then, just as in the case of Mrs Stenning, she was on the line a week before the Palladium show, offering Dawn free tickets for her performance. Another kind gesture?

For the television journalists it was now transparently obvious that this Palladium show – and by implication all other of Doris Stokes's public performances[7] – was nothing more than a set-up, with the audience, inevitably ignorant of the behind-the-scene arrangements, hapless dupes, and the Dawns and Marilyn Stennings grateful and trusting stooges. Enquiries with the manager of the London Palladium revealed that Doris Stokes booked the front three rows of the theatre for her own purposes. No longer was there need to believe that Doris's information in any way came from the dead. All the hard and really impressive material Doris produced during the show had been known or available to her beforehand. Even in the second, more free-for-all half of the programme a young woman called Georgina from Chigwell in Essex, for whom Doris produced an impressive series of names, turned out to have been specially invited to the show, with Doris's agent Laurie O'Leary as the best friend of someone she knew. It was no accident that Doris's second-half free-for-all messages for non-pre-arranged individuals were much less convincing. For these she had to rely on intelligent guesswork and 'fishing'.

Was Doris Stokes, then, just another 'black crow' along with so many of the others we have encountered? It is unfortunate that the very medium she mentioned as having most inspired her in her choice of career, Helen Duncan ('one of the greatest materialization mediums who ever lived'),[8] was one of Spiritualism's greatest frauds. During the 1930s, when Helen Duncan flourished, her 'ectoplasm' manifestations were variously established as cheesecloth, surgical gauze, and stuck-together lavatory paper. Two of her 'materializations' were so incontrovertibly exposed as herself that for the second offence, in 1944, she was prosecuted at the Old Bailey for 'conspiracy to pretend that she was in touch with spirits', found guilty, and sentenced to serve nine months in gaol.[9]

Can Doris Stokes, so grandmotherly and personable, really have been in the same mould? In February 1987 I travelled to Canvey Island, Essex, to question Dawn in greater depth on her experiences with Doris Stokes. She surprised me by relating some remarkable insights Doris had shown, quite unprompted, in her telephone dealings with her mother, Pat. Doris had said, 'It's Pat and John, isn't it?' referring to Pat's husband. Then she said, 'I have an elderly lady with me – she's telling me her name is Violet', the name of Pat's deceased mother. And she mentioned other personal details which deeply affected Dawn. So might Doris Stokes really have been a genuine medium, perhaps, if we really view her charitably, rigging her shows through sheer fear of facing a huge audience with no 'other-worldly' messages coming through? It is conceivable. But there is another, more prosaic possibility: that she simply obtained her information about Pat and her family from Pat's sister, Jean Wallington, whom Dawn acknowledged to be a prominent Canvey Island Spiritualist.

Whatever the truth, on the most charitable assessment Doris Stokes was not all she seemed, and the most serious question marks hang over her. Although she may have provided some comfort for the millions who believe in her, it was no service if that comfort was based on such a large measure of pretence. The further tragedy is that, if there really is some form of continuing experience after death, the world's many living Doris Stokeses only obscure the search for this. So having somewhat exhausted the worlds of reincarnation and spiritualism, is there left any other avenue or trail to explore?

# 7

# SPONTANEOUS TRANSMISSIONS

Ironically, after all the purported 'solid' evidence for afterlife that we have seen – the so scientifically attested 'past life' memories, and the so-convincing 'messages' from spiritualist mediums – perhaps the most truly substantial evidence for some form of continuance after death happens also to be the most insubstantial: the experiencing of ghosts. As Dr Johnson once remarked on the spirits of the dead appearing to the living: 'Reason says no, something else says yes.'

We have already seen in earlier chapters how the experiencing of the dead for people in antiquity seems to have been a very much more natural and accepted phenomenon than for ourselves; the greater the development of civilization, the more this faculty faded. But whatever the validity of this, even in the most materialist and rationalist of ages there seem certain circumstances in which what we call ghosts have been spontaneously experienced, quite uninvited by the living. The Romans, for instance, were hard-headed enough, and their first-century writer Pliny particularly so. Pliny none the less thought worthy to relate in one of his letters a ghost story that in its embodied features is a classic in more ways than one:

> There was at Athens a large and spacious but ill-reputed and pestilential house. In the dead of the night a noise resembling the clashing of iron was frequently heard, which if you listened more attentively sounded like the rattling of fetters; at first it seemed at a distance but approached nearer by degrees; immediately afterward a phantom appeared in the form of an old man extremely meagre and squalid, with a long beard and bristling hair, rattling the fetters on his feet and hands. The poor inhabitants consequently passed sleepless nights under the most dismal terrors imaginable. . . . By this means the house was at last deserted, as being judged by everybody to be absolutely uninhabitable; so that it was now entirely abandoned to the ghost. However, in hopes that some tenant might be found who was ignorant of this great

calamity which attended it, a bill was put up, giving notice that it was either to be let or sold.

It happened that Athenodorus the philosopher came to Athens at this time, and reading the bill ascertained the price. The extraordinary cheapness raised his suspicion; nevertheless, when he heard the whole story, he was so far from being discouraged, that he was more strongly inclined to hire it, and, in short, actually did so. When it grew towards evening, he ordered a couch to be prepared for him in the fore-part of the house, and after calling for a light, together with his pen and tablets, he directed all his people to retire within. . . . The first part of the night passed with usual silence, then began the clanking of iron fetters; however, he neither lifted up his eyes, nor laid down his pen, but closed his ears by concentrating his attention. The noise increased and advanced nearer, till it seemed at the door, and at last in the chamber. He looked round and saw the apparition exactly as it had been described to him: it stood before him, beckoning with the finger. Athenodorus made a sign with his hand that it should wait a little, and bent again to his writing, but the ghost rattling its chains over his head as he wrote, he looked round and saw it beckoning as before. Upon this he immediately took up his lamp and followed it. The ghost slowly stalked along, as if encumbered with its chains; and having turned into the courtyard of the house, suddenly vanished. Athenodorus being thus deserted, marked the spot with a handful of grass and leaves. The next day he went to the magistrates, and advised them to order that spot to be dug up. There they found bones commingled and intertwined with chains; for the body had mouldered away by long lying in the ground, leaving them bare, and corroded by the fetters. The bones were collected, and buried at the public expense; and after the ghost was thus duly laid, the house was haunted no more.[1]

There is no need for us to believe this story as necessarily accurate in all particulars. Pliny received it at second hand, and more than likely it had been embroidered more than a little before it reached him. But in its essential features it conveys that the experiences of ghosts that people reported two thousand years ago were very similar to those that continue to be reported to this day.

Among the elements in the Athenodorus story we may note that the ghost was heard approaching; that it was seen; that it did not speak; and that, at an unexpected point, it simply vanished. For a precise modern parallel we need look no further than a humdrum but strikingly similar experience of a ghost reported by former US Army anaesthetist Robert Puett in a recent *Newsletter* of Britain's Society for Psychical Research:

> It happened in a US Army hospital in Frankfurt, West Germany, about 3.30 a.m. on 17 October 1970. . . . On the evening of 16 October I was called to the operating theatre to assist with an emergency surgical procedure. The operation finished about 2 a.m. and the surgical team left the theatre except for myself and a technician. I decided to sleep in a chair in the coffee-break room as it was very late. The technician continued with his duties. All the entrances to the theatre had been locked and barred from the inside by then; I know that beyond a shadow of a doubt. . . .
>
> Suddenly I was awakened fully by the sound of footsteps coming down the hall. At first I thought it was the technician again, until I turned and saw him asleep in another chair across the room. I was alarmed that someone had broken into the theatre, so I stepped out into the hall . . . [to see] a 'person' at the far end of the hall walking towards me. I saw 'him' clearly except for his feet which seemed out of focus, that's the only way I can think of to describe it. I remember he was dressed in blue shirt and trousers which, as he came closer, appeared to be pyjamas. I called to him to stop, then said, 'Who is it, who are you?' He continued to approach for several more metres, then stopped. I don't know how long we just stood there looking at each other . . . then he turned, went toward the wall, and just disappeared. Believe me, it is difficult for me to write that last part because it sounds like nonsense, but he just ceased to be there.[2]

Here we see all the same elements as remarked on in the Athenodorus story. The technician, who emerged behind Puett from the coffee-room, corroborated that he too had seen the pyjama-clad figure 'walk through the wall'. Although the hospital's security was alerted and all doors were checked, no living intruder was found (Figure 6).

The archives of the Society for Psychical Research and similar bodies are so full of stories of this kind that certain broad outlines of the phenomenon can be sketched. According to the Oxford researcher Celia Green, for instance, 84 per cent of reported experiences of ghosts

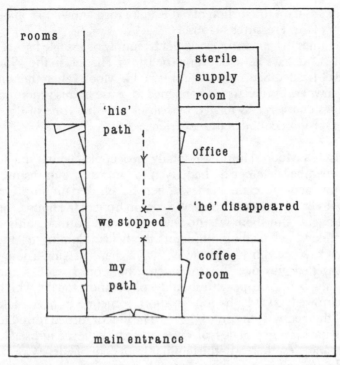

Fig. 6. Groundplan, by Robert Puett, of his viewing of the 'ghost' in Frankfurt's US Army hospital, 17 October 1970

involve the phantom being seen; 37 per cent entail some form of noise or speech; 18 per cent feature the sensation of a change of temperature, almost invariably to colder; and 15 per cent report the feeling of being touched.[3] Some hauntings consist of no more than the powerful feeling of the proximity of some 'presence'. On occasion, as in the case of Puett and the technician, a ghost may be seen by two or more people at the same time; but in other examples it may be experienced by just one person, perhaps a child, or even an animal, while others in the same vicinity observe nothing. Contrary to popular belief, ghosts usually appear convincingly solid rather than transparent.

Also paradoxically, ghosts are almost invariably reported wearing clothes, which can often help identify the particular period or individual with which they can be associated. Sometimes the apparition may be seen on a different level to that of the present day, as in the following case. A heating engineer, Harry Martindale, was mending pipes in the cellar of the medieval Treasurer's House in York.[4] He observed what seemed to him a whole troop of Roman soldiers 'marching thigh-deep in the floor', as if on the section of old Roman road known to run beneath the floor of the Treasurer's House.

Sometimes the apparition may not be simply of a single figure, but of a whole scene. At Cleve Court on the Isle of Thanet, in the 1930s, the very level-headed Scots physician Dr E. G. Moon, after attending the house's owner, Lord Carson, happened to pause in this much-haunted mansion's doorway. As related by Patrick Macrory, one of the few to whom Dr Moon confided the experience:

> His [Dr Moon's] mind was totally preoccupied with trying to remember whether he had given the nurse certain instructions about the medicines. Then he blinked in surprise. 'Surely there should be a yew hedge in front of the house', he thought. But there was no yew hedge and no road, only a muddy track leading out across the fields. Coming up the track, some thirty yards away, was a man carrying a long-barrelled gun over his shoulder, who wore breeches and riding boots, a cape with shoulder pleats and a top hat which narrowed towards the top. In short, someone from the late 18th or early 19th century. . . . The doctor turned round to assure himself that he really was where he believed himself to be and, yes, there was the familiar front door of Cleve Court. He turned again and there was the yew hedge, there was the road, the strange figure had vanished and he was once more in 1935.[5]

From cases of this kind some have postulated that there may not necessarily any longer be a sentient entity behind what are experienced as ghosts; that these may instead be no more than some form of holographic time-imprint etched into the fabric of buildings just like the voice of a singer is etched into a gramophone record or some visual scene and its sounds preserved on videotape. Among those to have suggested this have been Oxford Professor of Logic Henry H. Price, a one-time President of Britain's Society for Psychical Research. Price has envisaged a sort of 'psychic ether' permeating all matter and space, capable of retaining indefinitely impressions by the actions and even thoughts of the living.

The idea is an appealing one and it is possible that this may be *the* explanation for some of the more explicitly time-slip type experiences. Nor is it in any way undermined by the not infrequent feature of hauntings being associated with some historic tragedy, which arguably may 'imprint' more strongly. As we noted in the case of Athenodorus, his Athens ghost seemed to have been tragically left to die in his chains. The ghosts that populate Britain's historic houses are often those of individuals who have been put to death in tragic circumstances, as in the case of the ill-fated Katherine Howard, fifth wife of Henry VIII, whose ghost has been reputed to re-enact being dragged screaming down the Haunted Gallery of Hampton Court Palace after Henry had rejected her appeals for mercy. In England suicides have been so traditionally thought to engender ghosts that until 1821, when the practice was legally abolished, it was customary for suicides to be buried away from churches, generally on the highest crossroads, with the corpse impaled by a stake to prevent the ghost walking. The nineteenth-century novelist Thomas Hardy transcribed into his notebook an account of one such burial: 'Girl who committed suicide – was buried on the hill where two roads meet: but few followed her to her unblest grave: no coffin: one girl threw flowers on her: *stake driven through her body.*'[6]

But the interesting feature, indicative that something more than just time-slip may be involved, is that this type of haunting, what we may term the 'tragic ghost' type – typified by the apparition, although uncommunicative, appearing to be in some form of distress, and rooted to a particular site – seems often to be able to be stopped by a comparatively simple act of 'putting to rest'. As we noted in the case of Athenodorus, when the ghost's bones were dug up, and he was given a proper burial, he ceased to haunt any more. In both the Roman Catholic Church and the Church of England there are practitioners such as Canon Pearce-Higgins and the Revd Christopher Neil-Smith who can and do use the rite of exorcism to lay to rest the ghosts of haunted buildings, just as they use it to lay to rest instances of apparent 'possession' by the dead interfering in the lives of living people.

Just how simply such 'laying to rest' can be and has been brought about is best exemplified by the case of a ghost persistently reported at Abbey House, Cambridge, and experienced again by the family of university classics lecturer J. C. Lawson not long after they moved in, in 1903. Although, because the hauntings were mostly in darkness in the early hours of the morning, this particular ghost was never seen distinctly, she seemed to be of a woman of about thirty, dressed in a darkish robe, who would come into the Lawsons' bedroom up to three or four times a month. First there would be heavy footsteps, more like those of a policeman than a woman, then the Lawsons would both hear and in the darkness dimly see the figure tramp from the door towards the foot of their bed. Here she would pause for perhaps half a minute, then turn towards the window, where she would be at her most visible, then she would disappear through the curtains.

According to Mrs Lawson: 'I never felt in the least afraid or troubled by it. Sometimes I would wake and feel it staring and say to myself, "You can just go on staring. I'm bothered if I'll look up," but I always did in the end and then it moved on.'[7] Only when she was laid low by a prolonged illness did Mrs Lawson begin to find the visitations seriously disturbing: 'seeming to grudge me any comfortable long sleep and standing for so long at the foot of my bed and latterly sighing – the only sound I heard from it'.

At this point, Mrs Lawson was prompted to conduct an almost impulsive 'exorcism':

> At last one night I said, quite slowly and distinctly, 'In the name of the Holy Trinity, poor soul, rest in peace.' It went away to the curtain and I have never seen or heard it since. That same night it appeared to my husband who was sleeping in the bedroom upstairs . . . stared at him and disappeared. He had not seen it since.

The Lawsons would seem to have been trustworthy observers of what they described. As has been strongly affirmed by their son in a letter to psychical researcher Alan Gauld:

> I feel quite sure that neither was over-imaginative or predisposed towards belief in the supernatural. I am sure that prior to their own experiences they would have considered such events to have no place outside fiction or folklore. My father had considerable critical ability and would not have accepted his own experiences and recorded them without having carefully tested and cross-examined himself. My mother was a religious woman who would have been naturally unwilling to accept such events and would not have accepted them without considerable self-examination.[8]

Accordingly, if we are prepared to accept not only that some very level-headed people such as the Lawsons genuinely see ghosts, but also that those ghosts may cease to manifest themselves in response to certain intercessions made on their behalf, i.e. the prayer for eternal rest, then we have arrived at something very profound indeed: that at least some varieties of ghost, instead of being mere empty recordings, demonstrate a positive response to the living. In other words, the 'ghost' does seem to be the expression of an after death something that is somewhere, continuing to experience and benefit from actions made by the living on its behalf – the very same idea we saw so universally among the ancients in the earlier chapters.

While all this may well still appear highly tenuous, it can also be approached from another way. For if the distressed or unquiet dead do try to prompt the living to help on their behalf, are there also instances of dead persons, in the form of ghosts or similar, trying to help the living? If we are to expect this anywhere, it would perhaps be in the form of expressions of comfort from a dead husband to his grieving spouse, in which case we find ourselves confronted with a whole new field of ghostly experiences – those on the part of individuals known to the living, who may be positively reassured by their manifestations. In one of the few serious studies of this type of experience, conducted in mid-Wales in 1971 and published in the *British Medical Journal*, Dr W. Dewi Rees found that out of a total sample of 295 widows and widowers, no less than 137, or 47 per cent, admitted to having felt the presence of, seen, heard, spoken to, or been touched by their dead spouse.[9] Although some allowance may need to be made for the Welsh, as Celts, perhaps tending to be more partial to (or attuned to) such experiences than the average person, many of those in other areas who specialize in working sympathetically among the bereaved regularly find themselves being told of similar apparent encounters. The following, for instance, has been reported by Mrs Beryl Statham, a widow herself and a tireless counsellor of the bereaved in the Bristol region:

> Helen was in her nineties when I met her, living alone in an upstairs flat which she was unable to leave because her heart condition was such that on her bad days her lips went blue and she gasped for breath at the slightest effort. One day she said to me, quite suddenly, 'You wouldn't laugh at me if I told you something, would you?' I assured her that of course I would not, and she said, 'I can't lie down at night now and I sit in bed propped up high on my pillows. Sometimes I don't sleep at all, you know, and sometimes I can actually feel my husband's hand in mine and I know he is with me.'[10]

Another example is one of several collected by Celia Green of Oxford's Institute for Psychophysical Research:

> Our 8-year-old daughter died in 1967 and about two weeks after she died, as I sat down after my lunch, I distinctly saw her in the chair opposite, just as we always sat at this time. I was conscious of my brain questioning what my eyes saw,

and I was also conscious that there was no real solidity about what I saw, but that if I moved, the vision would fade. I was, of course, in some state of shock or grief, but was overjoyed to see my daughter so clearly.

I'm sure I'd have always doubted my own eyes, but for the fact that Rosemary spoke so clearly. She said in a matter-of-fact way, 'My foot is better', and swung the foot towards me. This was something that had worried her during her long illness in hospital, but she had so much else to contend with that we never told the doctors about it. Although she was sitting facing me, I realized that it was the affected foot she swung. I had forgotten about it in the grief of her death. [11]

The third example, which indicates that such occurrences can happen to those of the highest intellectual and critical calibre, and are not confined to immediate relatives, comes from the distinguished Church of England theologian Canon J. B. Phillips. Phillips claimed to have witnessed the ghost of the writer C. S. Lewis shortly after the latter's death in 1963. Here is his own account:

Let me say at once that I am incredulous by nature and as unsuperstitious as they come. . . . But the late C. S. Lewis, whom I did not know very well, and had only seen in the flesh once, but with whom I had corresponded a fair amount, gave me an unusual experience. A few days after his death, while I was watching television, he 'appeared' sitting in a chair within a few feet of me, and spoke a few words which were particularly relevant to the difficult circumstances through which I was passing. He was ruddier in complexion than ever, grinning all over his face, and as the old-fashioned saying has it, positively glowing with health. The interesting thing to me was that I had not been thinking about him at all . . . a week later, this time when I was in bed reading before going to sleep, he appeared again, even more rosily radiant than before, and repeated the same message, which was very important to me at the time. I was a little puzzled by this, and I mentioned it to a certain saintly bishop who was then living in retirement in Dorset. His reply was, 'My dear J—, this sort of thing is happening all the time.' [12]

A notable feature of this friendly, 'drop-in' type of ghostly visitation is its qualitative difference from those of the tragic type. The ghost, who appears to be free to pop up anywhere, converses with ease with the living person, appears to be happy (in the case of C. S. Lewis almost deliriously so), and manifests with no more apparent motive than to reassure or be of some benefit to the living.

The difficulty is the question of believing that the individual who reported the apparition genuinely saw something real, rather than was hallucinating. Unlike the tape recordings of 'past-life' experiences, a sighting of a ghost, even by so reliable an individual as Canon J. B. Phillips (he went to the same school as me), has nothing tangible to offer in the way of proof. Although perhaps we might find it more convincing if a photographer had happened to be standing by at the time of C. S. Lewis's manifestation, and could have provided a photograph perhaps showing a copy of that day's *Times* as proof of date, this might not only be expecting too much, it might be expecting the impossible.

For the history of 'ghost' photography is not an encouraging one. Of those photographs that have been put forward as of spirits, frauds abound. The great Sir Arthur Conan Doyle toted around for many years what appeared to be one of the best-ever photographs of a ghost, apparently taken on the night of 27 July 1909, when a group of Bristol University students held an all-night vigil at much-haunted Brockley Manor, a few miles to the south of Bristol. This appeared to show the figure of a monk, transparent against the Manor's panelling. However, to Sir Arthur's great discomfiture, one day in 1929 when he was showing the photograph while lecturing in Nairobi in Kenya, a member of the audience stood up to tell him that far from being a ghost the 'monk' was himself, who as a dental student at Bristol had posed for it as a prank. It had been created by nothing more than a simple double exposure, first of the student dressed in monk's garb against a plain background, then the Manor's panelling.[13]

Instead of any 'ghost' having some form of photographable reality, whenever and wherever it appears, there is a lot to suggest that a ghost is only 'in the mind'. Many hauntings seem to occur specifically when the percipient is not in what we may term a fully self-aware state of consciousness – as in the case of J. B. Phillips, who looked up from television and from reading, in that of Dr Moon, who had been trying to think about his instructions, and in that of the Lawsons, who saw their nun in the half-asleep, half-awake drowsiness of the early hours of the morning; for want of a better term, they were in the state of pre-consciousness which has so fascinated Princeton's Julian Jaynes. Consistent with this is the recurrence of two witnesses often perceiving the same apparition in slightly different ways, as for instance at the approach of the Abbey House nun, in which only Mr Lawson would hear her footsteps, and only Mrs Lawson would see the door open and close.

The same is suggested by a careful psychiatric and neurophysiological study recently made of a young woman patient, pseudonymously known as 'Ruth', who sought the help of psychiatrist Dr Morton Schatzman after repeatedly experiencing the ghost of her father, whom she knew to be still very much alive and three thousand miles away in the USA.[14] These experiences were so real to Ruth that she would see her father sit beside her on the bed, hear him speak to her, feel him when he touched her, and even smell soap on his body or alcohol on his breath. The trigger to such hauntings seems to have been obvious enough: that while she was still a child this father had cruelly raped Ruth, and mentally he was still 'possessing' her. But for Schatzman the particularly intriguing feature was the extraordinary 'reality' of Ruth's 'ghosts', which he was able to develop in her to the stage where she could eventually summon these in his presence, and then not only her father but anyone else on whom she chose to concentrate her mind. With the aid of St Thomas's Hospital neurophysiologist Dr Peter Fenwick, Schatzman linked Ruth to an electroencephalograph, set her before a television devised to evoke certain regular patterns of response in the brain, then asked her to summon her 'ghosts'. No camera was able to record what she 'saw'. But the electroencephalograph none the less registered her viewing of the television screen being blocked out just as if there was genuinely a figure in front of it.

From our point of view these researches by Dr Schatzman with Ruth are ambivalent. They show not only the futility of trying to photograph something that the subject registers in every way as a 'ghost', but also how easy it is for such a 'ghost' to be, as in Ruth's case, an undoubted illusion.

Is there any other way in which non-artificially produced 'ghosts' can be shown to be real communications from the dead, perhaps by the imparting of messages known to no one living? Interestingly, very occasionally a 'ghost' may impart a special message to the living, one known to no one else alive at the time. Perhaps nothing of this kind has been better attested than the strange case of the Chaffin family of North Carolina.

James L. Chaffin was a North Carolina farmer who at around the turn of the century had made a comfortable living for himself, his wife, and four sons John, James Junior, Marshall, and Abner. For reasons best known to himself, in 1905 Chaffin made out a properly witnessed will leaving all his property to his third son, Marshall, with all the rest of the family unprovided for. So far as any member of the family knew, this was James's final will, and when he died from a fall in September 1921 his estate uncontestedly went solely to Marshall.

By a strange quirk of fate, within a year of his father's death Marshall in his turn happened to die, his inheritance duly passing to his infant son, R. M. Chaffin, who was far too young to take up this legacy. At this stage the unprovided-for Chaffins still did nothing to contest the will because, as James Junior acknowledged, 'In all my life I never heard my father having made a will later than the one dated 1905.'

Then, in June 1925, James Junior began experiencing vivid dreams of his father appearing at his bedside. Initially in these James Senior said nothing, but then, in a new visitation described by the son in a sworn statement:

> He appeared at my bedside again, dressed as I had often seen him in life, wearing a black overcoat which I knew to be his own coat. This time my father's spirit spoke to me. He took hold of his overcoat this way and pulled it back and said, 'You will find my will in my overcoat pocket', and then disappeared. The next morning I arose fully convinced that my father's spirit had visited me for the purpose of explaining some mistake. I went to my mother's and sought for the overcoat but found that it was gone. Mother stated that she had given the overcoat to my brother John who lives in Yadkin County about twenty miles northwest of my home. . . . On the 6th of July . . . I went to my brother's home . . . and found the coat. On examination of the inside pocket I found that the lining had been sewn together. I immediately cut the stitches and found a little roll of paper tied with a string which was in my father's handwriting and contained only the following words:
> 'Read the 27th chapter of Genesis in my daddie's old Bible.'[15]

Bizarre as it sounds, it all seemed so compelling to James Junior that he felt he must pursue the trail. Knowing that the old Bible would be at his mother's home, he prudently decided that whatever discovery might be made should be in the presence of appropriately independent witnesses. Accordingly he invited a neighbour, Thomas Blackwelder, who lived on a farm about a mile away, to help him search for the old Bible at his mother's home, along with his own and Blackwelder's daughters. At this point Blackwelder, also in a sworn statement, takes up the story:

We made a search for the Bible and after some time we found it in a bureau drawer in the second storey of the house. We took out the Bible which was quite old and was in three different pieces. I took one of the three pieces out of the book and Mr Chaffin took the other two pieces, but it happened that the piece I had contained the Book of Genesis. I turned the leaves until I came to the 27th chapter and there found two leaves folded inward and there was a paper writing folded in these two leaves which purported to be the last will of James L. Chaffin.

On opening the document, all those gathered in the room read:

After reading the 27th Chapter of Genesis [which concerns how Jacob unfairly wrested his father's estate from his elder brother, Esau] I, James L. Chaffin, do make my last will and testament, and here it is. I want, after giving my body a decent burial, my little property to be equally divided between my four children, if they are living at my death, both personal and real estate divided equal; if not living, give share to their children. And if she is living, you must all take care of your mammy. Now this is my last will and testament. Witness my hand and seal.

James L. Chaffin
This January 16, 1919

In England such a will would have had no validity, because it had gone unwitnessed. But in North Carolina it could be considered legal so long as it could be proved to have been written by the deceased. Accordingly the Chaffins filed the will for probate, while at one and the same time gathering no less than ten individuals prepared to swear that it was the dead James Chaffin's own handwriting. For her part Marshall's widow, as legal guardian for her son, felt she had to protect his inheritance, resulting in the mustering of a most unusual court case, *Chaffin* v. *Chaffin*, which was set to be heard before a jury in December 1925.

In the event, during the trial's lunch interval Mrs Marshall Chaffin met up with the other members of the family, saw the documentation, and appears to have recognized that her case was hopeless. On assembly in the afternoon the court was therefore told that all parties had reached an amicable settlement, and there would therefore be no opposition to probate of the new will. There followed a judgement that must be one of the very few in which an after death message has played a significant part; the jury agreed that the document found in the family Bible was the valid will, positively superseding that made out in 1905.

Can the story be believed? In 1927, on behalf of a Canadian member of the Society for Psychical Research, the Chaffin affair was very carefully re-examined by J. M. N. Johnson, a North Carolina attorney-at-law. Johnson interviewed all the main witnesses, reporting that he was 'much impressed with the evident sincerity of these people, who had the appearance of honest, honourable country people in well-to-do circumstances'. He went on:

> I endeavoured with all my skill and ability by cross-examination and otherwise to induce some admission that possibly there was a subconscious knowledge of the Will in the old Bible, or of the paper in the coat pocket: but I utterly failed to shake their faith. The answer was a quiet: 'Nay: such an explanation is impossible. We never heard of the existence of the will till the visitation of my father's spirit.'

Here we have, then, if we really can accept it, a classic and relatively recent instance of just the sort of spontaneous communication of the dead via dreams and ghosts held by the ancient Egyptians, by the Makgabeng tribe of southern Africa, and by many others. The case does not stand alone. Directly from an individual whom I have known personally over several years, there is a related occurrence that is worth the telling. In 1985 the already mentioned Mrs Beryl Statham lent to a theological scholar friend, whom we will know as the Revd Black, a rare book on the Irvingite Church, made unique because of some marginal annotations made by her great-uncle, Heseltine Owen, who had been a prominent Irvingite. Beryl Statham had made arrangements with the Revd Black to collect the book, along with a couple of other items, on a particular Wednesday, only to be phoned that very morning to be told by a member of the family that the Revd Black had just died. A promise was made for the items to be sent to her, and in due course a packet arrived. But it did not contain the crucial book. In the circumstances Mrs Statham felt it would be too embarrassing to press the family over the omission. It was only much later, when the Revd Black's widow happened to ask whether she had received the book, that Beryl Statham felt bound to admit that she had not. Mrs Statham's account of the ensuing circumstances is as follows:

She [Mrs Black] was deeply distressed and worried. Her husband had a vast collection of books and papers, many of which had already been sorted, and finding this one at this stage would be difficult. I wished, after all, that I had told her sooner, or not at all. When, after a search, it could not be found, I tried to belittle the importance, but naturally she was very distressed, and I couldn't convince her that it didn't matter. Before her son left he and she had another check on books that had already been sorted, hoping to find the one they wanted, but they had no success. In fact, they did not know exactly what they were looking for, as they had not seen the book and I was unable to give them the precise title of it. . . .

The following morning, when she was alone again, she was making the bed of her tenant, in his bedroom which was next to her husband's study, when she heard the post arrive, as if a heavy package had been put through the letter-box and had fallen on the mat. She left her task and went downstairs to collect it, but there was nothing there. Surprised, as there had been no doubt in her mind as to what she had heard, she returned upstairs and as she reached the study she heard the movements of someone inside, and saw a shadow pass. Her immediate thought was that it must be her tenant, although he was not usually at home at that time of the day, and she wondered what he was doing in the study. She called him but there was no reply.

Certain that there was someone in the study, she went in. She was unafraid, but was moved to say a little prayer as she entered the room. There was no one there. Everything was in place, as they had left it, except that on the bottom shelf of the bookcase, isolated from all the other books, was *the* book. . . . It was the first thing she saw as she entered the room and it was laid out in full view . . . alone on the shelf, apart from the other books.[16]

According to Beryl Statham, Mrs Black's husband had said, before he died, that if he were allowed to let her know for certain that life continued after death, he would come to her. He in particular would have known the uniqueness of the book and would most certainly have wanted it to be returned. But more importantly he would have wanted to relieve his much-loved wife from her distress over the matter.

Was this a genuine experience of her husband on the part of the bereaved Mrs Black? And was this the Revd Black's non-intrusive way of indicating his continuing awareness of events in the world he had left behind? Along with the Chaffin case and all others of the 'drop-in' variety, it is at one level fragile and insubstantial, and therefore must constitute only the flimsiest of evidence. Yet at another level it has precisely that 'something else' remarked on by Dr Johnson, an intensely personal this-is-the-way-things-happen quality that carries with it a convincingness far greater than all the paraphernalia of mediumship. It may not seem very much to go on, as far as our search for evidence of experience after death is concerned; but it is a foothold on which we will now try to build.

# 8

# LEARNING FROM THE DYING

If something of us does survive into some other form of experience after the death of the physical body, then we might expect at least some hints of something special happening, something more than a mere disintegration into nothingness, during a dying person's last moments. In fact, such hints feature prominently in the folklore of peoples right across the world, and are today still attested to, on the part of the dying and those most closely associated with them.

One of the most striking indications that something of us is not solely confined to our physical bodies derives from the frequently reported instances of living individuals experiencing some form of intuition that a friend or relative, perhaps many miles away, either has died or is at the point of death. In Chapter 5 we noted how Swedenborg seemed to become aware of the murder, hundreds of miles away, of Tsar Peter III of Russia. I myself have never forgotten being at my parents' home one early morning in 1963 when the telephone rang and in the moments before answering it my mother, a school secretary not given to 'psychic' experiences, calmly announced:

'That will be the old people's home to tell us that Pop is dead.'

Since the previous evening I had personally driven 'Pop', my step-grandfather, the three miles back to the old people's home where he lived, the news was certainly not something we were expecting. The reason for my mother's assurance was that at six o'clock that morning she had awoken, vividly 'hearing' – she insists it was not a dream – Pop shouting her name 'Doris' through the house's letter-box. The phone call was indeed from the matron of the old people's home to tell us that Pop had died, specifically at 6 a.m., after shouting out and falling from his bed at the onset of a sudden fatal heart attack.

Before they became too corrupted by modern culture (not to mention *Crocodile Dundee*), such experiences were very commonly reported among Australian aboriginals, as attested by the anthropologist Ronald Rose:

My wife and I . . . collected numbers of such accounts
among detribalized aborigines on the north coast of New
South Wales. For example, Frank Mitchell, a full-blooded
Minyung (Queensland) native living on the government
station at Woodenbong, had had a number of unusual
experiences. We were told of one that had occurred about
three weeks before, by the then manager of the station, Mr J.
Foster.

'Frank's small son was in Kyogle Hospital,' said Mr Foster.
'He had been there for some time, and as far as I knew was not
in a dangerous condition. One morning, a few weeks ago
Frank came to my residence here before breakfast. "What's
the matter, Frank?" I asked, and he told me that Billie had
died in the hospital during the night. There is no way he
could have known this – Kyogle Hospital is over forty miles
away and my residence is the only place with a phone. I
didn't know what to make of Frank's statement; I told him I'd
ring the hospital later to reassure him. But before I had done
so, my phone rang. It was Kyogle Hospital; they told me that
Frank's son had suddenly taken a turn for the worse and had
died during the night.[1]

Ronald Rose and his wife Lyndon subsequently questioned the
aboriginal concerned. According to Rose:

He said that he and his wife had been lying in bed in their
shack on the station when he heard faltering footsteps on the
veranda. These they recognized as the spirit footsteps of his
deceased mother, and he heard the familiar tapping of her
walking stick. His wife Eileen also heard these noises, as
well as tapping on the window-pane. They interpreted
these as 'death signs', and concluded that little Billie had
died.

Such stories of death-knocks and rappings are commonplace in many
cultures, including the more rural communities of England, Ireland,
Scotland, and France. But even more spectacular are instances in which
an apparition of the dying or dead person is reported visiting the one
living. An early example is that of the nineteenth-century Scottish-born
peer Lord Brougham, Britain's Lord Chancellor between 1830 and
1834. Brougham described in his autobiography how, back in his
Edinburgh schooldays, he had made a pact with a friend, referred to as

'G', whereby whoever died first would try to appear to the other. During subsequent years Brougham lost all contact with 'G', and the shock was accordingly all the greater when 'G' seemed to fulfil the pact when Brougham was least expecting it, during a visit to Sweden. In Brougham's words:

> We set out for Gothenberg [apparently on 18 December], determined to make for Norway. About one in the morning, arriving at a decent inn, we decided to stop for the night. Tired with the cold of yesterday I was glad to take advantage of a hot bath before I turned in, and here a most remarkable thing happened to me. . . . I turned my head round, looking towards the chair on which I had deposited my clothes, as I was about to get out of the bath. On the chair sat 'G', looking calmly at me. How I got out of the bath I know not, but on recovering my senses I found myself sprawling on the floor. The apparition, or whatever it was, that had taken the likeness of 'G', had disappeared.[2]

Subsequent to his return to his native Edinburgh, Brougham learned that 'G' had died, four thousand miles away in India, on the very day that he saw the apparition in Sweden. To be noted in this as in so many other viewings of apparitions is how Brougham, on his own admission, was not in what one might term 100 per cent full consciousness: as he put it, 'relaxing in a warm bath' and unable, on 'recovering my senses', to recall the exact circumstances in which he subsequently found himself out of the bath and sprawled on the floor.

If it might be thought that Brougham's story is rather too old to be trusted, it can be supplemented by many parallel modern occurrences, including a particular one described to me at first hand as recently as 1986 by a 39-year-old London health visitor of Polish parentage, Krystyna Kolodziej. On the night of 21 March 1981, Krystyna was with a friend in her flat at Hackney, East London, waiting for news of her father, Kazimir, whom she knew to be dying fifteen thousand miles away in Australia. At this time she had not seen her father for some twelve or thirteen years, their relationship having been strained throughout most of her adult life because of his chronic drink problem. Knowing that he was dying, Kazimir had offered Krystyna the money to fly to Australia to visit him for the last time, but she had refused, largely because this would have meant her missing the B.Sc. examinations for which she had been studying during the previous three years.

Here is Krystyna's own account:

My friend had been with me a few hours and . . . she and I were sitting on my sofa talking at about 11 p.m., and she was describing to me some clothes she had bought recently. . . . Suddenly, and while still attending to her, my father's face appeared high on the wall to my left, just next to a large mounted picture. Indeed part of it occluded the picture. I saw it out of the corner of my eye, because my face was actually turned towards my friend, and the face imprinted itself onto my awareness in a way so real that I shook my head and looked away, as if trying to shake off the vision in disbelief. This time, I looked directly at the place and saw the face again, after which it disappeared almost instantly. The entire episode lasted only about ten seconds and my friend, absorbed in what she was saying, noticed nothing in my expression. I told her of it the next morning. My father did die within hours of my seeing him, and I awoke spontaneously just before the phone rang to tell me. . . .

What I remember most was the expression on my father's face – there was no expression. . . . If I had to describe the feeling the apparition imparted to me, it was as if seeing me, and perhaps being seen, was a duty my father had to perform.[3]

In this instance the one somewhat unsatisfactory feature, on Krystyna Kolodziej's own admission, was the fact that she knew her father was dying and could perhaps be argued to have 'hallucinated' seeing him, perhaps triggered by her conflicting emotions regarding travelling to Australia to visit him for the last time. But cases of these so-called 'crisis apparitions' occur too frequently (and often in too-unexpected circumstances, as in the case of my step-grandfather) for them all to be explained away so easily. Overall one is left with the eerie impression that at least some form of across-space communication really can be transmitted from a dying person to those with whom they wish to get in touch during their last moments.

But even if something of this kind does occur, does it necessarily imply a something of us actually surviving physical death? In this regard, inevitably because of the strong emotions surrounding death, one of the most neglected fields of study is that of the often quite remarkable phenomena associated with the dying themselves, phenomena which have only begun to be treated with renewed seriousness in recent years.

Among the several indications that the process of dying may involve something rather more profound than just complete and utter extinction is the repeatedly observed ability the terminally ill have to predict, quite calmly, when they are going to die, even when medically the final crisis may not be at all apparent. This has been noted from at least as early as the Middle Ages. As remarked by the French writer Philippe Ariès in his monumental *The Hour of our Death*,[4] there is an inscription of AD 1151 in the Musée des Augustins in Toulouse recording the death of the sacristan of Saint-Paul-de-Narbonne:

> *Mortem sibi instare cernerat tanquam obitus sui prescius.*[5]
>
> [He saw death standing beside him and knew that he was
>     about to die.]

Ariès also quotes a similar premonition reported of one of her contemporaries by Madame Dunoyer:

> The death [of Mme de Rhert] was no less amazing than her life. She arranged for the funeral herself, had her house draped in black, had masses said ahead of time for the repose of her soul, and had her funeral service – all this without feeling the least bit sick. When she had finished giving all the necessary orders to spare her husband the task that would have fallen to him without this foresight, she died on the day and at the hour that she had indicated.[6]

That this is not mere romantic fancy is clear from a serious study on terminal illness undertaken by British physicians Exton-Smith and Cantaub, and published in 1961 in the leading medical journal *The Lancet*:

> Seven patients had a premonition of death, and this was communicated to the nurses by such remarks as 'Goodbye, I am going' an hour before death. Another thanked the staff nurse who was doing the medicine rounds for all she had done, and said that she would not need tablets anymore after tomorrow. A man with congestive cardiac failure thanked all the nurses for their attention the day before his death, and a woman with rheumatoid arthritis, half an hour before she died, asked that her friend should be summoned. There is no doubt that these patients became aware that they were about to die, but the manner in which this knowledge was imparted to them could not be ascertained.[7]

The same has been observed on the other side of the Atlantic by Dr John Hunter Phillips, professor of medicine at Tulane University:

> I became interested in the mechanism of death in the elderly while serving in the nursing home, particularly in those patients who predicted that their death was imminent. They would say, 'I'm ready to die,' and there was very little the physician could do to prevent it. There was usually no obvious lethal disease process evident at the time, the electro-cardiogram might be normal, the chest X-ray normal, the screening blood tests all normal, and yet death would occur, usually within 24–48 hours once the positive statement was made. This made me very uneasy, and continues to make me uneasy when I sign the death certificate under the 'cause of death'. I don't really know *why* they died.[8]

Unpalatable though it might be to research the process of dying, intriguing special studies have been made which suggest that in a lingering death a patient's last moments may be far more meaningful and precious than is normally taken account of in modern hospitals. The earliest to involve himself in a study of this kind was Professor Sir William Barrett, a Fellow of Britain's Royal Society, and one of the founder members of the Society for Psychical Research, becoming its President in 1904. Fascinated by dying persons' apparent hallucinations of deceased relatives, Barrett made a careful collection of reports of these, aided by his surgeon-wife Florence. His short but pioneering book, *Death-Bed Visions*, was published in 1926, a year after his own death.[9]

The next person to take up the subject was Dr Karlis Osis, a Latvian born in Riga in 1917. On emigrating to the United States, Osis first worked with telepathy researcher Dr J. B. Rhine at Duke University, before becoming research director of the Parapsychology Foundation in New York. It was in this later post that he devised a questionnaire mailed to a random selection of 5,000 US physicians and 5,000 nurses specifically enquiring about patients' states of mind immediately prior to death: how many retained full consciousness up to the end, what emotions they exhibited, what hallucinations they appeared to experience. Osis received 640 replies, representing more than 35,000 observed death-bed scenes, and published his findings in an authoritatively statistical monograph, *Deathbed Observations by Physicians and Nurses*.[10]

The present-day individual with whom the study of dying has perhaps become most associated is Swiss-born Dr Elisabeth Kübler-Ross, a small, wiry, and intensely professional physician today resident in Virginia, USA. As a young woman just after the Second World War, Dr Kübler-Ross spent her summers in Poland helping the only-just-alive who had managed to survive the horrors of the Nazis' extermination camps at Auschwitz and Majdanek. The scenes she witnessed so extinguished in her any of the normal revulsions associated with death, that after marrying a young American doctor and moving to the United States where she became assistant professor of psychiatry at Chicago University, she saw the need for both doctors and terminally ill patients to be brought to terms with their feelings when confronted with the inevitability of death. Accordingly she began seminars for this purpose at Chicago University's Billings Hospital. As she openly admits, when she began there she was frankly agnostic and had no belief in a life after death, a view which was to undergo the profoundest change when she began to listen to what the dying had to tell her.

As already noted by Barrett and Osis before her, one of the several remarkable features of those near death, and seemingly closely akin to the already noted awareness of the imminence of death, is a paradoxical mood of elation. According to Elisabeth Kübler-Ross:

> Even the angriest and most difficult patients very shortly before death began to deeply relax, have a sense of serenity around them, and were pain-free in spite of perhaps a cancer-ridden body full of metastases. Also the moment after death occurred their facial features expressed an incredible sense of peace and equanimity and serenity which I could not comprehend since it was often a death that occurred in a stage of anger, bargaining or depression.[11]

Dr Karlis Osis has observed the same. To his question 'Have you observed a certain rise of mood to exaltation in a dying patient?' no less than 169 of those who answered his questionnaires responded positively, attesting to the incidence of this in no less than 753 individual patients' deaths. As Osis summed this up:

> A resident simply stated the facts: 'Great anxiety building up for days, that usually disappears one to three hours before death.' A hospital staff physician commented: 'Common to many is peace that occurs in spite of pain and discomfort previously seen. People (who were) in panic will often be serene in the last hour or so.' A general practitioner even

confessed that such observations had moulded his philosophy: 'There is such a resigned, peaceful, almost happy expression which comes over the patient – it is hard to explain, but it leaves me with the feeling that I would not be afraid to die.'[12]

Perhaps the most enigmatic yet consistently reported feature – the one which prompted Barrett in his study, and which Osis and Kübler-Ross have come across time and time again – is that of dying patients apparently 'seeing', and holding conversations with, deceased friends and relatives whom no one else present can either see or hear. This phenomenon has long been observed independently of the researches of the specialists. The nineteenth-century American physician Dr Wilson of New York, who attended the dying moments of his long-time patient, tenor James Moore, has left a particularly vivid account:

It was about four o'clock . . . when, as I bent over the bed, I noticed that his face was quite calm and his eyes clear. . . . Then something which I shall never forget to my dying day happened, something which is utterly indescribable. While he appeared perfectly rational and as sane as any man I have ever seen . . . he said in a stronger voice than he had used since I had attended him, 'There is Mother! Why, Mother, have you come here to see me? No, no, I'm coming to see you. Just wait, Mother, I am almost over. I can jump it. Wait, Mother.' On his face there was a look of inexpressible happiness, and the way in which he said the words impressed me as I have never been before, and I am as firmly convinced that he saw and talked with his mother as I am that I am sitting here. In order to preserve what I believed to be his conversation with his mother, and also to have a record of the strangest happening in my life, I immediately wrote down every word he had said.[13]

The evangelist Dr Billy Graham has described how on the day his grandmother lay dying she apparently sat up in bed even though she had been too weak to do so earlier. She then claimed seeing her dead husband Ben, who had lost a leg and an eye in the Civil War, with the words: 'There is Ben, and he has both of his eyes and both of his legs!'[14]

Among many other instances it has recently been reliably reported that on the death of the Duke of Windsor on 22 May 1972 his last words, murmured very quietly, were: 'Mama . . . Mama . . . Mama . . . Mama.'[15] Was he having his first encounter in decades with his deceased mother, Queen Mary, to whom in her lifetime he had caused such anguish as a result of his love for the American divorcee Wallis Simpson?

The inevitable objection to such experiences is that they are mere hallucinations of a dying person's last moments, perhaps the result of depletion of the oxygen supply to the patient's brain, or of some natural opiate in the brain that eases the final paroxysms of death. But although Barrett, Osis, and Kübler-Ross each in their turn considered this possibility, all ended up rejecting it on the basis of specific cases which seemed to rule this out; these were instances when the dying saw, as if 'beyond the grave', individuals whom they had not been told were dead.

For Barrett the classic case of this kind was one brought to his attention by his wife Florence, Lady Barrett, who worked as a gynaecologist at the Mother's Hospital in Clapton, East London. At this hospital in mid-January 1924 Lady Barrett happened to be called to a patient, Mrs Doris B., whose heart began to fail while giving birth. With Lady Barrett's help, the child was delivered safely, but it was obvious that Mrs B. was dying. After tending to the other patients on her round, Lady Barrett went back to the ward in case she could be of any further assistance. According to Lady Barrett's description of this:

> When I entered the ward Mrs B. held out her hands to me and said, 'Thank you, thank you for what you have done for me – for bringing the baby. Is it a boy or girl?' Then holding my hand tightly, she said, 'Don't leave me, don't go away, will you?' And after a few minutes, while the House Surgeon carried out some restorative measures, she lay looking up towards the open part of the room, which was brightly lighted, and said, 'Oh, don't let it get dark – it's getting so dark . . . darker and darker.' Her husband and mother were sent for.
>
> Suddenly she looked eagerly towards one part of the room, a radiant smile illuminating her whole countenance. 'Oh, lovely, lovely,' she said. I asked, 'What is lovely?' 'What I *see*,' she replied in low, intense tones. 'What do you see?' 'Lovely brightness – wonderful beings.' It is difficult to describe the sense of reality conveyed by her intense absorption in the vision. Then – seeming to focus her attention more intently on one place for a moment – she exclaimed, almost with a kind of joyous cry, 'Why, it's Father! Oh, he's

so glad I'm coming; he *is* so glad. It would be perfect if only W. [her husband] could come too.'

Her baby was brought for her to see. She looked at it with interest, and then said, 'Do you think I ought to stay for baby's sake?' Then turning towards the vision again, she said, 'I can't – I can't stay; if you could see what I do, you would know I can't stay.'[16]

Although Lady Barrett had to leave shortly after this, attendance on Mrs B. was continued by the hospital Matron, who added the following to Lady Barrett's account:

I was present, shortly before the death of Mrs B., together with her husband and her mother. Her husband was leaning over her and speaking to her, when pushing him aside she said, 'Oh, don't hide it; it's so beautiful.' Then turning away from him towards me, I being on the other side of the bed, Mrs B. said, 'Oh, why there's Vida,' *referring to a sister of whose death three weeks previously she had not been told.* Afterwards the mother, who was present at the time, told me, as I have said, that Vida was the name of a dead sister of Mrs B.'s, of whose illness and death she was quite ignorant, as they had carefully kept this news from Mrs B. owing to her serious illness.

(Signed) Miriam Castle
*Matron*

The crucial feature here is Mrs B.'s 'seeing', as if beyond the grave, her sister Vida, whom she did not know to be dead. The facts were corroborated by Mrs B.'s mother, Mrs Mary Clark, according to whom Vida, an invalid for some years, had died just two weeks and four days before Mrs B.

Dr Kübler-Ross, in her long experience of the dying, has similarly come across several cases of individuals seeing, as if beyond the grave, friends and relatives whom they did not know to be dead. She has quoted as one somewhat anecdotal example that of an American Indian girl, knocked down

by a hit-and-run driver on a highway when a stranger stopped his car in an attempt to help her. She very calmly told him that there was nothing else he could do for her except perhaps one day he might get near the Indian reservation where her mother lived about seven hundred miles from the scene of the accident. She had a message for her mother and maybe one day he would be able to convey this message to her. The message stated that she was OK, that she was not only OK, that she was very happy because she was already with her Dad. She then died in the arms of the stranger.[17]

According to Dr Kübler-Ross the stranger then drove seven hundred miles out of his way to visit the girl's mother, there to learn that the father had died of a coronary at the Indian reservation just one hour before the daughter had been killed in the car accident.

Particularly impressive is what Dr Kübler-Ross has learned from observation of dying children involved in multiple-death family car accidents, as can too often happen on US Fourth of July weekends, Labor Days, and similar. Of such occurrences, during which the dead and dying are often taken to different hospitals, Dr Kübler-Ross remarks:

> I have made it a task to sit with the critically injured children since they are my speciality. And being quite aware that they have not been informed about the number or names of the relatives who have been killed . . . [I have been] very impressed that they were always aware of those who preceded them in death. I sit with them, watch them silently, perhaps hold their hand, watch their restlessness, and then often shortly prior to death [observe] a peaceful serenity which is always an ominous sign. It is at this time that I ask them if they are willing and able to share with me what they experience. They share in very similar words: 'Everything is all right now. Mummy and Peter are already waiting for me.'[18]

As Dr Kübler-Ross makes clear, she may at this point already be aware that the child's mother has died in the accident, but may know nothing of the death of the child's brother, Peter. Then:

> Shortly afterwards I receive a call from the Children's Hospital that Peter had died ten minutes ago. In all the many years that we have collected this kind of data we have never met a child who in the imminence of their own death mentioned a person in their family that had not preceded them in death even if it was only by a few minutes.

To the sceptically minded, such accounts, even from an individual as clinical and pragmatic as Elisabeth Kübler-Ross, will almost certainly still be difficult to accept. Dr Karlis Osis has further complicated the issue by finding in his study that 28 per cent of those 'seen' by the dying are living relatives. However, since he derived his material largely from questionnaires, he has lacked Dr Kübler-Ross's facility to be able to distinguish at first hand those cases that carry the maximum conviction of the dying experiencing some realm beyond death.

But from here in Britain comes a case which seems very comfortably to negate even Dr Osis's careful qualification. In 1968 Mrs Janet T., wife of a Bristol accountant, gave birth to a baby daughter Jane, who sadly died of pneumonia two days later. Shortly after, some one hundred miles away in the village of Llangernyw near Abergele in North Wales, Janet's 96-year-old grandmother, Mrs Jane Charles, lay dying, attended by Janet's father, Mr Geoffrey Charles, a newspaper reporter.

Just as in the case of Mrs B., Mr Charles had carefully avoided telling his mother that Janet had lost her baby, not least because the infant had quite specifically been given the Christian name Jane in honour of her great-grandmother. So he had no idea of the bombshell that was about to strike when, just like the Barretts' Mrs B., Mrs Charles began to talk to apparent unseen visitors. Totally clear-headed, she first remarked on a woman who seemed to bother her. Then, just as in the cases observed by Barrett, Osis, and Kübler-Ross, she became 'calm and happy'. It was all right, she announced; she 'knew what it was all about now'. She very contentedly told her son that she had seen his father, her husband John, who had died in 1942. Then, with a puzzled expression, she remarked that the only thing she could not understand was that John *had a baby with him*. She said about this, very emphatically:

'It's one of our family. It's Janet's baby. Poor Janet. Never mind, she'll get over it.'[19]

Hard-bitten journalist though he was, Geoffrey Charles was dumbfounded and choking with emotion when he later telephoned the news to Janet. Mrs Charles's dying prediction came true; for although initially shattered, Janet did get over it, and now has a near grown-up son and daughter.

Janet T. is a thoroughly sensible teacher and housewife whom I have known for several years, and whose veracity on this deeply personal story I trust totally. Nor is the incident a tale that has grown with the years, for both she and her father wrote down what Mrs Charles said very shortly after Mrs Charles died. Neither Janet nor her father has read the works of Barrett, Osis, or Kübler-Ross.

There is still another major facet associated with the dying that as yet we have not even touched on, one so crucial to the case for after death experience that we will devote the next two chapters to it. It is best introduced by a story told by the controversial German cancer specialist Dr Josef Issels of a woman dying of cancer at his famous Ringberg Clinic in Bavaria:

> One day I experienced a remarkable happening. I was doing my morning round on Ward One, the ward reserved for the acutely ill. I went into the room of an elderly woman patient close to death. She looked at me and said: 'Doctor, do you know that I can leave my body?' I knew approaching death often produced the most unusual phenomena. 'I will give you proof,' said the woman. 'Here and now.' There was a moment's silence, then she spoke again: 'Doctor, if you go to Room 12, you will find a woman writing a letter to her husband. She has just completed the first page. I've just seen her do it.' She went on to describe in minute detail what she had just 'seen'. I hurried to Room 12, at the end of the ward. The scene inside was exactly the same as the woman had described it, even down to the contents of the letter. I went back to the elderly woman to seek an explanation. In the time I had gone she had died. It was the first, though not the last, time I experienced unusual happenings with seriously ill patients. [20]

Does this tell us that some part of us really is able to leave the physical body at the onset of death?

# 9

## TALES FROM THE RESUSCITATED

If there is something of us that separates from the physical body at the point of death, one of the oddities, as we have seen in the case of the dying, is why people should seemingly get a glimpse of an after death world even before they have made the transition. Surely there must be some firmly definable line between what is death and what is not death?

As it happens, it is perhaps the present generation's medical knowledge that has recognized more than any of its predecessors just how difficult that line is to draw. A few years ago death was pronounced when there was no detectable sign of respiratory activity, and the heart had stopped. Any all-too-rare individual who survived this particular state created newspaper headlines as having come 'back from the dead', and was a subject of almost reverential awe. Today all this has changed. With the present-day advances in surgical technology it is a matter of routine for the heart to be stopped for what may be hours during a complex heart operation. And although the electroencephalograph (EEG), for measuring brainwave activity, provides an extra instrumental guide to signs of life, there are patients who have registered a totally flat EEG reading who have still gone on to make a complete recovery.

Doctors have had to 'redefine' death, with few confident that they have yet reached any totally unimpeachable formula. Essentially they now see two broad categories of death. The first of these is clinical death, from which, although all signs of life may appear to be absent, prompt resuscitation methods may enable the patient to make a full recovery. In these circumstances the patient will be spoken of as having been 'near death' rather than actually dead. The second is biological death, which may have exactly the same outward features as clinical death, except the duration of this, concomitant with the onset of degradation of the physical organism, makes return to life impossible.

In the case of this second category, a moot question is the length of that duration before the body automatically becomes biologically dead. Although it has long been assumed that oxygen starvation will cause irreparable brain damage in anything over six minutes, it is now evident that in special circumstances this can be far longer. Off the coast of Alaska on 4 September 1983 a helicopter crew plucked from a freezing, tossing sea the body of three-year-old Misty Dawn Densmore, whose mother, shipwrecked with her, had watched her stop breathing, turn blue and 'die' some thirty minutes before. As recalled by the helicopter doctor, Flight Surgeon Martin J. Nemiroff:

> I wiped the sea foam from her and saw a blonde, well-built three year old with blue eyes staring out of a plump face. She was in full cardiac arrest – eyes fixed, pupils dilated, limbs chilled and blue, and no discernible heartbeat. I didn't feel like even attempting the resuscitation; I was ready to pronounce her dead.[1]

In the event, fired by the thought of his own three-year-old back at home, Nemiroff sucked a quart of seawater from Misty's lungs, and kept breathing into her. After having been 'dead' for some forty minutes, Misty spluttered back into life, to make a full recovery.

As Nemiroff has theorized, Misty probably owed her survival to the exceptionally cold water acting in some not yet fully understood way to conserve the oxygen in her brain. Her case illustrates the near impossibility of determining a fixed 'point' of death. Time and again throughout history doctors have bungled the task of certifying this. The fourteenth-century Italian poet Petrarch had been laid out in death, and would have been buried in four more hours, but for a sudden change of temperature which caused him to sit up and complain of the draught. He lived a further thirty years to write some of his best work. In late sixteenth-century England one Matthew Wall of Braughing, Hertfordshire, owed some extra years of life to one of his coffin-bearers tripping up and dropping him on the way to his funeral. The villagers of Braughing even to the present day commemorate his resuscitation. In the eighteenth century a Frenchwoman who had been buried in the cemetery at Orléans was revived by the shock of a grave-robber cutting off her finger while trying to steal her ring.[2] When medical knowledge dramatically improved in the nineteenth century the incidence of misdiagnoses of death increased. France's Dr Icard, reporting about a dozen cases of individuals wrongly adjudged dead, has described how one 'corpse' happened to regain consciousness during a funeral attended by several physicians.[3] Such mistakes continue to happen today, as we shall learn from cases to be explored later in this chapter.

So exactly what constitutes the barrier between life and death has long been blurred, and continues to be so. This raises the question what, if anything, do the resuscitated report of their experiences while clinically dead? Do they recollect anything of a process of seeming to leave the physical body? Do they report the same sort of elation and other-worldly encounters we have heard from the dying? Or do they recall nothing?

In fact, vividly recalled after death experiences have been reported from at least as early as the ancient Greeks. Plato in his *Republic* told the story of a Pamphylian soldier called Er whose body had been tossed in a heap along with all the other apparent fatalities when, just as the funeral pyre was about to be lit, he suddenly revived. According to Plato: 'He [Er] said that when his soul left the body he went on a journey with a great company, and they came to a mysterious place at which there were two openings in the earth.'[4]

In eighth-century England the monk Bede, in his *History of the English Church and People*, told the story of a Northumbrian man called Cunningham who 'died in the early hours of the night. But at daybreak . . . returned to life and suddenly sat up to the great consternation of those weeping around the body, who ran away.'[5] Cunningham described leaving his body to find himself in heavenly realms, accompanied by 'a handsome man in a shining robe', and was not at all happy to be told he had to go back to the land of the living:

> I was most reluctant to return to my body, for I was entranced
> by the pleasantness and beauty of the place I could see and
> the company I saw there. But I did not dare to question my
> guide and meanwhile I suddenly found myself alive amongst
> men once more.

In the early 1860s a Mormon who was badly injured in an accident told how

> His spirit left his body and stood, as it were, in the air above it.
> He could see his body and the men standing around and he
> heard their conversation. At his option he could re-enter his
> body or remain in spirit. His reflection upon his responsibil-
> ity to his family and his great desire to live caused him to
> choose to enter his body again and live. As he did so he
> regained consciousness and experienced severe pains
> incident to the injuries which he had suffered from the
> accident.[6]

Perhaps one of the most often quoted early cases of this kind is that of Dr A. S. Wiltse of Skiddy, Kansas, who 'died' of typhoid fever during the summer of 1889. His physician, Dr S. H. Raynes, pronounced him dead, and even the local church bells were rung to mark his passing. But as subsequently reported by Dr Wiltse some sort of awareness seemed to continue in him after this 'death':

> I . . . discovered that I was still in my body, but the body and I no longer had any interests in common. I looked in astonishment and joy for the first time upon myself . . . with all the interest of a physician. . . . I watched the interesting process of separation of soul and body.[7]

Wiltse recalled rising in some form of after death state, to observe as he did so a man standing by the door with whom he seemed to come in contact:

> To my surprise his arm passed through mine without apparent resistance. . . . I looked quickly up at his face to see if he had noticed the contact but he gave me no sign, only stood and gazed towards the couch I had just left. I directed my gaze in the direction of his and saw my own dead body . . . I was surprised at the paleness of the face . . . I know I attempted to gain the attention of the people with the object of comforting them as well as assuring them of their own immortality . . . I passed about among them . . . but found that they gave me no heed. Then the situation struck me as humorous and I laughed outright . . . how well I feel, I thought. Only a few minutes ago I was horribly sick and distressed. Then came that change called death which I have so much dreaded. This has passed now, and here am I, still a man, alive and thinking, yes thinking as clearly as ever, and how well I feel; I shall never be sick again. I have no more to die.

It is apparent that such reports are not mere hoary tales of an over-gullible past. They are corroborated by yet more dramatic examples from our own time. One such is the case of US Army Specialist Fourth Class Jacky C. Bayne, 'killed' in the early morning of 6 June 1966, while serving with the 196th Light Infantry brigade near Chu Lai, Vietnam. Trying to fire an anti-tank rocket during a fierce skirmish with the Vietcong, Bayne was near simultaneously machine-gunned in the hand, knocked backwards by the recoil of the rocket he was launching, and thrown forwards by a mortar exploding immediately behind him. When he regained awareness he seemed to be looking down on himself from above. As he has described this:

> I could see the Vietcong, I could see the guy that pulled my boots off. I could see the rest of them around picking up various things. They were taking rings . . . It was like I was looking right down on it right now. I could see me . . . it was just like I was looking at a manikin laying down there . . . I could see my face and I could see my arm. I was pretty well burnt up and there was blood all over the place . . . I could see an M-14 [rifle] about three or four feet away, and I was trying to get to it, but I just could not move . . . It was like being in a deep dream . . . When the guy was at my boots, I could see that and at the same time it was like waiting for him to get through so when he turned his attention I could get to my rifle, but I couldn't get my body to move. . . . It wasn't as if I could feel a broken leg or an amputation or a twisted back or something like that. It was just that I couldn't get that *manikin* to get to the rifle . . . I was trying to get that physical manikin over there to get that weapon. I was like *spectator* . . . like it was happening to someone else . . .
>
> It was about four or five in the afternoon when our own troops came. I could hear and see them too . . . It was quite obvious I was out of it, burnt up. All the top part of my garment was burnt off too. I looked dead . . . they put me in a bag . . . We were piled up on the amtrac . . . If I had seen any of them [the soldiers] afterwards, I would have been able to recognize them. . . . We were transferred to a truck and then taken to the morgue. And from that point, it was the embalming process. I then remember being on that table and that guy telling a couple of jokes about those USO girls . . . All I had on at that time was bloody undershorts. [I watched as] he just snatched those off and he placed my leg out and cut [into the left groin to expose the femoral vein to inject the embalming fluid] . . . He had already made a slight incision and when he stopped to laugh, he was just curious as to why there was that degree of blood. So he checked my pulse and heartbeat again and I could see that too, standing up about as if you were looking at a third party . . . He checked the pulse, and he wasn't sure so he asked someone else. He had decided he would stop cutting at that point. It was about that point I

just lost track of what was taking place . . . They apparently took me to another room and severed my hand off and maybe a few minutes after that surgical procedure, the chaplain was in there saying everything was going to be all right. . . . I was no longer outside looking at the situation. I was part of it at that point.[8]

A very similar experience – of observing, outside himself, his body being prepared for burial – has been described by an Englishman, former Church Army captain Edmund Wilbourne, who in 1949 'died' of pleurisy in Crumpsall Hospital, Manchester. After his doctors had declared him dead, a nurse was instructed to make his body ready for the mortuary, unwitting that an invisible something of Wilbourne was watching from a vantage-point that was certainly not his physical body. According to Wilbourne:

I can still picture the scene. I saw myself lying on the bed. I saw a young nurse. She was preparing me for the mortuary. I remember thinking at the time how young she was to have to do such a thing as getting me ready and even shaving me. [Like most laymen, Wilbourne had no idea of the hospital practice of shaving the dead.] I actually saw it taking place. I was detached from it, it was as if I was there watching and I was the third party. I felt no emotion, just nothing, like looking at a picture. I was clinically dead about two hours . . . and I woke up at the mortuary of Crumpsall Hospital and it was the mortuary attendant who nearly had a heart attack! I know it wasn't a dream.[9]

As some way to prove that it was not a dream, Wilbourne even has his signed death certificate. Such cases are so persistently reported and so difficult to ignore that it had to be only a matter of time before they would be treated with appropriate seriousness by individuals with suitable professional qualifications.

From this point of view a crucial moment was the dying, this time from double pneumonia, of a twenty-year-old US Army private, George Ritchie, in an isolation ward of the army hospital in Abilene, Texas, in 1943. Ritchie was pronounced dead by a duty medical officer, had a sheet pulled over his face, and would, like Wilbourne, have been wheeled to the morgue, but for the intervention of a conscientious ward orderly who thought he saw the hand of the 'corpse' move. Although the medical officer first re-confirmed death, on a second plea from the orderly he pumped adrenalin directly into Ritchie's heart. The result was that Ritchie, against all expectations, flickered back to life, to go on to make such a full recovery that he subsequently trained and qualified as a doctor, establishing himself with a flourishing psychiatric practice in Whitestone, Virginia.

With profound consequences for the future was the fact that Ritchie so vividly recalled the minutes that he was 'dead'. He unembarrassedly talked about these experiences to any medical colleagues and students who were prepared to listen. Although most tried to persuade him that he had simply been hallucinating, one who in the late 1960s happened to take him seriously was a young University of Virginia philosophy undergraduate called Raymond Moody, who during his subsequent training as a doctor made a special point of looking out for patients with stories similar to Ritchie's. He found that there were many, and without being particularly scientific about these, put them together in a book, *Life after Life*, published with an introduction by Elisabeth Kübler-Ross.[10] This swiftly became a major international best-seller, with popular tabloids claiming 'proof' of life after death, and large sums of money being offered for the most sensational and convincing so-called 'near-death' experiences.

Moody had not expected quite such success. As he quickly recognized, the problem was that those he most wanted to convince, his own medical profession, were unlikely to be encouraged by the popular clamour. He remarked:

> One of my concerns was that some of the sensational claims which were made . . . by others might have the effect of frightening off legitimate investigators from an area which I continue to believe has a profound significance for clinical medicine and human psychology.[11]

The justification for such concerns is typified by the initial reactions of one young physician, Dr Michael Sabom, who in the very year of *Life after Life*'s publication had just commented specialization as a cardiologist at the University of Florida, Gainesville. Sabom happpened to attend a talk on Moody's book given by a psychiatric social worker, Sarah Kreutzinger; as he has subsequently declared frankly, he felt

> less than enthusiastic. My indoctrinated scientific mind just couldn't relate seriously to these 'far-out' descriptions of afterlife spirits and such. Being the only physician present

that morning, I was asked for my opinion at the end of the class. The kindest thing I could find to say at the moment was 'I don't believe it.'[12]

Sabom felt this particularly strongly because in all his medical career up to that time none of his patients had ever mentioned any sensation of leaving their body, or the like. But at Sarah Kreutzinger's urging he was persuaded to at least try a modest survey among those at his hospital whom he knew to have had a medical crisis, if for no other reason than to report that he had been unable to corroborate anything of Moody's claims.

Sabom was astonished when, with merely the third patient he interviewed, he found himself listening to a middle-aged housewife from Tampa telling him of an experience that was classically of the Moody type. As he has recalled this:

> As soon as she was convinced that I was not an underground psychiatrist posing as a cardiologist, she began describing the first near-death experience I had heard in my medical career. To my utter amazement the details matched the descriptions in *Life after Life*. I was even more impressed by her sincerity and the deep personal significance her experience had had for her. At the conclusion of the interview I had the distinct feeling that what this woman had shared with me that night was a deep personal glimpse into an aspect of medicine of which I knew nothing.[13]

Thus fired to treat the subject constructively now, rather than destructively, Sabom's first concern was to be rather more scientific than his pioneering predecessor. As a cardiologist he was particularly well equipped for this in view of the high proportion of critically ill and resuscitated individuals whom he routinely came across during his daily work.

Sabom was not the only professional to begin seriously to tackle the near-death phenomenon at around this time. Largely as a result of experiences described by a patient who had dropped 'dead' in his office, fellow-cardiologist Dr Maurice Rawlings of Tennessee's Chattanooga Diagnostic Center collected his own somewhat limited pool of cases, and as early as 1978 hit the US bookstalls with *Beyond Death's Door*.[14] To the north-east, in Storrs, Connecticut, Professor of Psychology Dr Kenneth Ring conducted in-depth psychological interviews with more than one hundred patients who had come close to death, enshrining these in *Life at Death: A Scientific Investigation of the Near-Death Experience*, which he published in 1980.[15] Sabom, similarly with some one hundred cases, but more immediately derived from his direct personal experience, released his *Recollections of Death: A Medical Investigation* just two years later. And as if to prove that Captain Wilbourne's was not the only case outside the USA, English psychologist Margot Grey, prompted by the near-death crisis she had personally experienced in India in 1976, published her *Return from Death: An Exploration of the Near-Death Experience* in 1985.[16]

The remarkable feature of all these and related studies is the very consistency of the near-death experiences one with each other, attesting to something, whatever its nature, very much more profound than anything we came across in the case of purported 'past-life' memories.

Thus surrounding the apparent process of separation of a something of us from the physical body, the great majority of experiencers report such a feeling of ineffability that elation, the word we used of the dying as studied by Barrett, Osis, and Kübler-Ross, has to be an understatement. According to Dr Kenneth Ring's study, no less than 60 per cent of those resuscitated from near death describe such a sensation.[17] In the words of one of Ring's subjects who tried to commit suicide by throwing herself into a bone-chilling sea, her body being repeatedly hurled against the rocks of a cliff:

> This *incredible* feeling of peace [came] over me . . . all of a sudden there was no pain, just peace. I suppose it is because it is so completely unlike anything else that I have ever experienced in my life . . . a perfectly beautiful, beautiful feeling.[18]

Dr Sabom in his turn quotes the case of a 54-year-old construction worker from Georgia who needed cardiac attention so urgently that he had to have 'open-chest' heart surgery performed without anaesthetic. Describing his subsequent experience while 'unconscious', he reported: 'That was the most beautiful instant in the whole world when I came out of that body! . . . All I saw was extremely pleasant! I cannot imagine anything in the world or out of the world that could anywhere compare.'[19]

Just as, in the case of the dying mentioned in Chapter 8, many people exhibited a remarkably clear-headed awareness of the imminence of their deaths, so the resuscitated often, with equal clarity, seem to recall the realization of being dead. A 45-year-old man who had suffered a totally unexpected cardiac arrest told Sabom: 'I realized that I was dead . . . that I had died. [I thought,] I don't know whether the doctor knows it or not, but I know it.'[20]

One of Dr Ring's subjects called Margaret, who spent three days comatose after an apparent heart failure, told her interviewer:

> *Margaret*: I know that I had died, I know that I had died.
> *Interviewer*: Do you know . . . according to your medical records if you were declared clinically dead?
> *Margaret*: I've talked with Doctor — about it. He said, 'Margaret, I wouldn't have given two cents for your life. We were ready to give up so many times.'
> *Interviewer*: You felt at this time that you were dead, would you say? That you had died? This was your subjective feeling?
> *Margaret*: Yes. Yes. I did. I did.[21]

Particularly fascinating are the descriptions of separation from the body, and of floating above the scene of the apparent death. According to Ring's statistics, 37 per cent of resuscitated patients report some sort of awareness of this kind. The following, from a young Florida saleswoman knocked down by a speeding car in July 1964, is typical:

> A man yelled at me . . . apparently he was trying to warn me, and I was struck from behind. . . . That's the last thing I remember until I was above the whole scene viewing the accident. I was very detached. This was the amazing thing about it to me. . . . I don't remember hearing anything. I don't remember anybody saying anything. I was just viewing things . . . It was just like I floated up there . . . [up to the] roof-top or maybe a little higher . . . very detached. I think the thing that impressed me most was that I was devoid of emotion. It was as though I was pure intellect. I wasn't frightened. You know, it was very pleasant and obviously emotionally detached from the whole situation . . . [I remember] seeing my shoe, which was crushed under the car . . . I remember seeing the earring which was smashed. I remember wearing a new dress and I was wearing it for the second time – at that time I made all my clothes – and I thought: Oh, no. My new dress is ruined. And I wasn't even thinking about my body being possibly ruined too. This is an odd thing in that I don't think really that the seriousness of the

situation dawned on me. I don't think I really had the realization at the time that: Oh my God. I'm outside my body. What's happening to me? . . . My attention was called to my body when the attendants put it on the stretcher. . . . I saw myself in profile. I was actually towards the front and side of the car, viewing all of this. . . . I was viewing my body as they picked it up and put it onto the stretcher. It was from a distance away, actually. . . . I remember them looking at my eyes. I guess they were checking my pupils, I don't know. [22]

The 'floating above' viewpoint is so consistently described in such experiences and seems so positively distinct from anything that might be possible with the physical eyes, that it serves both to provide a cross-check on Dr Josef Issels's case of the dying woman, and to be consistent with Princeton's Julian Jaynes's argument that there is no theoretical reason for our self-awareness to be located in our brain-space. Here is how a British victim of a motor-cycle accident viewed his body:

I saw that 'I' (i.e. my head) was obscured by the head and shoulders of a man. 'I' was lying on my back, and although I could not 'see' my own face I recognised my clothing. I could see the heads and necks of about eight people peering over me. . . . Someone said, 'Leave him, he's dead.' I shouted from about fifteen feet above ground, 'No, I'm not!' [23]

This is how one of Dr Sabom's subjects, a 42-year-old woman from Missouri with a heart irregularity, described a lumbar disc surgical operation conducted on herself, during which her body lay *face-down* on the operating table:

What I recall . . . was it seems like I was just floating up near the ceiling. . . . It was sort of a funny feeling because I was up there and this body was below . . . It was a green room . . . They had surgical gowns on . . . I could see them operating on my back. . . . I came right down to the operation and I was amazed how deep my spine was in my back and how many layers with things clamped and all that sort of stuff. . . . Then I saw them reach in, I guess it was on my left-hand side, and get the disk out. [24]

In the case of one of Ring's subjects, also undergoing a surgical operation, she was even able to see the dirt on the operating theatre's light fittings:

> From where I was looking, I could look down on this enormous fluorescent light . . . and it was so dirty on top of the light. ['Could you see the top of the light fixture, then?'] I was floating above the light fixture. ['Could you see the top of the light fixture?'] Yes [sounding a little impatient with my question], and it was filthy. And I remember thinking, 'Got to tell the nurses about that.' . . . I don't know how long I was there [but] I could see what was going on in the cubicle next to mine. We were in a series of cubicles with curtains in between and I could see the woman in the cubicle next to me and she was asleep.[25]

As remarked by Sabom, for the vast majority of subjects whatever their separated 'self' was, it was not something that they could actually put a physical form to. According to Ring, more than 97 per cent of those who reported a definite near-death experience felt an absence of any form of body, and for nearly as many there was an absence of any normal concept of time. As described by a heart-attack patient interviewed by Ring: 'It seemed like I was up there in space and just my mind was active. No body feeling, just like my brain was up in space. I had nothing but my mind. Weightless, I had nothing.'[26]

Similarly, a woman subject of Ring's who had a cardiac arrest while undergoing a tonsillectomy reported:

> I was above. I don't know above what. But I was [pause] up. . . . It was like [pause] I didn't have a body! I was [pause] but it was me, not a body, but me! You know what I mean? . . . It was a me inside. The real me was up there; not this here [pointing to her physical body].[27]

And as another of Ring's patients responded when asked about his sense of time: 'My sense of time was way off. Time didn't seem to mean anything. . . . It was just, well, I don't know how to explain it, even.'[28]

Just as we noted in relation to 'ghosts', that while these might look solid, they are consistently reported to have no solidity to the living, passing through solid walls and even people, so in the near-death experiences whatever it is that seems to leave the physical body, sees the living as ghosts. As a US Vietnam War captain, who lost both legs and an arm when he stepped on a booby-trap bomb, recollects of his near-death experience while an army medical team tried frantically to save him:

> I really believe that I was dead . . . I actually remember grabbing the doctor. . . . Nothing [happened]. Absolutely nothing. It was almost like he wasn't there. I grabbed and he wasn't there or either I just went through him or whatever.[29]

The same idea of the unreality of the living was reported by the construction worker who so vividly described the sensation of ineffability:

> I could see they [doctors and nurses] were busy. In fact, one time a nurse I could see looked me right in the [non-physical] face just this far away [indicating one foot]. I tried to say something but she didn't say nothing. . . . She was like looking at a movie screen that can't talk back and that doesn't recognize you're there. I was the real one and she was unreal. That's the way I felt.[30]

The final feature, and one as astonishing as anything that has gone before, is the apparent facility of the separated something to travel anywhere it 'thinks' about. Sir Alexander Ogston, who seems to have had a near-death experience through typhoid during the Boer War of 1899–1902, noted:

> In my wanderings there was a strange consciousness that I could see through the walls of the building, though I was aware that they were there and that everything was transparent to my senses. I saw plainly, for instance, a poor RAMC surgeon, of whose existence I had not known, and who was in another part of the hospital, grow very ill and scream and die. I saw them cover over his corpse and carry him softly out on shoeless feet, quietly and surreptitiously, lest we should know that he had died, and the next night I thought take him away to the cemetery.[31]

Sir Auckland Campbell Geddes, a former physician and Britain's Ambassador to the United States from 1920 to 1924, told the Royal Medical Society in 1927 of a similar near-death experience: 'Gradually I realized that I was seeing not only "things" at home, but in London and in Scotland, in fact wherever my attention was directed.'[32]

A very similar sensation was reported by Dr Raymond Moody's mentor, George Ritchie. He experienced the sensation of crossing the United States during the period that his body had lain with a sheet over the face, on his return apparently recognizing his body only by the ring on its finger. Such experiences are also encountered among the subjects of both Sabom and Ring. A 52-year-old Florida night-watchman who suffered a cardiac arrest told Sabom:

> I could see anywhere I wanted to. I could see out in the parking lot, but I was still in the corridor. . . . It was just like I said, 'OK, what's going on out in the parking lot?' and part of my brain would go over and take a look at what's going on over there and come back and report to me.[33]

And as Ring was told by a woman near-death survivor who saw her sister, a hospital worker, being informed of her plight in a different part of the hospital to where she lay:

> I could follow her movements. . . . She walked in shortly after the alert was sounded and got to the emergency room where she worked and someone told her what was going on and she came ripping upstairs. I could see her doing it. I could see her coming up the elevator, telling people that they couldn't – and she told me this afterward and I shared that with her – get off the floor, that she used the emergency elevator and she went straight up to the floor.[34]

Could all these experiences be the exact counterparts of the so-called crisis apparitions of the dying to the living, as noted in Chapter 8? Do we have at least a clue to why Dr Issels's dying cancer patient was able to 'see' the woman writing the letter in the next ward, that something of her really did move into the next ward? As yet we have seen only one aspect of the tales of the resuscitated, their reports of their impressions while something of them, despite the 'thought-travel', seems still to be in an earthbound state. But for this alone the serious question is whether it can be believed. Is there *really* a something of us, after or around the time of death, which genuinely leaves the physical body and temporarily hovers near by? Or is everything that we have considered in this chapter no more than some form of hallucination? The right answer to this question is so important to the whole issue of the validity or otherwise of after death experience that we must now very carefully consider both the objections and the counter-objections.

# 10

# TRULY OUT OF THE BODY?

Just as in the cases of apparent 'past-life' memory that we examined, the claims of floating outside the body in near-death circumstances represent a substantial corpus of evidential material upon which a reasoned judgement should be possible. From this material we should be able to find some means of establishing either that something of us genuinely does separate from the physical body, or that there is some other rather more prosaic explanation.

One explanation that appears to be readily discountable for at least the vast majority of claimed cases is any form of conscious fraud. In marked contrast to, for instance, Dr Ian Stevenson's Asian 'reincarnation' cases, those who describe near-death experiences have usually had to be sought out and virtually coaxed to talk, due to fear that their story either will be ridiculed or will cause questions to be raised about their sanity. As Dr Sabom's security-guard subject told him:

'You're the only person [I've told] . . . People will think I'm crazy. . . I've lived with this thing for three years now and I haven't told anyone because I don't want them putting the straitjacket on me.'[1]

Similarly the collectors of these cases are in no way self-deluded, wholly-headed occultists. Those whom we have quoted are all professionals in the medical and psychology fields, and scarcely dismissible as on the lunatic fringe of these. Dr Michael Sabom is vigorous, brawny, and extrovert, assistant professor in cardiology at Emory University, still youthful and with a young family. Dr Kenneth Ring, professor of psychology at Connecticut University, is similarly young, and sufficiently humorous and light-hearted in his approach that he and his wife have dubbed their Ashford, Connecticut, home the 'Near-Death Hotel' because of the number of near-death experiencers and researchers to whom they find themselves offering hospitality.

None the less the seriousness with which Sabom, Ring, and others treat cases of the kind we have studied is as yet a long way from any similar acceptance by the general consensus of medical practitioners and psychologists. So what other possible explanations are offered?

One suggestion from the field of psychiatry has been a condition known as 'autoscopy', in which individuals, without necessarily being in any form of life-threatening situation, see a mirror replica of themselves, quite separate from their physical bodies, in the form of a 'double'. This condition is principally found among schizophrenics and sufferers from depressive illnesses, and has been carefully studied by Dr Lukianowicz of Barrow Hospital, a psychiatric hospital just to the south of my own city of Bristol. As Dr Lukianowicz has observed of one of his patients, this man would see

> an image of his own face 'as if looking at it in a mirror'. This phantom face would imitate all his facial expressions and D. [the patient] would frequently 'play with it', forcing it to copy his mimicking. The patient's attitude toward his double was overtly sadistic . . . For instance, he would often strike the phantom on its head.[2]

Yet as evident even from this limited description, the autoscopic condition appears demonstrably different from the experiences described by the subjects of Sabom *et al.* Whereas the autoscopic experiencer stays within his physical body and sees his 'double' as a form of ghost, the near-death experiencer consistently has no image of his non-physical body and recognizes his 'dead' body as retaining its original physical substance, the unreality of which he is well aware of. Furthermore the autoscopic 'double' mimics the actions of its 'real' counterpart instead of lying prone in death. And there is none of the feeling of ineffability.

Another objection frequently raised, and one particularly pertinent to individuals whose near-death crisis has occurred during a surgical operation, is that as a result of inadequate anaesthesia patients may appear to be deeply unconscious yet still have some awareness of the work being done on their bodies. The sense of hearing is especially well known to be the last to succumb to anaesthesia; in recognition of this, trainee surgeons are specifically advised not to make anxiety-raising remarks during surgical operations. As case studies have found in the past, careless remarks can sometimes be unconsciously remembered, causing untold psychological distress.

In this context just how much such awareness may continue during operations has been made clear by several recent court cases in Britain. These have concerned pregnant mothers who have received rather too finely judged anaesthesia prior to undergoing caesarian-section operations. Mrs Margaret Ackers of Liverpool was in 1985 awarded £13,000 compensation following a caesarian-section operation, because, although she had been given enough anaesthetic to render her unable to move or to speak or in any other way to register distress, the dosage did not render her unconscious. According to her own description:

> It was just like being trapped inside your own body or being buried alive. I couldn't scream. I couldn't move a muscle. I couldn't do a thing. I felt as if I was going to die. I kept thinking, 'I'll go to sleep in a minute', but they made the incision and it felt like a red-hot poker. I felt a lot of movement in my abdomen and I felt lighter as they lifted the baby out. There was scraping, then I felt the stitches going in and being pulled tight. It seemed to go on for ever.[3]

Again, however, there is a substantial qualitative difference between a case of this kind and those of the near-death variety. Instead of any 'on-the-ceiling' viewpoint or sense of being able to move anywhere, part of the horror of Mrs Ackers's experience was specifically the sensation of being trapped in her own body. Rather than the peace and painlessness so consistently reported by Sabom and Ring's patients, hers was a nightmare of physical pain of the most excruciating kind. In fact, one of Sabom's near-death experiencers who some years previously had similarly been semi-consciousness during surgery has provided an independent first-hand differentiation between surgical semi-consciousness and a near-death experience:

> Several years back, I was in an auto accident. . . . I was laying there [in the emergency room] and I could hear two nurses there and they were trying to get my blood-pressure. One says to the other, 'You know, I can't get a reading on this', or something like that, and she said, 'Well, try the other one.' And I heard all this and I knew they were there but I couldn't communicate with them . . . But I didn't see nothing. I just heard. This other time with the cardiac arrest [and near-death experience], I was looking down from the ceiling and there were no ifs, ands or buts about it.[4]

Another possible explanation of the experiences is that they are a form of dream. Undeniably some dreams involve the sensation of flying or floating through the air, and some can seem very vivid. But whereas most dreams involve disjointed or unreal elements and fade very quickly unless they are written down immediately, among the many consistent features of near-death experiencers' reminiscences are their total reality and apparently effortless recall even years later. Sabom was told by a Georgia business man who suffered a cardiac arrest:

> It's reality. I know for myself that I didn't experience no fantasy. There was no so-called dream or nothing. These things really happened to me. It happened. I know. I went through it. Even though I was in a blackout stage I know myself I went through it.[5]

As a 46-year-old labourer, also from Georgia, put it:

> I *know* it was real. I *know* that I was up there. . . . And I *know* that I seen me down there. I could swear on a Bible that I was there. I seen things just like I seen them now. I can't prove it to none of those people there because they didn't see me. There's no way you can prove it, but I was there.[6]

Yet another explanation that has been put forward is that of wish-fulfilment, or prior expectation of an afterlife on the part of the religiously inclined. Since both Doctors Sabom and Rawlings's patients derive from the so-called Bible Belt southern sector of the United States, this is a possibility that has to be treated with due seriousness. Furthermore, since all the modern researchers have conducted their enquiries after the publication and huge media attention accorded to Moody's book, it must also be considered that some subjects' stories have been influenced by this.

Aware of such concerns, Sabom in particular made a careful note of the religious affiliations and strength of belief on the part of all his subjects, and whether they had previously heard of the so-called near-death experience. His tabulations show that nearly a third of his subjects either were agnostic or never attended any church, and less than half of his subjects attended church with any sort of regularity (monthly or more). Since most of his interviewing was conducted before news of *Life after Life* had percolated to the rural populations of northern Florida (from where most of his subjects derived), only 12 per cent of those describing a near-death experience claimed to have heard of the phenomenon beforehand.

Even this does not exhaust the possible explanations, however. Another of the most common to be advanced, suggested by Dr Richard Blacher in a 1979 issue of the *Journal of the American Medical Association*, is that the near-death experiences derive from hypoxia, a sort of delirium brought about by a diminishing oxygen supply to the brain at the onset of the death process:

> People who undergo these 'death experiences' are suffering from a hypoxic state, during which they try to deal psychologically with the anxieties provoked by medical procedures and talk . . . we are dealing here with the fantasy of death.[7]

On the other hand, the effects of hypoxia are well known from high-altitude mountaineering expeditions, and were carefully studied during the 1930s by a Columbia University physician, Dr R. A. McFarland,[8] who accompanied an international expedition to the Chilean Andes. They are characterized by sluggishness, irritability, fogginess of thought, and poor memory recall, a far cry from the euphoria and clarity so consistently reported in near-death experiences. The inapplicability of this has been further indicated by one of Dr Sabom's patients whose blood-oxygen and carbon-dioxide levels were being monitored at the time of his near-death experience. His oxygen level was well above normal at the time.

A rather more plausible suggestion has been that the effect of pain-killing narcotics administered to the patients, or some natural opiates released during the dying process, may act in a manner akin to hallucinogenic drugs. This idea has been cogently put forward by a British psychologist well known to me, Dr Susan Blackmore of Bristol University's Brain and Perception Laboratory, who personally experienced a vivid sensation of being outside her physical body as a result of the effects of cannabis. As she has described in her book *Beyond the Body*, she accepted a small quantity of cannabis one evening that she spent with two friends, Vicky and Kevin, listening to music in the room of an Oxford college. She was feeling 'terribly tired'; then, according to her own account:

> As I sat, listening to the music, the voices of my friends seemed a very long way off. If I thought about my own body it did not seem to be firmly on the hard floor but rather indistinct, as though surrounded by cotton wool. In my tiredness my mind seemed to follow the music into a scene of a tree-lined avenue. . . . The whole was like a tree-lined tunnel and I was hurtling through it . . . simultaneously with this experience I was aware of Vicky asking if I would like some coffee. Kevin answered but I did not . . . It is to Kevin's credit that he both initiated and helped me with the next

stage. Quite out of the blue, and I have no idea why, he asked, 'Sue, where are you?' This simple question baffled me. I thought; struggled to reply; saw the road and leaves; tried to see my own body; and then did see it. There it was below me. The words came out: 'I'm on the ceiling.' With some surprise I watched the mouth – my mouth – down below, opening and closing and I marvelled at its control.

Kevin seemed quite calm at this pronouncement and proceeded to question me in detail. What was it like up there? What could I see? What was 'I'? . . . Again, as I formulated answers, the mouth below spoke. . . . From the ceiling I could apparently see the room quite clearly. I saw the desk, chairs, window, my friends and myself all from above. Then I saw a string or cord, silvery, faintly glowing and moving gently, running between the neck of my body below and the navel, or thereabouts, of a duplicate body above. . . . With encouragement I moved out of the room, myself and my cord moving through the walls, another floor of rooms and the roof with ease. I clearly observed the red of the roofs and the row of chimneys before flying on to more distant places. . . . I visited Paris and New York and flew over South America.[9]

Impressive though this experience was to Susan Blackmore, she was too much of a scientist to blind herself to the signs that it was really a fantasy. For instance, when she went out next day and studied the roofs of the houses over which she had theoretically 'flown', she noted that these were in fact grey, not the red that she had 'seen' while under the influence of the cannabis. Furthermore there were none of the chimneys that she had seen during her 'trip', which had also involved her passing through a completely illusory floor of rooms. So if cannabis can induce the illusion of separateness from the physical body, why should one believe that such an experience on the part of the dying should be any more real?

However, yet again this experience of Dr Blackmore's incorporates features qualitatively different from those of the Moody/Sabom/Ring pattern. For instance, she unequivocally describes a 'duplicate body', whereas, as we have seen, the vast majority of medically attested near-death experiencers report no awareness of any form to the something of them that separates from the physical body. Similarly, she refers to a silver cord seeming to link her physical body and the 'spirit' one. While such silver cords are commonly referred to in Spiritualist literature, they are almost completely absent among the medical collections of near-death experiences. There is also the suggestion of sluggishness in her description. In other words, while there is no doubt that Susan Blackmore's cannabis experience was just a hallucination, it would be quite unjustified to suppose that near-death-type descriptions of being out of the physical body should be dismissed in the same way. Furthermore, as noted by Dr Sabom and others, there are many instances of near-death experiences in which the patient received no form of drugs or other medication; and others in which medication actually appears to have blocked what might otherwise have been a near-death experience.

But what does become clear from Susan Blackmore's line of thinking – and she published her book before Sabom had published his – is the importance of trying to isolate information given by near-death-experience patients that can be demonstrated to have been impossible for them to have obtained with their normal physical senses. For instance, in Chapter 9 we noted how one patient saw dust on top of the lights high on the ceiling of the operating theatre while her physical body lay on the operating table below. Although this particular item of information is inadequate because it is too general and might so easily be guessed at, is there any else that might be construed as rather more specific?

A tantalizing field for potential verification has been alluded to by Dr Elisabeth Kübler-Ross, who along with Doctors Moody, Sabom, Ring, *et al.* has assembled her own collection of near-death experiencers. Among these have been some totally blind individuals, of whom Dr Kübler-Ross says:

> We asked them to share with us what it was like when they had this near-death experience. If it was just a dream fulfilment those people would not be able to share with us the colour of the sweater we wear, the design of a tie, or minute details of shape, colours and designs of the people's clothing. We have questioned several totally blind people who were able to share with us in their near-death experience and they were not only able to tell us who came into the room first, who worked on the resuscitation, but they were able to give minute details of the attire and the clothing of all the people present, something a totally blind person would never be able to do.[10]

Regrettably Dr Kübler-Ross has tended to be too committed to her patients to spend time publishing these cases in the proper depth to prove her point. It would have been helpful to be told, for instance, whether some or all of these people had been blind since birth; one can only assume not, since anyone blind since birth would need to learn the recognition of colours.

Other sources do seem to back Dr Kübler-Ross up. For instance, the very patient of Ring's who remarked on the dust on the operating-theatre lights happened to have as her anaesthetist a physician who often worked with children. In order to amuse and relax young patients prior to their being operated on, this man habitually wore a yellow surgical hat ornamented with magenta butterflies. In 1974 when the woman patient went into shock as a result of post-surgical complications, she heard a doctor mutter, 'This woman's dying'; then, in her own words:

> Bang, I left! The next thing I was aware of was floating on the ceiling. And seeing [the anaesthetist] down there, with his hat on his head . . . it was so vivid. I'm very near-sighted, by the way, which was another of the startling things that happened when I left my body. I see at fifteen feet what most people see at four hundred. . . . They were hooking me up to a machine that was behind my head. And my very first thought was, 'Jesus, I can see! I can't believe it, I can see!' I could read the numbers on the machine behind my head and I was just so thrilled. And I thought. 'They gave me back my glasses.'[11]

This woman claimed to have purposefully remembered the numbers on the machine, and had she had these independently verified, and obtained some form of signed statement to this effect, it would have been particularly evidential. Unfortunately not all these requirements were fulfilled. According to Ring:

> This woman later told me that after she recovered she asked permission to return to the operating room to determine whether the numbers she had seen on the machine were correct. She claims that this was indeed so, and that she told her anaesthiologist at the time, but since he is no longer practicing in Connecticut and she has lost track of him, it was not possible for me independently to corroborate her story.

None the less, case after case attests that in principle *real* recall of information beyond the reach of the physical senses is achieved. The already mentioned Dr Maurice Rawlings has described the case of one of the nursing staff who had attempted suicide at the hospital where he worked. Rawlings himself found the young woman's body, hanging from a coat-hook on the back of her bathroom door, from which she had suspended herself using a neck-strain collar as an impromptu noose. Rawlings writes: 'her face, tongue and eyes were bulging and swollen. Her face had a dark, bluish tinge. The rest of her body had a death pallor. She had long since stopped breathing.'[12]

Sending the girl's room-mate for help, Rawlings took off his jacket, loosened his tie, and immediately began external heart resuscitation and mouth-to-mouth ventilation. As soon as the proper resuscitation equipment arrived, he switched to administering oxygen and intravenous drug injections. The young woman was then taken on a stretcher to intensive care, where after remaining in a coma for four days she eventually made a full recovery. According to Rawlings:

> About the second day after recovery from her coma, I asked her if she remembered anything at all. She said, 'Oh, I remember you working on me. You took off your plaid brown coat and threw it on the floor, and then you loosened your tie. I also remember that your tie had white and brown stripes in it. The nurse who came to help you looked so worried! I tried to tell her I was all right. You told her to get an Ambu bag and also an intracath to start an IV [intravenous injection]. Then the two men came in with a stretcher.

Rawlings comments: 'Recall with me – she was in deep coma at that particular time, and remained in a coma another four days! At the time I took off my brown plaid coat, only she and I were in the room. And she was clinically dead.'

Perhaps even more precisely evidential is a case reported by Professor Kimberly Clark of the University of Washington, Seattle, in respect of a patient called Maria who suffered cardiac arrest while in the hospital where the Professor worked:

> She said, 'The strangest thing happened when the doctors and nurses were working on me: I found myself looking down from the ceiling at them working on my body.'
> I was not impressed at first. I thought that she might know what had been going on in the room, what people were wearing, and who would be there, since she had seen them all day prior to her cardiac arrest. . . .
> She then told me that she had been distracted by some-

thing over the emergency room driveway and found herself outside, as if she had 'thought herself' over the emergency room driveway and, in just that instant, she was out there. At this point, I was a little more impressed, since she had arrived at night inside an ambulance and would not have known what the emergency room area looked like. . . .

But then Maria proceeded to describe being further distracted by an object on the third floor ledge on the north end of the building. She 'thought her way' up there and found herself 'eyeball to shoelace' with a tennis shoe, which she asked me to try to find for her. She needed someone else to know that the tennis shoe was really there to validate her out-of-the-body experience.

With mixed emotions I went outside and looked up at the ledges but could not see much at all. I went up to the third floor and began going in and out of patients' rooms and looking out their windows, which were so narrow that I had to press my face to the screen just to see the ledge at all. Finally, I found a room where I pressed my face to the glass and saw the tennis shoe! My vantage point was very different from what Maria's had to have been for her to notice that the little toe had worn a place in the shoe and that the lace was stuck under the heel and other details about the side of the shoe not visible to me. The only way she would have had such a perspective was if she had been floating right outside and at very close range to the tennis shoe. I retrieved the shoe and brought it back to Maria; it was very concrete evidence for me. [13]

Of all the researchers in the near-death field it is perhaps Dr Michael Sabom who has made the greatest efforts to pin-point such potentially convincing items of information and to try to cross-check these. In *Recollections of Death* he published six in-depth descriptions by patients of their surgical operations as purportedly viewed by them while out of the body, comparing these wherever possible with the surgeon's notes and other independent eyewitness testimony. In some of these the difficulty is both to marry laymen's observations with clinical surgical descriptions and to isolate information that could not have been gleaned from operations viewed in hospital dramas and documentaries as seen on television. Typical, for instance, are the following extracts from a Florida night-watchman's account of his open-heart surgery at the University of Florida in January 1978:

*Patient*: My head was covered and the rest of my body was draped with more than one sheet, separate sheets laid in layers.

*Surgeon*: The patient . . . was prepped from the chin to below the ankles and draped in the customary sterile fashion.

*Patient*: I could draw you a picture of the saw they used.

*Surgeon*: The sternum was sawed open in the midline.

*Patient*: . . . the thing they used to separate the ribs with. It was always there . . . It was draped all around, but you could see the metal part of it. . . .

*Surgeon*: . . . . A self-retaining retractor was utilized over wound towels.

*Patient*: He cut pieces of my heart off. He raised it and twisted it this way and that and took quite a bit of time examining it and looking at different things.

*Surgeon*: An incision was made over the most prominent portion of the aneurism after the heart had been turned upside down in the pericardial wall. . . . The entire aneurism was resected.

*Patient*: . . . They injected something into my heart. That's scary when you see that thing go right into your heart.

*Surgeon*: Air was evacuated from the left ventricle with a needle and a syringe.[14]

Although all this might seem too unspecific, one feature that did impress Sabom was the patient's classic description of what he could see of his heart:

Shaped something like the continent of Africa, with it being larger up here and tapered down . . . [the surface was] pinkish and yellow. I thought the yellow part was fat tissue or something. Yucky, kind of. One general area to the right or left was darker than the rest instead of all being the same color.[15]

Another intriguing item of information, however, was uncheckable:

All but one doctor had scuffs tied around his shoes and this joker had on white shoes which had blood all over them. I was wondering why this one doctor was in a pair of patent-leather white shoes in the operating room when the nurses and everybody had green covers that they put their shoes into. . . . I'm morbidly curious about that. It seemed so odd . . . I thought it was unsanitary.[16]

More promising, not least because of the profession of the subject, is Sabom's record of his questioning of a former US Air Force pilot who had his near-death experience while being resuscitated from a massive heart attack sustained in 1973, at the age of thirty-nine:

*Pilot*: I remember them pulling over the cart, the defibrillator, the thing with the paddles [contact discs for the electrical shock method of restarting the heart] on it. I remember they asked for so many watt-seconds or something on the thing, and they gave me a jolt with it.

*Sabom*: Did you notice any of the details of the machine itself or of the cart it was sitting on?

*Pilot*: I remember it had a meter on the face. I assume it read the voltage, or current, or watt-seconds or whatever they program the thing for.

*Sabom*: Did you notice how the meter looked?

*Pilot*: It was square and had two needles on there, one fixed and one which moved.

*Sabom*: How did it move?

*Pilot*: It seemed to come up rather slowly, really. It didn't just pop up like an ammeter or a voltmeter or something registering.

*Sabom*: And how far up did it go?

*Pilot*: The first time it went between one-third and one-half scale, and the third time it was about three-quarters.

*Sabom*: What was the relationship between the moving needle and the fixed needle?

*Pilot*: I think the fixed needle moved each time they punched the thing and somebody was messing with it. And I think they moved the fixed needle and it stayed still while the other one moved up.

*Sabom*: Did the moving needle ever pass the fixed needle?

*Pilot*: I don't think so, but I don't specifically remember.[17]

As Sabom commented, the pilot's information was made all the more weighty by his career and life having been geared to accurate instrument-reading:

I was particularly fascinated by his description of a 'fixed' needle and a 'moving' needle on the face of the defibrillator as it was being charged with electricity. The movement of these two needles is not something he could have observed unless he had actually seen this instrument in use. These two needles are individually used (1) to preselect the amount of electricity to be delivered to the patient ('they moved the fixed needle and it stayed still') and (2) to indicate that the defibrillator is being charged to the preselected amount ('[the moving needle] seemed to come up rather slowly, really. It didn't just pop up like an ammeter or a voltmeter or something registering'). This charging procedure is only performed immediately prior to defibrillation, since once charged, this machine poses a serious electrical hazard unless it is correctly discharged in a very specific manner.[18]

Perhaps the most compelling of all was the story Sabom obtained from a retired labourer from Michigan of how he had 'seen' members of his family while his body was being frantically resuscitated from a cardiac arrest. Here is the patient's description:

I remember seeing them down the hall as plain as could be – my wife, my oldest son and my oldest daughter and the doctor. . . There was no way, being out, that I could have seen anybody . . . I knew damn well they were there . . . I didn't know what was going on. I didn't know why they were crying.[19]

As Sabom established from interviewing this man's wife, he had been expected to be discharged from hospital the next day, and therefore she had not originally planned to visit him. She decided to do so only because her eldest son and daughter had happened to call, the three arriving at the floor of her husband's hospital room just in time to see him being wheeled away from them down the corridor towards intensive care, with a whole team of doctors frantically working on him. His face was pointed away, so that she only recognized him by a glimpse of his grey hair. Yet when she was able to talk to him three days later he told her, as she informed Sabom:

He seen everything. He seen them working with him. And he told me he seen us standing down at the end of the hall. And he couldn't have seen us because his head was facing us [i.e.

the face pointed the other way]. He couldn't have seen us. . . . He swore he'd seen us, and I said he couldn't have. And even if he had just been laying there in the hall without the heart attack or anything he couldn't have recognized us from the distance. . . . And what was funny was that I wasn't always with the same people. We have six children, and they're all grown. So when we went to see him, it was never the same. One time one daughter would go or another daughter or son would go or me. So he couldn't have known who I was with or that I was even there. And he told me who was there. . . . He said he seen us standing there talking to the doctor. And we were. . . . And when he told me the different things that he had seen, it's always the same. He never changes it.[20]

None of all this range of evidence constitutes proof, and ideally there will be future cases yet more evidential than those cited. But that at the onset of what we call death something of us really can and does move outside the confines of the physical body seems to be very powerfully demonstrated by everything that we have seen, whatever afterlife construction we may care to put on it. However, as we are about to see, this is merely the easiest aspect of near-death cases to accept. For, as was remarked by the very last patient we have cited: 'And then I went further . . . I went to a different world.'

# 11

# INTO THE LIGHT . . .

In the Palace of the Doges at Venice is a tall, rather over-varnished panel painting created about five hundred years ago, around the time that Columbus discovered the New World. Entitled 'The Ascent into the Empyrean', it is from the brush of the visionary Flemish painter Hieronymus Bosch, and shows an extraordinary scene of the souls of the dead floating upwards through darkness, helped by aerial beings, then being drawn like moths towards a spiralling tunnel of radiant light. At the far end of this tunnel, conveyed by an orb of pure yellow, is the just discernible human shape of a Being who seems to be the source of all light.

For his inspiration Hieronymus Bosch is thought to have derived much from fourteenth-century mystical treatises such as Netherlander Jan van Ruysbroeck's *Adornment of the Spiritual Marriage*, which speaks of the privileged dead being drawn via an abyss or chasm towards the divine radiance: 'some immense effusion of essential light which encircles and attracts us'.[1]

What is most intriguing about the image Bosch created all those years ago is how closely it conveys in pictorial form the 'other-worldly' journey described by some near-death experiencers either in the wake of their apparent hovering over their physical bodies, or alternatively to this latter. According to Dr Kenneth Ring, some 23 per cent of all near-death survivors he interviewed described the sensation of leaving the physical dimension and hurtling fearlessly and effortlessly in darkness through some form of void or tunnel towards a source of extraordinary light.

This is how it was remembered by one of Dr Maurice Rawlings's subjects, a woman in her mid-twenties, who 'died' as a result of uncontrollable bleeding following childbirth:

> Next I was hurtling down this dark tunnel at a high speed, not touching the sides. It made a sort of swishing sound. At the end of the tunnel was this yellow-white light. And then I said, 'This must be what it feels like to die. I feel no pain at all.'[2]

One of Dr Ring's patients, a young woman who suffered a near-fatal asthma attack, particularly remarked on the tunnel's pipe-like appearance:

> I do remember thinking to myself that I was dying. I felt I was floating through a tunnel. . . . When I say tunnel the only thing I can think of is – you know, those sewer pipes, those big pipes they put in? It was round like that, but it was enormous. I couldn't really see the edges of it; I got the feeling that it was round. ['What kind of feeling did you have as you were floating through this tunnel?'] Very peaceful, almost as if I were a raft in the ocean, you know?[3]

Other descriptions are similar. A subject of Dr Raymond Moody noted, just as in Bosch's painting, that the tunnel seemed to spiral:

> I found myself in a tunnel, a tunnel of concentric circles. Shortly after that I saw a TV programme called *The Time Tunnel*, where people go back in time through this spiralling tunnel. That's the closest to it I can think of.[4]

Again, just as in the Bosch painting, virtually all near-death experiencers report at the end of the tunnel what seems to be an extraordinary light. According to one of Dr Ring's female patients: 'It was like – hard to believe – like you were going from dark to light. I can't explain it . . . all of a sudden there was light.'[5]

And as described by a 35-year-old former fireman subject of Dr Michael Sabom:

> At the end of that tunnel was a glowing light. It looked like an orange – you've seen the sunset in the afternoon? From the light it makes up an orange glow with a yellow tint in a circle. That's what it looked like at the end of the tunnel.[6]

A consistent description of this light from all subjects was that once you arrived in it, while it seemed to have a form of brightness, 'it didn't hurt your eyes'. Dr Sabom's 54-year-old construction-worker patient tried to explain it in this way:

> This light was really the absence of darkness. We're not used to that concept because we always get a shadow from a light

unless the light is all around us. But this light was so total and complete that you didn't look at the light, you were *in* the light. See what I'm saying?[7]

A patient of Dr Ring's put it in almost identical terms:

[The light] wasn't centred on anything; it was, like, all around me. It was all around me . . . it was not bright. . . . You know what it was? Like someone had put a shade over the sun. It made me feel very, very peaceful. I was no longer afraid. Everything was going to be all right.[8]

Could it be that it was the experiencing of this very same unearthly light which was the cause of all the elation and exaltation noted on the faces of the dying by researchers Barrett, Osis, and Kübler-Ross?

We now reach a stage reported by only about one in five of all those describing a near-death experience. To anyone of a sceptical disposition what follows becomes the most difficult of all to take at face value. Having entered the light, the resuscitated now report finding themselves in extraordinarily beautiful surroundings that are unequivocally stereotypes of popular concepts of 'heaven'. To quote from some of Dr Sabom's subjects: 'clouds . . . gray-white clouds', 'beautiful flowers in a flowerbed', 'steps leading to the Golden Gates of Heaven', a 'beautiful park with hill, trees and flowers', 'just another world . . . bright, sunny . . . real beautiful', 'still stream of water . . . rainbow colors in background', 'beautiful blue sky . . . field of flowers of different colors', 'a place of beautiful light that pulsated with exquisite music', 'a fence dividing extremely scraggly territory from the most beautiful pasture scene', 'flowers, trees of all kind, beautiful flower gardens, the sun was beautiful . . . a tremendous happiness thing'.[9]

Similar imagery was used among Dr Rawlings's subjects, as in this description by a seventy-year-old accountant who suffered a near-fatal heart attack:

I . . . saw on the other side this beautiful, brilliantly lit city, reflecting what seemed to be the sun's rays. It was all made of gold or some shiny metal with domes and steeples in beautiful array, and the streets were shining, not quite like marble, but made of something I have never seen before. There were many people all dressed in glowing white robes with radiant faces. They looked beautiful. The air smelled so fresh. I have never smelled anything like it.[10]

A woman patient of Dr Ring, who according to him had the most profound experience he had encountered, also experienced a marble-like 'other world':

> All I could see was marble all around me; it was marble. It looked like marble, but it was very beautiful. And I could hear beautiful music; I can't tell you what kind, because I never heard anything like it before. . . . The whole thing was just very good, very happy, very warm, very peaceful, very comforted, very – I've never known that feeling in my whole life.[11]

But what was usually the real surprise for the experiencers at this point, although it is a feature now already familiar to us from our earlier studies of the dying, is their 'seeing' and meeting up with deceased relatives and other dead individuals well known to them. The woman patient of Dr Ring who saw all the beautiful marble, for example, met her mother:

> Then suddenly I saw mother, who had died about nine years ago. And she was sitting – she always used to sit in her rocker, you know – she was smiling and she just sat there looking at me and she said to me in Hungarian [the language her mother had used while alive], 'Well, we've been waiting for you. We've been expecting you. Your father's here and we are going to help you.'[12]

The night-watchman patient of Dr Sabom felt himself in the presence of his brother:

> [With me was] my older brother who had been dead since I was a young fella. I couldn't see, but I knew he was right by me, even patting me on the shoulder, saying, 'It's entirely up to you – you can do anything you want to do . . . I'll be right by your side and everything is going to be fine.'[13]

Usually where such relatives could be 'seen', they looked physically healthier than at the time of their death. According to a retired-labourer patient of Dr Sabom's:

> My grandmother had been ninety-six. She never did look old, she looked perhaps forty or forty-five. My mother was

sixty when she died and way overweight, and she looked trim and a good general-health look, happy and healthy. Everybody looked healthy, real, real healthy.[14]

As for Dr Rawlings's accountant patient: 'My mother was an amputee and yet that leg was now restored! She was walking on two legs!'[15]

Dead friends and acquaintances also figure in these experiences, the presence of these sometimes, as in the case of Dr Sabom's night-watchman, being more felt than seen in the conventional sense. One of Dr Moody's patients said:

> A good friend of mine, Bob, had been killed. Now the moment I got out of my body I had the feeling Bob was standing there, right next to me. I could see him in my mind and felt like he was there, but it was strange. I didn't see him as his physical body. I could see things but not in the physical form, yet just as clearly, his looks, everything. Does that make sense? He was there but he didn't have a physical body.[16]

Dr Sabom's US Army captain subject, blown up in a booby-trap explosion in 1969 while serving in Vietnam, reported something very similar. In this instance a large number of his dead comrades were involved:

> What makes this so real was that the thirteen guys that had been killed the day before, that I had put in plastic bags, were right there with me. And more than that, during the course of that month of May, my particular company lost forty-two dead. All forty-two of those guys were there. They were not in the form we perceive the human body, I can't tell you what form they were in because I don't know, but I know they were there. I felt their presence. We communicated without talking with our voices.[17]

Intriguingly this apparently telepathic means of communication recurs repeatedly though by no means universally in the descriptions of near-death experiencers' meetings with the deceased. It also seems to extend to the yet more remarkable 'encounter' sometimes reported, that with a mysterious 'Being' associated both with the unearthly light and with the whole question of whether or not the near-death experiencer would stay on this non-earthly plane. As one of Dr Ring's subjects,

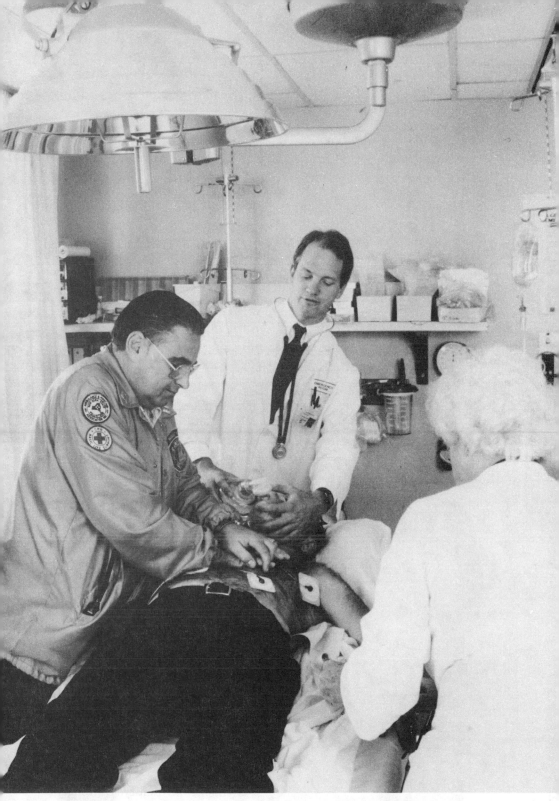

Modern medical technology being applied to the resuscitation of a heart-attack victim. A significant proportion of those brought back 'from the dead' report viewing those working on them from 'out-of-the-body'

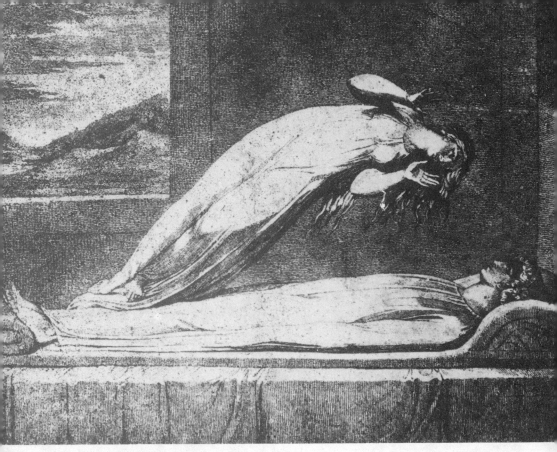

The concept of some after-death element floating over the body precedes modern resuscitations. An engraving of the late eighteenth-century English artist–visionary, William Blake

American cardiologist Dr Michael Sabom, Assistant Professor of Medicine at Emory University, and one of the leading researchers into so-called 'near-death' experiences

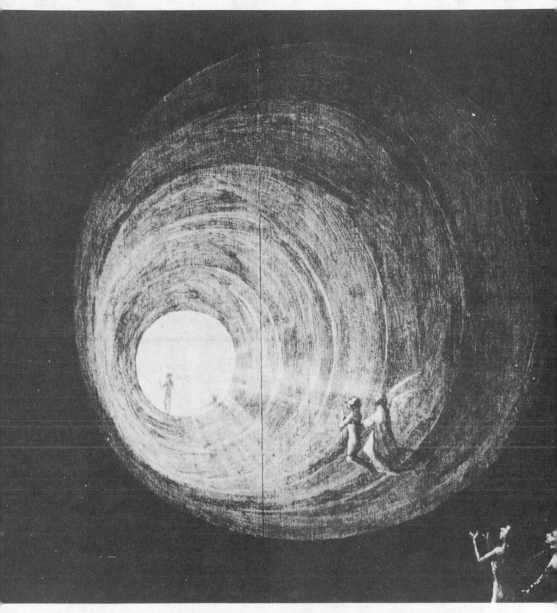

How the idea of the dead being drawn into a spiralling tunnel dates from well before the present day. Fifteenth-century Flemish artist Hieronymus Bosch's *Ascent into the Empyrean* from the Doge's Palace, Venice

Bristol electronics engineer, David Ayre. After 'committing suicide' in the toilet of his home, he recalls going 'through the wall', then meeting his dead father and a 'Being of light' in some after-death realm

*(Opposite)* The Earl and Countess Spencer. Earl Spencer says he heard and remembered everything his wife said to him while he lay comatose and apparently insensible after a brain haemorrhage in 1979

(*Above*) Dr Susan Blackmore, who has researched those who claim 'out-of-the-body' experiences in non-death-threatening circumstances. The validity of these is doubted

(*Above*) Psychologist Margot Grey of London. She had her own near-death experience in India in 1976, and has subsequently studied many British cases of a similar kind

Dr Wilder Penfield, the pioneering Canadian neurosurgeon who firmly believed in the existence of some form of 'mind' as distinct from the physical brain

Exposed brain of patient operated on by Dr Wilder Penfield, with numbers showing points at which electrical stimulation produced apparent 'recording-trace' memories

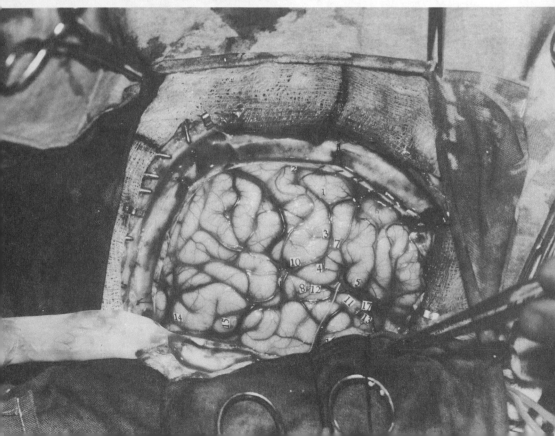

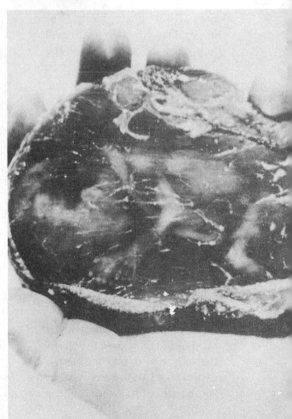

(Above, left) The late Dr Robert Thouless, who died leaving behind a special cipher, the key to which he hoped to communicate from beyond the grave. No spiritualist medium has yet succeeded in decoding the cipher

(Above, right) Dr Robert Morris, the first Koestler Professor of Parapsychology at the University of Edinburgh. Might he be the first to establish genuine scientific evidence for some form of after-death existence?

Baby, eleven weeks after conception, pictured in the womb. Although already aware of and reacting to the external world, legally such babies can be killed by abortion. The murder of a soul?

Despite the degradation of impending death, the evident happiness of a patient at the St Joseph's Hospice, Thornton, near Liverpool. With hospice care, many 'find' their true selves for perhaps the first time in their lives

Dr Colin McCallum, shortly before his death. His widow is convinced that in his dying moments he experienced and was received into some form of heaven. . . .

a woman who had suffered cardiac arrest during a tonsillectomy, described her encounter with this presence:

> I was above – and there was a presence. It's the only way I can explain it – because I didn't see anything. But there was [pause] a presence and it may not have been talking to me but it was like [pause], like I *knew* what was going on between our minds.[18]

Such a 'Being', although often thought by Christians to have been Jesus or God, would appear to be one encountered even by non-Christians. In the words of one of Dr Rawlings's patients, a non-Christian: 'I was stopped by this brilliantly lighted person. He knew my thoughts and reviewed my life. He told me to go back – that my time would come later.'[19]

This 'life review', as researchers tend to describe it, is another constantly recurring element of the whole gamut of near-death experiences. According to one of Dr Moody's subjects:

> When the light appeared, the first thing he said to me was, 'What do you have to show me that you have done with your life?' or something to this effect. And that's when these flash-backs started. I thought, 'Gee, what is going on?' because all of a sudden I was back in my early childhood. And from then on, it was like I was walking from the time of my very early life, on through each year of my life, right up to the present . . . the things that flashed back came in the order of my life, and they were so vivid. The scenes were just like you walked outside and saw them completely three-dimensional, adding colour. And they moved. For instance, when I saw myself breaking the toy [an incident from her kindergarten days in which she had smashed a toy that she had liked], I could see all the movements. It wasn't like I was watching it all from my perspective at the time. It was like the little girl I saw was somebody else, in a movie, one little girl among all the other children out there playing on the playground. Yet, it was me. I saw myself doing these things, as a child, and they were the exact same things I had done, because I remember them.[20]

Again no matter who is the researcher, the subjects appear to recall this life review in almost identical terms. This was how it was described by one of Dr Ring's subjects called Frank, who nearly died in a car accident:

> It was like I got to view my whole life as a movie, and see it and get to view different things that happened, different things that took place . . . somehow it's very hard on words describing . . . basically it was like watching a movie . . . although it is speeded up, probably to show you it all. [21]

In what may now be seen as a phenomenon with a recurring pattern or structure, the next phase seems to involve a decision. The subject is either given a choice of returning to earthly life, or, as in some instances, is roundly commanded to do so, sometimes by the 'Being of light', sometimes by deceased relatives, and sometimes by another authority figure.

Dr Ring's subject Frank described what happened immediately after his life review:

> The next thing was a voice coming to me after all this and saying, very compassionately – it was like an all-knowing voice, something that at the time I took to be the voice of Jesus, but I can take it to be the voice of any one God as far as the whole universe is concerned . . . It was like a voice I knew and it said to me, 'You really blew it this time, Frank.' . . . and I looked down at this scene and that scene compared with the fact that I had seen this view of my life and I said, 'No, I want to live.' [22]

In the case of another of Dr Ring's patients, a woman whose near-death experience was due to a severe asthma attack, the voice was that of a Mrs Friedrich, a wealthy and much loved woman for whom she had once worked. Mrs Friedrich had died nine years previously, and had been responsible for the building of part of the hospital in which the patient was. According to the patient's account:

> Then I heard, I heard Mrs Friedrich. She had been dead for nine years at that time. I heard, in her very distinctive voice – she spoke slowly and every word was brought out strong – and she had a low voice, and she said, 'Miss Harper, *Miss Harper* . . . I want you to live.' And she appeared not distinctly, but . . . it's hard to explain . . . I don't think I saw her face; it was there but it was more of a [pause] . . . she was

dressed in black. I don't think I could see her feet, but I could
see the middle part of her, and it was almost as if you would
look at the side of a tree, a straight tree . . . but she was there,
and she said, 'Miss Harper, Miss Harper! I want you to live!'
. . . and finally I answered in my mind, 'I'll try, Mrs
Friedrich, I'll try.'[23]

An almost universal feature of the subsequent phase is that there is no
sensation of returning down the original tunnel, only a very abrupt
'waking-up' back in the original body, usually to be aware of some
resuscitation procedure having been successfully carried out, accompanied by all the physical body's original pains. It is common for patients
at this point to feel an intense annoyance at having been brought back
from such a pleasurable state to one where all the pain and anguish
which they thought they had left behind has now returned along with
their rejoining of the original body.

Almost invariably the psychological impact of the experience will
have been profound, particularly in respect of a loss of fear of dying. As
one of Dr Ring's patients remarked, 'The one thing I most distinctly
remember is that it left me, where I had been terrified by death before, it
now left me with a total lack of fear of death.' One of Dr Moody's patients
remarked in similar vein:

> Now I'm not afraid to die. It's not that I have a death-wish, or
> want to die right now. I don't want to be living over there on
> the other side now because I'm supposed to be living here.
> The reason why I'm not afraid to die, though, is that I know
> where I'm going when I leave here, because I've been there
> before.[24]

Perhaps one of the most interesting features is that even those without
any prior religious beliefs have returned believing in a life after death. As
one of Dr Ring's patients who had suffered a cardiac arrest during
surgery commented:

> I would say – and not being religious at all – that there must
> be something after death which I never believed in before. I
> always believed that when you were dead, they put you in the
> ground and you stayed there. But I'm not too sure about that
> anymore.[25]

Such reactions are by no means confined to the credulously religious – nor, as we are about to see, to the uneducated. Among Dr Ring's subjects has been a noted anthropologist, Professor Patrick Gallagher, who was a complete agnostic when, at the age of 46, he 'died' in, of all places, Death Valley, California. As a result of a car crash Professor Gallagher was catapulted some fifty feet into the air. He was airlifted to Los Angeles with a badly fractured skull and numerous other injuries that left him unconscious for several weeks. He has no idea at what stage his near-death experience occurred during this time, but on his recovery he was left with the following memory:

> [It] seemed to be in a sequential nature, more or less, I say more or less because time itself seems to have disappeared during this period. But the first thing I noticed was that I was dead and . . . I sort of had the perspective that I was dead in the same way that you see in television movies where the sheriff will say, 'Yup, he's gone.'

Dr Ring asked him whether he could see his body:

> Oh, yes, quite clearly. I was floating in the air above the body . . . and viewing it down sort of a diagonal angle. This didn't seem to cause any consternation to me at all. I really was completely dead but that didn't cause emotional difficulties [for me].
>
> Then, after that, I realized that I was able to float quite easily, even though I had no intention of doing that. . . . Then I very quickly discovered also that not only was I floating and hence free from gravity but free also from any of the other constrictions that inhibit a flight. . . . I could also fly at a terrific rate of speed with a kind of freedom that one normally doesn't experience in normal flight, in airplanes, but perhaps experiences a little more in hang-gliding and things like that. . . . But I noticed that I could fly at a phenomenal rate of speed and it seemed to produce a feeling of great joy and sense of actually flying in this total fashion.
>
> . . . Then I noticed that there was a dark area ahead of me and as I approached it I thought that it was some sort of a tunnel and immediately, without further thought, I entered into it and then flew with an even greater sense of the joy of light. . . .
>
> [After] what now I would imagine to be a relatively short

period of time – although again time was dispensed with – I
noticed a sort of circular light at a great distance which I
assumed to be the end of the tunnel as I was roaring through
it . . . and the light – the nearest thing I can barely approxi-
mate its description to is the setting of the sun at a time under
ideal circumstances when one can look at this object without
any of the usual problems that staring at the sun causes . . .

The fact is, this seemed like an incredibly illuminating sort
of a place, in every sense of that word, so that not only was it an
awesome brightness . . . with a tremendous beauty, this kind
of yellowish-orange colour, but it also seemed a marvellous
place to be. And so this increased the sense of joy I had about
this flight. And then I went through the tunnel and seemed to
be in a different state. I was in different surroundings where
everything seemed to be similarly illuminated by that same
light, and, uh, I saw other things in it, too . . . [a] number of
people . . . I saw my father there, who had been dead for
some twenty-five years. . . .

I also felt and saw of course that everyone was in a state of
absolute compassion to everything else. . . . It seemed, too,
that love was the major axiom that everyone automatically
followed. This produced a phenomenal feeling of emotion to
me, again, in the free sense that the flight did earlier, because
it made me feel that . . . there was nothing *but* love. . . . It
just seemed like the real thing, just to feel this sense of total
love in every direction.

[Later] I did feel, because of my children and the woman I
was married to then, the urge to return . . . but I don't recall
the trip back.[26]

As can be seen, Professor Gallagher's account is a classic example of
most of the main elements: floating out of the body, the ability to move
at a phenomenal speed, the tunnel, the realm of light, meeting with
deceased relatives, even the lack of recall of how exactly he returned to
the land of the living.

However incredible Professor Gallagher's story might seem, it is one I
accept completely as having been genuinely experienced by him (whatever its actual nature), due to an almost equally 'other-worldly' one,
with yet more detail, which has been described to me at first hand by a
44-year-old electronics engineer from Bristol, David Ayre. As David
told me in the course of a long interview, his wife left him in 1978, and
during the weeks that followed, burdened as he was with stress of a

pending divorce, he resolved that his only solution lay in committing suicide. Being by nature a methodical and caring individual, he planned his death to be as painless and unobtrusive as possible. The method he therefore chose was to swallow a large quantity of pain-killers and sleeping-tablets, drink two full bottles of whisky, and turn a large portable gas cylinder full on in what he wryly describes as the smallest room in the house. He had previously switched off all appliances that might cause an explosion and, so far as he was able, carefully sealed the room he was in in order for the gas to have maximum effect.

Unlike Gallagher, David had a modicum of Christian faith and indeed prayed both before and during all his elaborate suicide preparations. But nothing had prepared him for the experience that followed when, after what became completely involuntary gulping in of more and more gas, so that he felt he ought to explode, 'something seemed to snap inside . . . like an over-stretched elastic band'. As in so many of the previous experiences we have studied, David became aware of a tremendous feeling of peace and warmth, then a sense of being dead. He specifically recalls telling himself: 'This must be it; yes, this is it.' Then he seemed to come out of his crumpled body 'like the thought bubble of a cartoon character', finding the detached 'consciousness' part of him seemingly trapped up in the corner of the tiny room, 'clearly looking down on myself . . . completely detached from it and completely at peace'.

After experiencing some form of preliminary life review, David recollects the clear thought: 'Oh God, what happens next?' This was immediately followed by a feeling of annoyance with himself that, having so carefully sealed the room in which he had decided to commit suicide, he had not allowed any way for his out-of-the-body self to get out. He briefly imagined he might have to remain earth-bound as a ghost. However, hardly had this thought occurred to him when, in his own words, he 'went through the wall'. First he found himself soaring on a very precise trajectory over the roof-tops of Bristol, then spiralling in what seems to have been the same 'tunnel' experience reported in so many other cases.

Precisely as in the usual pattern, David became aware of a light at the end of the tunnel, then of other beings seemingly around him. As he told me: 'I can't describe them – it was just that I was aware of the presence of others.' Then he seemed to find himself on some form of grand staircase on which there were little groups of people at different points all the way up, some seeming to have a guide with them. Just as described by the other experiencers, everything seemed to be of a lovely golden colour, as from the light. But for David the oddity was that, unlike everyone else, he seemed to be heading straight to the top. Then, in his own words: 'I got to the top of the stairs and, surprise, surprise, surprise, surprise, there was my father who had died some two years before. I wasn't expecting any of this. . . . He was there and he stood quite calm.'

Although David's father had died at the age of 73, he now looked substantially younger and healthier, particularly in his complexion. As David further recalled:

> I might well have expected some reproof or something like that. In fact I did expect that. But no such thing. There was just compassionate communication, no reprimand or anything, and just telepathic . . . It was incredible, as if he knew everything I knew, and I knew everything he knew.

After moving through more people, all 'very radiant', David then had the most difficult-to-accept encounter of all: 'I came into the presence of the "Being of light".' On David's own admission, this was 'absolutely incredible . . . a total peace, an indescribable total peace. . . . It was like being inside a soft gold neon tube, you were enveloped in this . . . one I don't hesitate to call God.'

David seems again to have been shown a life review, during which he saw 'without any apparent condemnation' episodes in his life along with the effect of these on others, on which the 'Being' seemed to comment:

'So you see what you did, then? That wasn't very helpful, was it?'

Then David recalls hearing what seemed to be these very words: 'Now will you go back?'

Having barely mumbled an acceptance, David's next awareness, without any apparent journey back, was of finding himself back in his original body 'in an absolutely incredible state . . . collapsed on the floor', but with the motivation now to try to live. After collapsing several times, he managed to reach his telephone and dialled 999. Although he subsequently lapsed into unconsciousness several more times, he managed to impart sufficient information for police and ambulance men to break into his home, leading to his recovery.

David's story is as incredible as any we have come across, and it has to be acknowledged that in his case there are some unsatisfactory features. For instance, were it an isolated story it could easily be dismissed as mere hallucination resulting from the effects of the gas and drugs he had taken. David had some Christian faith, so it could also be argued to be some form of wish fulfilment. On his own admission, nine months after the 'suicide' David became a patient at Bristol's Barrow Hospital, having suffered a mental breakdown. This was however purely temporary, and without any prior personal or family history of such problems, and he has long since fully recovered.

But David's story is not alone. It is one we can now see to be part of a consistent pattern recurring in individuals widely separated in time and space. As noted by Dr Sabom, one in five all near-death experiences incorporate *both* out-of-the-body and out-of-this-world elements. And ringing down through well over a thousand years is the striking similarity of the Northumbrian Cunningham's 'other-worldly' experience, not least his unwillingness to return to the earthly world, as preserved in the writings of the Anglo-Saxon monk Bede: 'I was most reluctant to return to my body, for I was entranced by the pleasantness and beauty of the place I could see and the company I saw there. But I did not dare to question my guide.'[27]

How can we evaluate such experiences? Should we simply dismiss Professor Gallagher, David Ayre, and the rest as nothing more than the victims of their own hallucinations. Or is it possible that we are now *really* dealing with glimpses of a world beyond death?

# 12

# TRULY OUT OF THIS WORLD?

Although Britain has been slower than the United States to take a serious interest in near-death experiences, perhaps the most outstanding individual to be an exception to this is a very articulate and well-presented woman psychologist, Margot Grey, who had her own near-death experience in India in 1976. She now lectures on the subject, and has assembled her own collection of cases of British individuals who have had apparent 'other-worldy' experiences in the wake of a near-death crisis.

One of Margot Grey's most intriguing (if most problematic) cases is that of an elderly cockney lady, one who might have stepped straight out of the cast of the television soap opera *East-Enders*, who had a near-death experience as the result of a heart attack. As she told Margot, on 'dying' she found herself standing in front of a 'nice prefab' (a temporary, prefabricated dwelling of the kind provided to British families made homeless by the bombing raids of the Second World War). In her own words:

> There was a path leading up to the [prefab's] front door with masses of nasturtiums on either side. I thought, 'That's funny, my mum always wanted a prefab and she always loved nasturtiums.' . . . I could see my Uncle Alf inside; I never cared for him much in this life. They seemed to be getting ready for a visitor, as if they were expecting someone. I said, 'Can I come in?' It looked so nice and welcoming, but my mother said, 'No, you can't, it's not your time to stay.' I said, 'Please, Mum, it's so lovely here. I don't want to go back.' But she was very firm and would not allow me to cross the threshold.
>
> I said, 'You seem to be expecting someone; if it's not me, then who are you expecting?' She said, 'We are getting ready for your Auntie Ethel. She is expected shortly.' I begged once again if she would let me come in, as it was so warm and sunny and I felt really happy and at peace there. I did not

want to go back, but she would not allow me to come in. The next thing I remember is finding myself back in bed at the hospital. I had been unconscious for three days. The nurse said to me, 'You gave us a real scare, we all thought you were a goner.'

A day or two later my family were allowed to see me and they all looked very glum. I said, 'I don't know what you are all looking so glum for, I haven't died yet, you won't get rid of me so easily.' They said they had some bad news and didn't know if they should tell me as I had been so ill, nearly dying and all. So I said, 'You might as well tell me now that you've said that much.' And they said that since I had been in hospital my Auntie Ethel had unexpectedly died of a sudden heart attack. I thought, well I could have told them that, as I already knew.[1]

Margot Grey enthuses over this story because of the cockney lady's chirpy ordinariness and her unquestioning and matter-of-fact acceptance of the experience completely at face value. But there are two conflicting elements to it which epitomize the problem posed by near-death experiences of the 'other-worldly' variety. On the one hand the story intriguingly and perhaps persuasively suggests that in her near-death moments the cockney lady was privileged to a particular item of foreknowledge – the impending death of her Aunt Ethel – not available to the living. We may recall something of the same in the case of the dying 96-year-old Mrs Jane Charles back in Chapter 8, who correctly prophesied that granddaughter Janet T. would 'get over' the loss of her 2-year-old baby daughter. Primitive peoples often cherish the same idea of the dead and dying possessing powers to see into the future, as in the case of the Australian aboriginals studied by anthropologist Ronald Rose:

Some strange beliefs have developed around the fact of dying. One, for example, is that the dying man becomes suddenly invested with clairvoyant ability of the most extraordinary kind. His last hours are thus likely to be filled by intense cross-examination on a wide variety of subjects. Even the sophisticated native believes that the one occasion during his life on which he can know the answer to any question is three days after his mother's death. He must stand at the foot of the grave and ask his question.[2]

On the other hand the more-difficult-to-take feature of the cockney lady's story is her vision of a heaven consisting of her dead relatives sitting in a cosy 'prefab' with nasturtiums growing in the garden. For the rationalist-minded, including myself, it does seem to be asking a great deal to believe that the afterlife might take such a prosaically 'earthly' form. Yet what is intriguing is that precisely similar problems of disbelief have arisen among the near-death experiencers themselves, even, as some recollect, while actually having the experience. As Dr Sabom was told by a 23-year-old college-student patient who saw her deceased father in a near-death experience arising from complications following a kidney-removal operation: 'Even then my mind was saying, "But I can't be seeing Daddy and talking to him – he's dead." . . . Yet I could see him perfectly.'[3]

This is consistent with the already remarked expressions of delighted, near-disbelieving astonishment on the faces of the dying who 'see' their deceased relatives and similar 'other-worldly' scenes. Lady Florence Barrett was told by her dying patient, Mrs Doris B.: 'I can't stay; if you could see what I do, you would know I can't stay.' Death-bed researcher Dr Karlis Osis observed of dying patients: 'Surprise – the eyes of the patient open wide, staring at something very surprising, reaching out.'[4]

And as Dr Sabom similarly heard from the night-watchman subject who described meeting his dead brother:

> People will think I'm crazy. I wouldn't dare tell my wife. She would have me as a candidate for the second floor [psychiatric ward]. But you've expressed an interest in it and you seem sincere. I'm not telling you everything, Doctor. Just enough so that you won't get too uptight with me. Maybe later, when I know you better and know how serious you really are about this thing. It's a pretty kinky experience.[5]

So if we accept, on the basis of the arguments advanced earlier, the inadequacy of the most ready-to-hand 'rational' explanations, how then are we to understand such experiences? Perhaps one of the most helpful guides to the way we should be thinking comes from a classic near-death account related by an American Catholic priest, Father Louis Tucker, who happened to have his experience and set it down on paper before most if not all the present-day generation of near-death researchers had even been born.

In 1909, while at Baton Rouge, Louisiana, Father Tucker 'died' from ptomaine poisoning. He subsequently recorded in his book, *Clerical Errors*, his first encounter with the 'other-worldly' tunnel:

The sensation was not quite like anything earthly; the nearest familiar thing to it is passing through a short tunnel on a train. There was the same sense of hurrying, of blackness, of rapid transition, of confused noise, and multiform, swift readjustment.[6]

Next he met his father:

I emerged into a place where people were being met by friends. It was quiet and full of light, and Father was waiting for me. He looked exactly as he had in the last few years of his life and wore the last suit of clothes he had owned.

The crucial feature of interest in Father Tucker's account is his explanation of why his father should be seen in an earthly-domain suit of clothes: 'I knew that the clothes Father wore were assumed because they were familiar to me, so that I might feel no strangeness in seeing him, and that, to some lesser extent, his appearance was assumed also.' Father Tucker made a particular point of explaining why he knew this; apparently, in common with other near-death experiencers, he shared some form of telepathic rapport with his dead father:

I knew all these things by contagion, because he did . . . I discovered that we were not talking, but thinking. I knew dozens of things that we did not mention because he knew them. He thought a question, I an answer, without speaking; the process was practically instantaneous.

This is an almost identical description to the communication process reported by Dr Sabom's subject 'killed' by a Vietnamese booby-trap bomb, who described meeting the forty-two fellow soldiers who had preceded him in death during the same month:

All forty-two of those guys were there. They were not in the form we perceive the human body. I can't tell you what form they were in because I don't know, but I know they were there. I felt their presence. We communicated without talking with our voices.[7]

What Father Tucker's deceased father seems to have tried to convey was that the actual images of a near-death experience – particularly those of the 'other-worldly' variety – may simply be visual components necessary for the dying person to have some meaningful experience of the 'other side'. In other words, people's appearance, clothes, and surroundings might be nothing more than projections to convey a feeling of familiarity, rather than the 'other side' necessarily being a 'real' realm – in the case of the cockney lady, of bungalows and nasturtiums. This would explain why not all subjects actually 'see' their deceased friends and relatives but sometimes instead 'feel' their presence in a way they find hard to explain.

An almost identical concept of after-death experience is explained in the Tibetan *Bardo Thodol*, or *Book of the Dead*: 'It is quite sufficient for you [i.e. the deceased] to know that these apparitions [i.e. images of the dead and an after death realm] are [the reflections of] your own thought forms.'[8]

As explained by the modern authority on the Tibetan book, Dr Evans-Wentz:

> Accordingly, for a Buddhist . . . as for a Hindu, or a Moslem, or a Christian, the *Bardo* [after death] experiences would be appropriately different: the Buddhist's or the Hindu's thought-forms . . . would give rise to corresponding visions of the deities of the Buddhist or Hindu pantheon; a Moslem's, to visions of the Moslem Paradise; a Christian's, to visions of the Christian heaven, or an American Indian's to visions of the Happy Hunting Ground.[9]

These difficult-to-grasp ideas would almost certainly find ready support from former Society for Psychical Research president George N. M. Tyrrell.[10] He postulated a 'producer' and a 'stage carpenter' element within the percipient's own unconscious mind as being reponsible for something of the viewing of ghosts – even though he also believed there to be some genuine underlying reality to these.

If we can then even begin to accept such ideas (inevitably a big and heavily qualified 'if'), what is remarkable is how the whole gamut of near-death experiences begins to assume at least some rationality, potentially the threshold to a genuine understanding of how and in what form something of us might survive physical death. Rather than dismissing the out-of-the-body descriptions merely as some modern fad, we therefore begin to see that they underlie after death concepts dating back thousands of years, and from the most diverse of cultures. For example, the great nineteenth-century anthropologist J. G. Fraser recorded of the Melanesian peoples of the Pacific:

Fig. 7. The *ba* flutters over the deceased, from the Egyptian Book of the Dead, Papyrus of Ani

All the central Melanesians believe that man is composed of a body and a soul . . . they imagine that as soon as the soul quits the body at death, it melts into a tree where there is a bird's-nest fern, and sitting there amongst the ferns it laughs and mocks the people who are crying and making great lamentations over the deserted tabernacle. There he sits, wondering at them and ridiculing them. 'What are they crying for . . . whom are they sorry for? Here am I.'[11]

The more recent anthropologist J. Goody has noted that the Lodagaa tribe of West Africa have almost the identical idea that the after death 'soul' sits among the tree-tops.[12] The Egyptian concept of the *ba* was of an after death, bird-like something which fluttered over the body of the deceased (Figure 7). Modern near-death experience subjects typically 'look down' from a similar elevation, in the manner described by a subject of Dr Ring's: 'I viewed myself from the corner of the hospital room, looking down at my body which was very dark and gray. All the life looked like it was out of it. . . . And my Italian girl-friend at the time was crying at the foot of the bed.'[13]

Whoever wrote the *Bardo Thodol*, the Tibetans' *Book of the Dead*, back around AD 800 seems to have known something of the confusion experienced by those modern individuals who find themselves out of the body, like this subject of Dr Moody's:

I thought I was dead . . . but I just couldn't figure out where I was supposed to go. My thought and my consciousness were just like they are in life, but I couldn't figure all this out. I kept thinking, 'Where am I going to go? What am I going to do?' And, 'My God, I'm dead! I can't believe it!'[14]

According to the *Bardo*:

When the consciousness principle gets outside the body it says to itself, 'Am I dead or am I not dead?' It cannot determine, it sees its relatives and connections as it had been used to seeing them before, it even hears the wailings.[15]

Swedenborg, writing in the eighteenth century, expressed the sense of confusion thus:

When a man comes into the other life he is not aware that he is in that life but supposes that he is still in the world, and even that he is still in the body. So much is this the case that when he is told that he is a spirit, wonder and amazement possess him, both because he finds himself exactly like a man, in his senses, desires and thoughts, and because during life in this world he had not believed in the existence of the spirit.[16]

Earlier in the book we noted how the Egyptians believed the death-surviving element of the individual to be able to pass through physical barriers, including the false door of the tomb-chamber, in order to partake of those offerings provided for it in the outside world. Is this not exactly the same as the ability to pass through walls and ceilings claimed by near-death experiencers? In the words of a Georgia-labourer patient of Dr Sabom's: 'I could float anywhere I wanted to. I could float through the wall or whatever I wanted to do.'[17] And as I was personally told by Bristol would-be suicide David Ayre 'I went through the wall.'

If we look for early parallels to the 'tunnel' concept, already remarked on is the extraordinary image of this in Bosch's painting of five hundred years ago. But early experience of this same motif may also be implicit in the very architecture of houses of the 'living dead', such as Egypt's pyramids and, even more so, Ireland's Newgrange. Is it perhaps of more than passing significance that one of the pyramids' key features is a long tunnel, fraught with pitfalls, leading off the abode of the dead? And we may recall from Chapter 1 how, in the fourth millennium BC, an Irish community living near the river Boyne went to incredible lengths to construct as an integral part of their Newgrange monument a 70 foot tunnel through which the light of the sun would shine just once a year, on the shortest day. Whatever the validity of this, such tunnels are a special feature of many other of the prehistoric 'passage-graves'.

The idea of the 'life review' is also one of extraordinary antiquity and universality. It was expected by every ancient Egyptian for the moment when he would be required of give an account of himself before ancient Egypt's equivalent of the 'Being of light', the god Osiris, according to the *Book of the Dead*'s prescribed 'negative confession':

> Hail to you, great god, Lord of justice! . . . I have not done
> falsehood . . . I have not deprived the orphan of his property,
> I have not done what the gods detest . . . I have not caused
> pain, I have not made hungry, I have not made to weep, I
> have not killed, I have not made suffering for anyone. . . . I
> am pure, pure, pure, pure![18]

Medieval Christians believed from their own observations of the dying that life reviews were flashed before their eyes on their death-beds (Figure 8). And such experiences have been too often noted by those who survive 'death' falls for them not to have some profound underlying truth and relevance.

Perhaps the most compelling parallel of all, however, is the antiquity of the idea of meeting up with deceased ancestors. From Arab ambassador Ibn Fadlan, resident with a Viking community living on the Volga *c.* AD 922, has come a graphic description of a Viking chief's burial during which a slave woman about to die with her master was three times hoisted up on a special frame from which she declared herself able to see her master and her parents beyond the grave. According to Ibn Fadlan's account of the woman's utterances, as translated for him by his interpreter:

> The first time they lifted her she said: 'Look! I see my father
> and mother.' The second time she said: 'Look! I see all my
> dead relatives sitting around.' The third time she said: 'Look!
> I see my master sitting in paradise, and paradise is beautiful
> and green and together with him are men and young boys.
> He calls on me. Let me join him then!'[19]

Other cultures similarly have accounts of individuals seeming to visit the land of the dead, in precisely the manner of a near-death experience.

Fig. 8. Medieval man torn between heaven and hell as, in his dying moments, he sees a panoramic view of his life. From a fifteenth-century *Ars moriendi* (Art of Dying)

Anthropologist Irving Hallowell made studies of Canada's aboriginal Salteaux Indians of the Berens River to the north of Winnipeg, (published in 1940, well before anyone had heard of Raymond Moody).[20] Hallowell found that the Salteaux's beliefs in life after death derived largely from the apparent experiences of those thought to have been dead yet who revived. Among the descriptions given by these individuals were feelings of extraordinary bliss; the sensation of being out of, or separated from, the physical body; and, not least, the meeting with deceased loved ones and friends in some form of 'spirit realm'.

There even seems to be a universally understood rule that, while the dead may eat food provided by the living, it is death for the living to eat the food of the dead. According to nineteenth-century anthropologist Robert Codrington's study of the Melanesians, a woman who visited her dead brother in Panoi, the Polynesian 'other world', was cautioned by him 'to eat nothing there, and she returned'.[21] The New Zealand folklorist Edward Shortland, who made a study of the Maori peoples, recorded a Maori woman who visited the 'other world' in a trance and met there her dead father.[22] He likewise forbade her to eat any of the 'other-world' food, so that she might be able to return to the land of the living in order to care for her child. Mary Eastman, who made an early study of the Sioux Indians of Dakota, told yet another story of the same kind.[23] This involved an Indian called Ahak-tah who had seemed to die during a period of forty-eight hours, recovered, and described having been to a beautiful land of tall trees and singing birds. In the beautiful land, Ahak-tah met the spirits of his forefathers and his uncle. But although he had felt hungry there, and had seen a tempting dish of wild rice, his uncle would not allow him to eat this. According to Ahak-tah: 'Had I eaten of the food of spirits, I should never have returned to earth.'

Does this not all sound remarkably similar to what we heard in the near-death experience described by the chirpy cockney lady to Margot Grey?

> They seemed to be getting ready for a visitor, as if they were expecting someone. I said, 'Can I come in?' It looked so nice and welcoming, but my mother said, 'No, you can't, it's not your time to stay.' I said, 'Please, Mum, it's so lovely here. I don't want to go back.' But she was very firm and would not allow me to cross the threshold.[24]

A problem remains, however, in that all this perhaps sounds rather too trite and wish-fulfilling, too good to be true. Why, for instance, does no one claim a taste of anything like hell?

The straightforward answer to this matter is that some actually do. Rare, but none the less on the record, are instances of individuals reporting experiences of terrors that certainly seem to them at least to be those of hell. Dr Maurice Rawlings's entrée into near-death experiences was specifically because of a male patient whose heart had stopped and for whom Rawlings had to arrange immediate emergency procedures including the insertion of a pacemaker wire into the vein leading directly to his heart. In the course of these efforts the patient revived but then 'died' again several times. What astonished Rawlings was what the man told him during his moments of recovery:

> Each time he regained heart-beat and respiration the patient screamed, 'I'm in hell!' He was terrified and pleaded with me to help him. . . . He then issued a very strange plea: 'Don't stop!' You see, the first thing most patients I resuscitate tell me, as soon as they recover consciousness, is, 'Take your hands off my chest; you're hurting me!' I am big and my method of external heart-massage sometimes fractures ribs. But this patient was telling me, 'Don't stop!'
>
> Then I noticed a genuinely alarmed look on his face. . . . This patient had a grotesque look on his face, expressing sheer horror! His pupils were dilated, and he was perspiring and trembling – he looked as if his hair was 'on end'.
>
> Then still another strange thing happened. He said, 'Don't you understand? I am in hell. Each time you quit I go back to hell! Don't let me go back to hell!'[25]

Difficult though this may be to believe – along with Margot Grey's cockney lady's prefabs with nasturtiums growing in the garden – experiences of this kind have also to be taken as a fact of life among some near-death experiencers. Margot Grey has come across other 'hell' reminiscences not unlike Dr Rawlings's patient's, remarking particularly on their point-for-point parallels with those of the 'heavenly' variety: in place of elation, the emotions of fear and panic; similar though less pleasant sensations of being out of the body; the plunging into a totally black void instead of an end-lit tunnel; and not least, a sense of an overwhelming proximity of forces of demonic evil.

Similar experiences have also been reported by researchers of the dying, as particularly observed by one of the respondents of Dr Karlis Osis: 'The patient had a horrified expression, turned his head in all directions and said, "Hell, hell, all I see is hell." Another had the terrifying feeling of being buried alive.'[26]

So yet again we are faced, as suggested by Mr Tucker Senior (father of the Father Tucker quoted on p. 154), and by the *Bardo Thodol*, with those who are near death having experiences which (if they are to be accepted as having any form of reality) are more likely to be projections or reflections of their own unhappy or unhealthy state of mind. But can we really be sure all this is not mere hallucination rubbish, that those receiving both pleasant and unpleasant apparent afterlife experiences are not merely regurgitating their prior expectations of what may happen to them after death, deriving perhaps from what they may have read about such experiences in the case of others, or been warned of in hell-fire sermons?

One of the several indications against this possibility is the now well-observed fact that even very young children who have suffered clinical death, and who are most unlikely to have read books such as *Life after Life*, have reported experiences similar to those of adults. In Seattle, paediatrician Dr Melvin Morse of the University of Washington has made a special study of young patients at Seattle's Children's Orthopedic Hospital and Medical Center.[27] Of seven youngsters who had suffered clinical death or something close to it, mainly through either cardiac arrest or drowning, four subsequently described distinct memories of what they had experienced while unconscious.

Just as in the case of adult out-of-the-body memories, one eight-year-old diabetic girl who had suffered a sudden near-fatal coma recalled vividly and in full colour seeing herself lying on an operating table, while another something of her floated above. According to Morse 'She could look down on her body below, as well as see two male doctors around her.' A six-year-old boy whose heart had stopped during an operation to remove his tonsils similarly remembered leaving his body and floating above the operating table, remarking in particular 'I had a tube in my mouth.' In addition he recollected, according to Morse, 'travelling in a long tunnel that was lined with brightly coloured lights of every hue, similar to "airplane landing lights".' This particular boy's parents never attended church, and had taught him no ideas about any form of afterlife. And in a striking parallel to David Ayre's story, a sixteen-year-old boy whose heart had stopped while undergoing a kidney operation told his (Mormon) parents on regaining consciousness: 'I have a wonderful secret to tell you. I have been half-way to heaven.' The experience 'felt wonderful and peaceful. I was on a dark staircase and I climbed upwards.' Apparently on getting half way up the stairs he decided to turn back because he had a young brother who had previously died, and did not think it was his time to die yet.

As a form of cross-check Morse studied the cases of some thirty children who had been treated for unconsciousness in the hospital's intensive care unit at around the same time as the others, but had not been on the brink between life and death. Of these, twenty-four had to be excluded because of impaired subsequent mental functioning, but of the remaining six none reported any near-death-type memories. The experience therefore would seem to be specific to those either very near to death, or actually clinically dead, irrespective of age or culture.

But the detractors of the near-death experience have not denied that there is a certain particularity and universality to the phenomenon. As acknowledged by the Californian psycho-pharmacologist Dr Ronald K. Siegel:

> The experience of dying involves common elements and themes that are predictable and definable. These elements and themes arise from common structures in the brain and nervous system, common biological experiences, and the common reaction of the central nervous system to stimulation. The resultant experience, universally accessible, is interpreted by self-referential humankind as evidence of immortality, which is little more than a metaphor to describe a common subjective state of consciousness.[28]

So are there any other ways in which 'other-worldly' experiences can be shown to be something more than Siegel's 'common subjective state of consciousness', jargon on his part for what he might more bluntly and honestly have labelled mere hallucinations? We noted in Chapter 8 certain instances in which the dying person seemed to 'know' of the death of individuals of whose demise he or she had not been told. There was the case of Lady Florence Barrett's patient, Mrs Doris B. and the death of her sister Vida, and 96-year-old Mrs Jane Charles and the death of her great-granddaughter Jane T. In similar vein Margot Grey, in a lecture to the British Society for Psychical Research, has described an intriguing near-death experience involving a little Pakistani girl living in Britain who 'met', as if beyond the grave, a great-grandfather whom she had never seen before, not even in photographs. As described by Margot:

> [The Pakistani girl] 'died' of a very unpleasant toxic condition. . . . Luckily her father was a doctor and he came back at lunch-time to find out how his little girl was and realised that she was beginning to turn blue. . . . He was able to resuscitate her and . . . able to bring her back [to life].
> What happened in her case was that she said she found

herself in a most beautiful garden, and there were fountains and pomegranates (it was very much the kind of thing you would expect coming from her culture). . . . And she said, 'There was a very lovely old man, a kindly old man, who came up and greeted me and picked me up and sat me on his knee. And he talked to me and he said, "Do you want to stay, or do you want to go back? Because if you want to stay there is someone we have to go and see and ask their permission."' And she said, 'No, I think Mummy and Daddy would be very sad if I didn't go back, so I think I'd really like to go back.' But she stayed with him for a while in the garden, and was very happy, before being sent home. And she was resuscitated by her father. . . .

Now about six or nine months later some relatives came over from Pakistan to visit the family, and they brought with them some photograph albums, and the family were gathered together as families will, and they were looking at the photograph album. And suddenly the little girl got frightfully excited and said, 'Oh look, that's the old gentleman I met up with in the garden.' It was her great-grandfather, and she had never either seen him nor had she ever seen a picture of him.[29]

This case is a little more anecdotal than one would wish, so how can we be assured that the little girl really did 'see' her dead great-grandfather beyond the grave?

Dr Kenneth Ring has quoted something similar:

A woman respondent informed me that her father, as he lay dying, saw a vision of two of his brothers, one of whom had been dead for years, while the other had died only two days previously – a fact unknown to her dying father. The father, however, decided to 'return' when he heard his (living) wife call to him, and only afterward learned of his brother's demise.[30]

Even this story, however, is also rather too anecdotal. But as it happens there is another case, from that potential 'white crow' among the mediums, Mrs Osborne Leonard (see Chapter 6), that is more compelling and better attested than either of the last two related. On 17 and 19 November 1917 Mrs Leonard gave sittings to a widow, Mrs Hugh Talbot, of whom, according to Mrs Talbot, the medium could have had no prior knowledge: 'Mrs Leonard at this time knew neither my name nor address, nor had I ever been to her or any other medium before in my life.'[31]

Via the squeaky-voiced 'control' Feda, the deceased Mr Talbot seemed to be reached. Again as related by Mrs Talbot:

> [All] that he [Mr Talbot] said, or rather Feda for him, was clear and lucid. Incidents of the past, known only to him and to me, were spoke of: belongings, trivial in themselves, but possessing for him a particular personal interest of which I was aware, were minutely and correctly described and I was asked if I still had them.

But then Feda/Mrs Leonard began to talk of a book with a special message in it, a form of demonstration of mediumistic powers of which Mrs Leonard made somewhat of a speciality. According to Mrs Talbot:

> Feda began a tiresome description of a book. She said it was leather and dark, and tried to show me its size (about 8 to 10 inches long and 4 or 5 inches wide). Feda said: 'It is not exactly a *book*, it is not printed, Feda wouldn't call it a book, it had writing in.'
>
> It was long before I could connect this description with anything at all, but at last I remembered a red leather note-book of my husband's, which I think he called a log-book: and I asked: 'It is a log-book?' Feda seemed puzzled at this and not to know what a log-book was and repeated the word once or twice, then said: 'Yes, yes, he says it might be a log-book.' I then said: 'Is it a red book?' On this point there was hesitation. They thought possibly it was, though he thought it was darker.
>
> The answer was undecided and Feda began a wearisome description all over again, adding that I was to look on page twelve for something written . . . there, that it would be so interesting after this conversation. Then she said: 'He is not sure it is page twelve, it might be thirteen, it is so long, but he does want you to look and to try to find it. It would interest him to know if this extract is there.'

Although Mrs Talbot thought she remembered the book, she was not sure what had happened to it. Rather off-handedly she told Feda she would see what she could do to find it. But Feda in her characteristic squeakiness became very emphatic: 'There are two books, you will know the one he means by a diagram of languages in the front – Indo-European, Aryan, Semitic languages and others.'

Still unconvinced it was anything more than a waste of time, Mrs Talbot made a search the same evening, eventually finding two of her husband's old notebooks at the back of a top bookshelf. One of these seemed to accord with Feda's description, and on opening it she was astonished to read: 'Table of Semitic or Syro-Arabian languages.' But yet more astonishing, for us perhaps even more so than for Mrs Talbot, was the book's page thirteen. On this Mr Talbot had transcribed, some time in his life, the following passage from a book called *Post Mortem*, published anonymously in 1881:[32]

> I discovered by certain whispers which it was supposed I was unable to hear and from certain glances of curiosity or commiseration which it was supposed I was unable to see that I was near death. . . . Presently my mind began to dwell not only on happiness which was to come, but upon happiness that I was actually enjoying. I saw long-forgotten forms, playmates, schoolfellows, companions of my youth and of my old age, who one and all smiled upon me. They did not smile with any compassion, that I no longer felt I needed, but with that sort of kindness which is exchanged by people who are equally happy. I saw my mother, father and sisters, all of whom I had survived. They did not speak, yet they communicated to me their unaltered and unalterable affection. At about the time when they appeared, I made an effort to realise my bodily situation . . . that is, I endeavoured to connect my soul with the body which lay on the bed in my house. . . . The endeavour failed. I was dead.

Was this Mr Talbot's way of trying to tell his wife, from beyond the grave, what he had experienced on passing into an afterlife? So many of the features of what we have been calling a near-death experience (but in this instance can legitimately call an after death experience) are here. There is the 'hearing' and 'seeing' while out of the body; the life review; the encountering of deceased relatives; the communication without words. And all this from a passage written nearly a hundred years before Raymond Moody had written *Life after Life*. Surely this was the 'something written' which, through Feda/Mrs Leonard, the deceased Mr Talbot appears to have felt his wife would find 'so interesting after this conversation'. Since Mrs Talbot had no prior knowledge of this passage – and everything in her account was independently corroborated for the Society for Psychical Research by members of her family[33] – there are really only two alternative explanations. Either some confederate of Mrs Leonard's secretly gained entry to the Talbot household, rifled through the bookshelves, and lighted upon this passage to regurgitate during the sitting (very difficult to sustain in view of Mrs Leonard's apparent lack of any prior knowledge of Mrs Talbot; also that according to Mrs Talbot's niece the notebook was covered in dust). Or Mr Talbot really was communicating through Mrs Leonard. This particular medium – and I continue to hold the strongest views against mediums in general – would then perhaps legitimately earn William James's appellation of a 'white crow', that is, the one to disprove the rule that crows are always black just as mediums are always fraudulent.

None of this yet constitutes proof that 'other-worldly' experiences are genuinely what they seem. But since we find them from times before drugs, and among positively unmedicated patients, pharmacological explanations are found wanting.[34] Since they occur among patients without high body temperatures, they cannot be dismissed as mere feverish delirium.[35] Since they occur specifically in circumstances of actual rather than merely feared life-threat, they are difficult to attribute just to psychological crisis mechanisms such as depersonalization.[36] Furthermore on the positive side there seem to be such strong links between Moody-type near-death experiences, the Kübler-Ross-type phenomena associated with the dying, and the 'friendly'-type apparitions of the dead that, if there is any validity to these, then there is validity to all of them. They stand or fall together.

So we are faced, if still so tenuously, with a phenomenon which perhaps really is *the* after death experience: the underlying factor to our human make-up which, perhaps more than any other, has been responsible for such powerful historical beliefs that the dead really do live on, and that deceased loved ones really can be but a whisper away. But such is our curiosity, we have to know more, not least that if something of us does *not* go on to tend nasturtiums in prefabs in the sky, then how are we to understand it? What part of us might survive?

# 13

# WHAT MIGHT SURVIVE?

The medium Doris Stokes in her autobiography *Voices in my Ear*
described how as a patient in hospital she once sat with a doctor
watching the dying moments of an elderly patient in the opposite bed:

> I glanced across and saw a wisp of mist, like smoke, coming
> from the crown of the old woman's head. 'It's starting to take
> place,' I said. . . . 'Any minute now she'll see her husband.'
>
> And at that very moment she brushed her hand across her
> face, pushing off the mask and said, 'Oh 'enery. That you,
> Henry?'
>
> 'Oh bloody hell,' said the doctor.
>
> As I watched I saw the spiritual body, which is exactly the
> same as the physical body, even appearing in the same
> clothes, but lying face down, hovering above the woman.
> She was chattering away to Henry.
>
> The spiritual body rose a little higher and I could see it was
> attached to the physical body by a silver cord, like an
> umbilical cord. 'I should think it'll be about another twenty
> minutes,' I told the doctor. . . .
>
> The minutes ticked by. After a while the spiritual body rose
> till the cord was stretched to its fullest extent, then slowly the
> spiritual body tilted and the cord broke.
>
> 'Now she's gone,' I said.
>
> And the doctor, his fingers on her pulse said, 'My God, she
> has.'[1]

While Doris Stokes's account of this woman's vision of her already
deceased husband Henry might happen to be along the same lines as
everything we have noted, there the affinity ends, and with it any
compatibility between Doris Stokes's claims and what I regard as the
altogether more serious evidential material assembled by Dr Sabom and
others.

For although, as we noted in relation to Dr Susan Blackmore's cannabis 'trip', the concept of a 'silver cord' linking the physical body and the 'spirit' is a common one in Spiritualist circles, it certainly does not figure in the descriptions of those resuscitated from clinical death. These might surely have been expected to be aware of such a cord – not least as something of an encumbrance – in reported instances of 'thought-travel' down hospital wards, or to the other side of the United States. But even when specifically questioned, they have reported nothing of the kind.[2] Similarly among these there is almost invariably no awareness of anything along the lines of Doris Stokes's 'spiritual body'. As described by one of Dr Ring's patients who suffered a heart attack: 'It seemed like I was up there in space and just my mind was active. No body feeling, just like my brain was up in space. I had nothing but my mind.'[3]

Dr Moody reported of one of his subjects: 'He felt as though he were "able to see everything around me – including my whole body as it lay on the bed – without occupying any space", that is, as if he were a point of consciousness.'[4]

And, as a 48-year-old Florida fireman subject of Dr Sabom's put it: 'There was no feeling of being . . . If you think about it, you can feel your clothes against your skin. But there was nothing there like that.'[5]

Such remarks are also readily compatible with some parallel British studies by Celia Green of Oxford's Institute of Psychophysical research.[6] Green has reported that 80 per cent of the out-of-the-body experiencers she studied similarly felt themselves to be a 'disembodied consciousness' rather than inside a second body.

So what is it that – conceivably – survives? Even if there is no recognizable form, as 'seen' by Doris Stokes, but pure mind or consciousness, we still need to ask what mind might truly be to constitute the real 'us'? It is, of course, the deepest and most difficult question of all to answer, but broadly there are two theories. There is the mechanistic or monist theory, which proposes that we are no more than totally self-contained machines, and that everything we do, say, think, etc. derives from physical and chemical processes which we are becoming increasingly capable of understanding. Our 'minds' are thereby no more than finite prisoners of the particular machine into which they have been born. Then there is the interactionist or dualist theory, which proposes that mind and body are separate, interacting elements, of which the mind, of some nature yet to be determined, is not necessarily permanently contained by the body, and therefore theoretically capable of surviving it.

Of these two the mechanistic theory is to all intents and purposes still the received wisdom of our times, the very linchpin of our science and medicine. It satisfies because it can be demonstrated to work. Put a patient on a course of drugs, and his or her depression may be relieved, or the more bizarre behaviour of a 'mental' patient may be arrested. Since the early part of the twentieth century the field of psychology has been dominated by the similarly mechanistic 'behaviourist' thinking of Americans John B. Watson and B. F. Skinner, with their arguments that only what is directly measurable and observable is truly worthy of study, and therefore insubstantial concepts such as consciousness are best avoided. To mechanistic and behaviourist theory, the belief that anything of us survives after death is both unnecessary and incompatible with the idea that each of us is a single unit, a single machine.

However, what has continued to give at least some thoroughly level-headed scientists room for credence in interactionist theory is that mechanistic theory, for all its demonstrability, by no means explains everything, and certainly not the very clear-headed, though so difficult-to-prove, attestations of detachment from the physical body as claimed by the subjects of Doctors Sabom, Ring, Moody, *et al*. In subject after subject describing the near-death experience 'detachment' is the very word used, as in Dr Sabom's road accident victim: 'I was above the whole scene viewing the accident. I was very detached . . . I was just viewing things. It was just like I floated up there . . . [up to the] rooftop or maybe a little higher . . . very detached.'[7]

Even long before Dr Moody had been heard of, one for whom such questions proved a source of fascination throughout his long and distinguished career was the neurosurgeon Dr Wilder Penfield, founder of the Montreal Neurological Institute and Hospital, and a pioneer both in modern brain surgery techniques and in mapping the functions of different areas of the brain. Although more conversant than most with the mechanics of brain and body as a working machine, Penfield to the end of his life sided himself firmly with dualist/interactionist theory; he based this stance, more than most, on direct observation of the workings of the human brain.

For instance, Penfield noted among his patients that any who suffered seizures focused in the brain's frontal or temporal cortex (for Penfield the seat of the 'mind mechanism') effectively became 'automatons' or, quite literally, ones who had 'lost their mind'. In such circumstances, according to Penfield:

> The patient becomes suddenly unconscious, but, since other mechanisms in the brain continue to function, he changes into an automaton. He may wander about, confused and aimless. Or he may continue to carry out whatever purpose

his mind was in the act of handing on to his automatic sensory-motor mechanism when the highest brain-stem went out of action. Or he follows a stereotyped, habitual pattern of behaviour. In every case, the automaton can make few, if any, decisions for which there has been no precedent. . . . He will have complete amnesia for the period. [The automaton is] a thing without that indefinable attribute, a sense of humor. The automaton is incapable of thrilling to the beauty of a sunset or of experiencing contentment, happiness, love, compassion. These, like all awarenesses, are functions of the mind.[8]

Penfield was also very much aware that among the many mysteries of the brain, if as required by mechanistic theory this fully contains the mind, not least is where or how this organ stores its memories. For while it is well known that damage to certain areas of the brain can severely impair or destroy memory function, looking for some form of storage system for all our memories, conscious or unconscious, seems to be to pursue the invisible. As Harvard University's professor of psychology, Karl Lashley, remarked frustratedly back in 1950: 'I sometimes feel, in reviewing the evidence on localization of the memory trace, that . . . learning is not possible.'[9] In the thirty-seven years since Lashley wrote those words, little further progress has been made.

Accordingly, what for Penfield made this question all the more fascinating was his personal discovery, while working on a particular treatment of epileptic patients, of the existence of what seems to be almost a 'black box' recording-track of our life's experiences, far more extensive than anything to which we have conscious access. To treat certain epileptic cases he had devised a procedure of opening up a patient's skull, using merely local anaesthetic, then electrically exploring exposed areas of the brain while the patient remained fully conscious. While doing this he found he could bring long-forgotten memories back into the patient's 'mind', even though the areas stimulated could not be construed as ones for memory storage. This occurred in the case of one patient, Mary (pseudonym),[10] who had her operation on 25 September 1952; the moment Penfield applied a three-volt current to her temporal lobe, she responded: 'I heard something. I do not know what it was.'

On a new stimulus from Penfield, she went on: 'Yes, sir, I think I heard a mother calling her little boy somewhere. It seemed to be something that happened years ago. . . . It was somebody in the neighbourhood where I live.'

When Penfield moved the electrode to a neighbouring point on the cortex, she said: 'I heard voices down along the river somewhere – a man's voice and a woman's voice calling. . . . I think I saw the river.'

Asked what river, she replied: 'I do not know. It seems to be one I was visiting when I was a child.'

Penfield then reactivated the current in the same place, and Mary told him: 'Yes, I hear voices. It is late at night, around the carnival somewhere. Some sort of travelling circus . . . I saw lots of big wagons that they use to haul animals in.'

After further explorations Penfield took an electrode insulated down to the tip, and, after inserting this deep into a cleft of Mary's brain known as the fissure of Sylvius, again reactivated the electric current: 'Oh! I had the same, very, very familiar memory, in an office somewhere. I could see the desks. I was there and someone was calling to me. A man leaning on a desk with a pencil in his hand.'

Sometimes such patients relived the very emotions of the original incident, as in the case of one who cried out: 'There they go, yelling at me. Stop them!' Yet, as Penfield carefully noted, they – or something of them – still retained awareness of their real-time, real-life location in his Montreal operating theatre; this was seemingly an indication that there was some form of detached, observing higher consciousness ('mind'?) over and beyond the workings of the physical brain.

Penfield marvelled at the mystery recording-track's apparent sheer totality. Indicative of this was how the incidents described were almost invariably the trivia of life: laughing with friends, listening for whether a baby was awake, or grabbing a stick from a dog's mouth. Whatever point of life was tracked back to, this was always experienced in 'forward play' mode, never backwards. If the memory track involved listening to music, then this was heard at what would have been the precise original tempo, the patient being able to hum this is a way they would claim themselves incapable of in normal consciousness. This was effectively confirming exactly what we remarked on in Chapter 4 concerning hypnotic 'past-life' memories, that there is an apparent astonishing ability of something within us to record absolutely everything, even though we have no direct access to it.

Why should nature have provided such an extensive track-record of all our experience, yet seemingly not provided us with the key to gain normal conscious access to it – unless this has some purpose, conceivably, since it is of no apparent earthly use, beyond life itself? Tenuous though this might seem, giving fuel to the idea that there is something death-associated with this track is the frequently observed fact of something like it spontaneously impinging on the consciousnesses of individuals who believe themselves to be facing certain death, as in mountaineering and parachuting accidents. According to scientific surveys, in nearly a third of these cases survivors really do describe having their lives 'flash before them'.[11] In the words of one American who miraculously survived after his parachute failed to open during a fall from 3,500 feet:

> It is like a picture runs in front of your eyes, from the time you can remember up to the time, you know, what was happening [that is, the present]. . . . It seems like pictures of your life just flow in front of your eyes, the things you used to do when you were small and stuff: stupid things. Like, you see your parents' faces – it was everything. And things that I didn't remember that I did. Things that I couldn't remember now, but I remember two years ago or something. It all came back to me, like it refreshed my mind of everything I used to do when I was little . . . it was like a picture, it was like a movie camera running across your eyes. In a matter of a second or two. Just boom, boom [snaps his fingers]! It was clear as day, clear as day. Very fast and you can see everything. It was, like, wow, like someone was feeding a computer or something, like putting a computer in your head and programming you, that's what it was like. . . . It was like starting in the beginning and working its way up to the end, what was happening. Like clockwise, just going clockwise. One right after another.[12]

Another indication of the apparent death-crisis-generated nature of this recording-track is the case of a seventy-year-old Englishwoman who in 1902 very nearly died from bronchial pneumonia and was saved only by a nick-of-time intervention by her physician, Dr Henry Freeborn. As Dr Freeborn subsequently reported in the journal *The Lancet*, the woman lapsed into a delirium during which those around her became aware that she was speaking in what seemed a completely unintelligible language – until a visitor happened to recognize it as perfect Hindustani.[13] According to the translator, her ramblings were all about going to the bazaar to buy sweets, and she seemed also to recite Hindustani poems. These went on for about twenty-four hours, after which she began talking English, later mixed with some French and German.

Only on the woman's recovery to full consciousness about a week later did an explanation become available. Although consciously she could recall scarcely a word of Hindustani, during the first three years of her life, seemingly as the result of the death of her mother, she had been brought up in India exclusively in the care of native *ayahs* or nursemaids who had spoken to her in nothing but that language. She had then been shipped back to England, where inevitably she spoke only English, subsequently learning French and German during youthful travels and residence on the European continent. It was all as if at the point of death her theoretical recording-track had wound back to the time of her birth, then, during the course of her recovery, progressively advanced in a 'slow forward' mode to take her back to the real-life present.

Further evidence suggesting something genuinely above, beyond, and detachable from the physical machine of body and brain is the increasingly recognized fact that while a person may be in the deepest coma, and continually fail to respond to any normal stimuli, *some* part of them appears to be listening.

For instance, from Father Peter Rinaldi, for many years the parish priest at Port Chester, New York, and personally well known to me, has come a story of how he was one day telephoned by a mystery woman asking him to go urgently to the bedside of a Catholic man, also unknown to him, dying at Port Chester's United Hospital. Faithful to his calling, Rinaldi dutifully arrived at the hospital, to be told by the nursing staff that the patient in question had suffered a massive stroke and was most unlikely to be reached. Undaunted, and with his usual priestly calm, Rinaldi began the time-honoured administration of the Last Rites, whispering in the patient's ear to squeeze his hand if he could still hear him. Initially he received only the most barely perceptible response, until the point where the sign of the cross is made in oil on the palm of the dying person's hand, when according to Rinaldi:

> The unexpected happened. As I turned his [the patient's] right hand over, he slowly moved it back to its former position, palm down. Again and again, as gently as I could, I turned his hands over, first the right, then the left, only to see him turn them back to the palms-down position. . . . Then suddenly it all came to me in a flash. 'Are you a priest?' I asked him, as I held his hand. He clasped mine as he opened his eyes with a hint of a nod. It is not generally known, but when the Last Rites are administered to a priest, his hands are anointed on the back, since the palms received the anointing on the day he was ordained.[14]

As tears of relief and gratitude welled in the dying man's eyes, Father Rinaldi deduced that this 'priest' had to have been one who had broken his vows – presumably by a sexual liaison with the mystery woman caller for there was no information about a priestly calling on his medical record. But the remarkable feature was that his mind in his last moments, despite the desperate infirmity of his body, had retained the most intense concern to receive the correct absolution by which he could die at peace.

A similar example is provided by the case of Johnnie Earl Spencer, father of Diana, Princess of Wales, who on 9 September 1979 collapsed with a brain haemorrhage in the courtyard of his ancestral home, Althorp in Northamptonshire.[15] Despite Johnnie lying comatose and near to death for many months, his wife Raine, the Countess Spencer, kept determinedly talking to him at his bedside, firmly believing that with sufficient stimulus the comatose can be restored to consciousness. At last one day, as Raine played him a tape recording of his favourite operatic aria, 'One Fine Day' from Puccini's *Madama Butterfly*, Johnnie opened his eyes. He told Raine afterwards that throughout the months of his coma, 'I knew you were there, and I heard everything you said to me.'

Dr Gerald MacKenzie, a former Registrar at London's National Heart Hospital, has also described to me how his own sister-in-law, who suffered a severe brain haemorrhage and was thought to be irrecoverable, clearly recalled her two sisters' visits, including parts of their conversation, and went on to make a full recovery.

This point is further reinforced by instances of severely brain-damaged individuals who, although perhaps unable to speak or control their movements, and perhaps appearing even imbecilic, have been found to possess fully competent and even exceptional mental powers if some means of communication can be found for them. One such has been Christopher Nolan from Dublin in Eire, whose motor cortex was so severely damaged at his birth that he was left unable to control his movements, to speak, walk, swallow properly, sit unsupported, or even hold up his head for any length of time.[16] During his early childhood his family thought they could detect signs of intelligence – he was sometimes the first to laugh at jokes – but it was only in 1977, when Christopher was eleven, that the combination of an anti-spastic drug and a 'unicorn' device fitted to his head enabled him to communicate by pressing the keys of an electric typewriter. When he did, what poured from him, seemingly fully developed, was a literary talent of a maturity far exceeding that of any normal eleven-year-old. His recently published autobiography *Under the Eye of the Clock* makes clear the sharpness of his mind, despite such an unpromising exterior.

That brain and body can thus be inhibitors of an altogether more intelligent something else struggling to express itself has been further suggested by apparent remarkable recoveries of mentally sick patients shortly before their death. As reported by Dr Karlis Osis in his death-bed study:

> In two cases . . . one of severe schizophrenia and one of senility, the patients regained normal mentality shortly before death. The schizophrenic had been out of touch with reality for two years, according to the informant. Naturally the two cases vary a little, but if the observations are accurate they would indicate an extremely important area for psychiatrists to explore. [17]

The implications are that 'we', our minds, consciousnesses, or whatever we may like to call them, may be something very much more subtle and complex than indicated by mechanistic theory. Nevertheless, the true criterion has to be whether, independent of all out-of-the-body evidence we have seen, there is other evidence that we are not confined to the shell of our physical bodies. For this perhaps the most crucial question is whether there is any *real* evidence that one mind, without the aid of any physical contrivance such as radio or telephone, can communicate with another mind across space – i.e. by some means akin to what is labelled telepathy. If any such leap of communication can genuinely be demonstrated to take place between two persons over several thousand miles, this would suggest that there really is something in us that transcends the physical cage of our 'machine' or human body, something thereby arguably capable of surviving death. But can this be demonstrated?

In this course of this study we have seen at least some suggestions of a process along these lines. We noted how Swedenborg seemed to be able to 'see' the fire happening hundreds of miles away in Stockholm. We noted how Australian aborigines appeared to be able to receive some form of transmission of the death of a relative. Further examples have been cited by Professor Hornell Hart in his book *The Enigma of Survival*. [18] Hart has described how one Scottish sportsman, David Leslie, wanting to know what had happened to eight Kaffirs who had gone out many miles away on a hunting expedition, learnt precise details of their movements from a Zulu witch-doctor. Similarly Commander R. Jukes Hughes, serving in the Transkei, was told by local natives the blow-by-blow details of a running battle taking place three hundred miles away.

But are there other, perhaps more readily substantiable indications? One such is suggested by naturalists' observations that creatures which live in communities, such as ants, termites, and wild bees, appear to have some form of communication between them that transcends physical barriers. If there is injury, for instance, to a termite queen, who spends her life sealed away in a dark tomb laying eggs, then the activity of the whole termitary becomes immediately disrupted, even if, for experimental purposes, the queen has been screened off from outlying parts of her community by sheets of steel.[19] It is just as if some near-death type of 'thought-travel' has taken place.

Perhaps the most striking indication of this same apparent faculty indicates that its nature is something deeper and subtler than mere thoughts transmitted like radio waves. This evidence comes from a number of well-researched instances of rapport between identical twins separated from each other since birth, and subsequently unaware of each other's existence.

One classic instance of this happens to have involved not simply twins but triplets. Three American boy babies were parted from each other for adoption purposes at birth in 1961, and grew up totally unknown to each other in three separate families as Bobby Shafran, Eddy Galland, and David Kellman.[20] In 1977 and 1978 all three underwent psychiatric treatment, quite independently, for little better reason than that each felt there was something missing in his life and did not know what this was. Neither they nor their adoptive families had been told that they had been separated triplets, and the respective psychiatrists put it down to the fact of having been adopted, even though all three boys had been brought up in loving and supportive families.

The penny began to drop only when in September 1980 Bobby began attending a college in New York State, to find himself repeatedly mistaken for a mysterious someone called Eddy. Eddy turned out to have been a student at the same college the previous year, and when another student who had known him arranged for him and Bobby to meet there was no mistake. Bobby recalled the moment, after a three-hour drive, when he waited on Eddy's doorstep for the door to open:

It seemed forever. . . . After that, I said, 'Oh, my God' – and simultaneously *saw* myself saying, 'Oh, my God.' I scratched my head – and saw myself scratching my head. I turned

away, and saw myself turning away. Everything in unison, as
though professional mimes were doing this. We started
shaking hands, and wound up hugging.[21]

Subsequent newspaper publicity brought to light the third triplet,
David, with whom there was a similarly extraordinary reunion. All three
said in unison, 'I can't *believe* this!' followed by the equally simultaneous
'I can't believe you *said* that!' before falling into each other's arms.

Predictably David, Bobby, and Eddy turned out to have a whole series
of characteristics in common, smoking the same brand of cigarettes,
enjoying wrestling, Italian food, and the company of older women. But
perhaps the really significant feature is that each had dreamed of having
an identical-looking brother, and experienced sufficient emotional
turmoil associated with this that in each case psychiatric help was
deemed necessary. It is as if, below the level of consciousness, each
somehow did know of the others' existence all along.

This is no one-off, over-sensationalized freak. During the past few
years American psychologist Dr Tom Bouchard of the University of
Minnesota, Minneapolis, has carefully assembled a remarkable collection of cases of separated twins with particular accent on their shared
characteristics.[22] One such example is that of James Lewis and James
Springer, separated in 1940 at only five weeks old. On becoming
reunited in 1979 they discovered that, besides arguably genetics-related
similarities such as fingernail-biting and weak hearts, while at school
both had owned a pet dog whom they had named 'Toy'. In their adult
life, both had married a Linda, divorced her, and got remarried to
women called Betty. Both had called their first-born son James Allan,
James Lewis's choice of this being differentiated only by a single 'l'
spelling. In respect of their occupations both had worked as petrol-
station attendants, as employees of the McDonald's fast-food chain, and
as part-time deputy sheriffs.

Case after case from Dr Bouchard's files repeats such oddities, and of
course a lot must be put down to coincidence, genetics, and other
factors. But there also continually recur, as in the triplets case, instances
in which some form of below-the-level-of-consciousness transmission
between minds seems the *only* explanation. In one example, British
twin sisters Bridget Harrison and Dorothy Lowe, having been separated
only weeks after their birth in 1945, and not knowing of the other's
existence until 1979, both kept a diary for the year 1960 (and only for
that year), both chose for this the same make, the same type, and the
same colour, and both made entries on exactly the same days, leaving
the identical others blank.[23] While two other British twins, Irene Reid

and Jeanette Hamilton, were being studied in Minneapolis, Irene, when actually with Dr Bouchard, reported the feeling that Jeanette was in trouble, to be telephoned half an hour later by Bouchard confirming that this was indeed the case. Two days later this happened the other way round; Irene became poorly, and Jeanette was the one to sense this.[24]

Such examples would seem to indicate not telepathy in the normally understood sense of some radio-type transmission between two independent machines but something altogether deeper, a process in which two minds meet as one across space, without necessarily even any awareness of this on the part of the operating consciousness. Almost certainly the phenomenon is at its most evident among twins simply because of the closer biological bonds between them. But it also seems to indicate, in the strongest possible terms, that what we call ourselves, or 'us', really is something rather more than just the finite assemblage of physics, chemistry, and genetics that the mechanists would have us believe – something that arguably survives beyond physical death.

Shortly before his death in 1976 Dr Wilder Penfield put together a book which was essentially the concluding reflection on his career. In this book, *The Mystery of the Mind,* he did not shrink from tackling the issue of the mind's survival after death:

> When death at last blows out the candle that was life, the mind seems to vanish, as in sleep. I said 'seems'. What can one really conclude? What is the reasonable hypothesis in regard to this matter, considering the physiological evidence? Only this: the brain has not explained the mind fully. The mind of man seems to derive its energy, perhaps in altered form, from the highest brain-mechanism during his waking hours. In the daily routine of a man's life, communication with other minds is carried out indirectly through the mechanisms of the brain. If this is so, it is clear that, in order to survive after death, the mind *must* establish a connection with a source of energy other than that of the brain. If not, the mind must disappear forever as surely as the brain and body die and turn into dust. If, however, during life, when brain and mind are awake, direct communication is sometimes established with the minds of other men . . . then it is clear that energy from without can reach a man's mind. In that case it is not unreasonable for him to hope that after death the mind may waken to another source of energy.[25]

If Penfield is right – and everything we have explored certainly suggests this – then what can that energy be? Not, I would suggest the 'spiritual body' duplicate, with its 'silver cord', as envisaged by Doris Stokes. Are there any other indications? It may be a side-track, but among Celtic peoples, so prone, as many seem to be, to flashes of that pre-consciousness state postulated by Julian Jaynes, there recur persistent claims of the ability to see the departing spirits of the recently deceased in the form of what are popularly described as 'death candles'. Dr Evans-Wentz, who conducted special researches among the Celts of Wales during the early part of the twentieth century, related a particular case of an exclusively Welsh-speaking spinster from Pembrokeshire who had lived all her life in the same house as generations of her ancestors. She told him:

> I have seen more than one death candle. I saw one death candle right here in this room where we are sitting and talking. . . . The death candle appears like a patch of bright light; and no matter how dark the room or place is, everything in it is as clean as day. The candle is not a flame, but a luminous mass, lightish blue in colour, which dances as though borne by an invisible agency, and sometimes it rolls over and over. If you go up to the light it is nothing, for it is a spirit. . . . The man you saw here in the house today, one night as he was going along the road near Nevern, saw the death-light of old Doctor Harris, and says it was lightish green. [26]

Evans-Wentz was told by his informant's nephew and niece that the death candle seen in the woman's house

> took an untrodden course from the house across the fields to the grave-yard, and that when the death of one of the family occurred soon afterwards, their aunt insisted that the corpse should be carried by exactly the same route; so the road was abandoned, and the funeral went through the ploughed fields.

Such experiences are not confined to the British Isles. Dr Kenneth Ring was told by one survivor of a near-death experience:

> Five years ago my brother, aged 52, passed away. At 4 a.m. that day I was awakened by a soft, luminous light, at the foot

of my bed. It slowly ascended up and then disappeared. Half an hour later, I was notified of his passing, exactly at 4 a.m. While the light was present I felt extremely tranquil and didn't move. [27]

A very similar experience, though this time a light of an apparently hostile nature, has been directly described to me by a former Royal Air Force driver from Cardiff, Ken Watson. In 1945, when Ken served in Burma, he was driving some fellow RAF men through dangerous territory late at night when his truck was suddenly fired upon by unseen terrorists. Ken managed to accelerate safely away while his companions fired randomly into the darkness, but shortly after all were astonished to see on the road ahead what Ken describes as 'a round white light within a few feet of the ground, as if the moon had suddenly come down; only there was no moon'. Ken stopped the truck, and his companions got out, guns at the ready; but the light, which seemed to have something eerie and sinister about it, gradually disappeared. Ken was subsequently told by Welsh folklorist Bertram Griffiths:

> It is very probable that the luminous cloud you saw on the Burma road was an attempted materialization by some poor chap who had been killed. . . . These appearances take the following shapes – balls, masses (both called clouds). [28]

Before such manifestations are dismissed as ball lightning, or just plain balderdash, let us consider an interesting and puzzling feature of prehistoric and ancient places of the dead, which are frequently decorated with incised or painted motifs in the form of spiral balls. The great Egyptologist Sir Flinders Petrie went so far as to call these 'the main feature of primitive decoration', and the spirals are found extraordinarily far afield, in locations as widely scattered as Scandinavia, Asia Minor, China, New Zealand, Australia, India, and North and South America.

Although no one seems to be sure of the motif's exact meaning, its particular association with places of the dead is evident from the fact it forms the main decoration of the great entrance stone (and of some of the interior stones) at Newgrange, the prehistoric Irish 'house of the dead' (Figure 11); it features as the main ceiling decoration of Malta's prehistoric hypogeum of Hal Saflieni, where many thousands were buried, and recurs at the entrances of many other early tombs. A message from an Egyptian widow, Merti, to her deceased son – 'May Osiris, first of the western ones [the dead], give you millions of years by blowing wind [fresh air] into your nostrils and bread and beer for

Fig. 9. Early man's image of the souls of the dead? Spiral motifs from the Newgrange passage grave, County Meath, Ireland

nourishment' – was written on a shallow bowl in the form of a spiral. Might the spiral have been for the ancients a universally understood symbol for the souls of the dead?

With Dr Wilder Penfield it is perhaps safest and wisest to conclude that at present 'Science can make no statement . . . as to the question of man's existence after death, although every thoughtful man must ask that question.'[29] Yet Penfield goes on:

> But when the nature of the energy that activates the mind is discovered (as I believe it will be), the time may yet come when scientists will be able to make a valid approach to a study of the nature of a spirit other than that of a man.

Can we foresee such a time? Is it possible that the energy in question – if it indeed exists – may be fitted into our understanding of the physics of the universe? It is time to consider the physics of the non-physical.

# 14

# PHYSICS OF THE NON-PHYSICAL

If the late Pope Paul VI had one particularly cherished personal possession, it was his bedside alarm-clock. A perfectly ordinary alarm-clock with lacquered brass frame and Roman numerals on a white face, for fifty-five years he almost obsessionally insisted on taking it with him wherever he travelled. It was never known to be fast or slow, and was always set by him to give its tinny ring at precisely 6.30 a.m., just as it did on the morning of the last day of his life, Sunday, 6 August 1978, the Feast of the Transfiguration.

Throughout that day, as physician Mario Fontana and other aides and officials watched Paul's life ebb away, the clock ticked steadily at his bedside, neither reset nor rewound. The Last Rites were given, and at 9.40 that evening, just after Paul had feebly recited but failed to finish the Lord's Prayer, Fontana listened to his chest, felt his pulse, and announced, 'It is over.' At that precise moment, to the utter astonishment of all present, Paul's ancient alarm shrilled throughout the bedroom.

If we could understand exactly what happened in that extraordinary and well-attested moment,[1] and in particular whatever something of the Pope's passing had sufficient energy to trigger that alarm, then the nature of any possible afterlife might be rather more encompassable within accepted science than it is at present. The search for a scientific base for 'soul' or 'mind' was high on the priorities of those who so enthusiastically founded the British and American Societies for Psychical Research back in the 1880s. A generation later the great American inventor Thomas Edison, developer of the first successful incandescent electric light, confidently claimed:

> I am inclined to believe that our personality hereafter does affect matter. If we can evolve an instrument so delicate as to be affected by our personality as it survives in the next life, such an instrument ought to record something.[2]

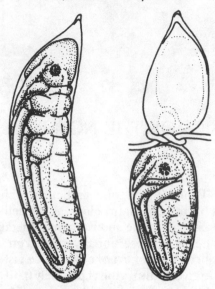

Fig. 10. Driesch's entelechy hypothesis demonstrated. Left: a normal embryo of the dragonfly. Right: a small but complete embryo formed from the posterior half of an egg ligated around the middle soon after laying

Yet even a hundred years after the Society for Psychical Research's foundation, as has recently been acknowledged by its current President, Cambridge criminologist Professor Donald West: 'We do not seem to have got very far.'[3]

The situation is by no means as bleak as it might at first appear, however. Not long after the Society's foundation, biologist Hans Driesch, at that time working at the Marine Zoology Station in Naples, carried out an experiment with a sea-urchin's embryo in which he killed one cell at the two-celled stage and found that the surviving cell produced not half a sea-urchin but a perfect one half the usual size.[4] Driesch's deduction from the experiment was that the living cell aims at some sort of wholeness, a principle he dubbed 'entelechy' (Figure 10). In 1926 Driesch became President of the Society for Psychical Research and in his presidential address propounded the theme that the development of organisms was directed by 'a unifying non-material mind-like something . . . an ordering principle which does not add either energy or matter' to what goes on.' This principle, he hypothesized, might exist outside time and space.

A generation later Driesch's ideas were enthusiastically taken up by the great English biologist Sir Alister Hardy, Oxford University's

Linacre Professor of Zoology from 1946 to 1961 and President of the Society for Psychical Research during the years 1965–9. Personally convinced of the actuality of something along the lines of telepathy, Hardy considered the idea 'that individual organisms are somehow in psychical connexion across space' to be one of the greatest scientific breakthroughs of all time if it could be established.[6] In his last years he set up at Oxford a special Religious Experience Research Unit with this among its aims. As recently as 1981 Hardy's ideas were followed up by the young English biologist Dr Rupert Sheldrake with a pioneering book *A New Science of Life*.[7] Sheldrake argues that the characteristic forms and behaviour of physical, chemical, and biological systems are determined by invisible organizing fields, dubbed 'morpho-genetic fields', apparently capable of transcending both space and time, yet without any mass or energy of their own.

Such ideas – with their possible relevance to whatever substance-less, space-and-time-transcending something of us might survive physical death – find remarkable echo in some of the most recent findings in theoretical physics. A few decades ago physicists had assembled such an impressive set of apparent classical laws for the universe that many thought they were genuinely close to knowing all the answers. But in recent years one after another of the old concepts (the nature of matter, the directionality of time, the relation between space and time, and the geometry of space) have all had to undergo drastic revision. The exact implications of exotic new theoretica such as 'black holes', 'worm-holes' in space, backwards causality, positive entropy, neutrinos, negative mass, imaginary mass, and others (that I don't pretend to understand) all still need to be worked out.

For instance, it is now long recognized from the work of Einstein and others that items which may appear to us as very solid and 'physical' are in fact no more than concentrations of energy. When analysed in terms of their constituent electrons, protons, neutrons, etc., these items are ultimately little more substantial than what appear to us to be insubstantial or non-physical phenomena, such as waves of light.

In a manner not unfamiliar to the problems for psychical research, we are even obliged to believe in these basic constituents of matter without the apparent evidence of being able to 'see' them. As pointed out by Einstein's contemporary Heisenberg, to 'see' anything requires illumination, and even if one could capture a stationary electron and put it under some sort of super-microscope, the first photon (particle of light similar in size to an electron) from the microscope's light to try to light the electron would collide with it and knock it out of the way.

Another factor of considerable potential relevance to the existence of 'minds', and to the idea of these being able to communicate across space (and perhaps time), has been a problem arising out of Einstein's theory of relativity and Max Planck's quantum theory, the assertion that radiant energy is emitted in 'discrete atomic quantities', or quanta. According to quantum theory there are certain conditions under which, in the case of two very distant subatomic particles, if the behaviour of one is altered the other can be expected to change instantaneously in exactly the same way, despite no apparent force or signal linking them. It is as if each particle 'knows' what the other is doing. Einstein always rejected this on the grounds that, since there could be no harmony without some signal passing between the two distant particles, a signal of this kind would have to travel faster than the speed of light, and his theory of relativity did not allow for this.

For a long while the difficulty was one of finding any way of checking whether Einstein or quantum theory was correct. Professor David Bohm of Birkbeck College, London, tried by measuring the polarization of twinned pairs of photons from a common light source. He encouragingly found that, whenever the first of these was measured, the twin behaved as though it too had been disturbed. But he could find no precise way of determining whether the process was genuinely instantaneous, and therefore faster than the speed of light.

A French team, headed by Alain Aspect of Paris's Institut d'Optique Théorique et Appliquée, has recently come on to the scene. The French researchers have simply added to Bohm's experiment a switch to block any signal between the paired photons *except* one travelling faster than light, and have found this experiment to work. Professor Bohm has commented:

> All we can do is to look at several possible interpretations. . . . It may mean that everything in the universe is in a kind of total rapport, so that whatever happens is related to everything else. Or it may mean that there is some kind of information that can travel faster than the speed of light. Or it may mean that our concepts of space and time have to be modified in some way that we don't now understand.[8]

This is extremely interesting in relation to our recent remarks on apparent telepathic phenomena and on the correspondences between separated twins. But it does nothing to help prove the existence of 'soul', 'mind', or any afterlife dimension except from the negative, 'Hamletian' point of view that there could be more things in heaven and earth than are yet dreamed of in our theoretical physics.

If there is to be any breakthrough in scientific verification of after death experience, there have been encouraging recent developments here in Britain providing the groundwork. One individual who as much as anyone this century was fascinated by the challenge of the nature of mind and the possibility of this surviving death was the late Arthur Koestler. Koestler had his own mind concentrated wonderfully on the question when in 1937 he was imprisoned under sentence of death for ninety-six days during the Spanish Civil War, watching hundreds of fellow prisoners go to their execution while awaiting his own.[9] From having been a relatively 'popular' journalist, Koestler devoted much of the rest of his life to grappling with scientific paradoxes and life-after-death issues. In March 1983, debilitated and depressed by Parkinson's disease, he committed suicide with his third wife Cynthia, leaving his entire estate for the endowment of the first professorial chair in the field of parapsychology (effectively the science of whether or not we have some form of soul) at any suitable British university prepared to accept this on its curriculum.

Only the University of Edinburgh and University College, Cardiff, proved willing to accept the offer on Koestler's terms. Edinburgh was chosen by the executors, and in May 1985 the university formally announced the appointment of American psychologist Dr Robert Morris as first professor of a subject previously virtually without academic status in Britain. In his mid-forties, married, with twin daughters, at the time of writing Dr Morris is still in the process of setting up his department, but has already shown himself to have a far more enlightened approach than his much longer-established counterpart in the United States, the already mentioned Dr Ian Stevenson of the University of Virginia. In very much the spirit of Britain's Society for Psychical Research, Professor Morris claims no personal 'party line' on his subject, his priority being to try to develop the right framework by which any conceivable future breakthrough – such as some un-impeachable means of contact with the dead – can be scientifically demonstrated.

Morris's root difficulty, inevitably, is that of finding a means of establishing the existence of something no one can be sure exists. As he is well aware, the history of psychical research is all too littered both with the spurious and with the failure or at best 'not-proven' nature of many initially enthusiastically offered hypotheses.

For instance, in 1906 a Dr Duncan MacDougall of the Massachusetts General Hospital hypothesized that if there was some form of entity, such as a soul, which genuinely left the body on physical death, conceivably this departure might be measurable by a perceptible loss of body weight. With the prior consent of six dying patients, Dr Mac-Dougall devised an experiment whereby on the imminence of their deaths these would be lifted on to a specially lightweight bed, then set on finely balanced platform scales to provide a continuous record of any weight lost. MacDougall carefully chose patients whose deaths were likely to be peaceful rather than violent; the vibration of instruments would otherwise upset his calculations. On the demise of his first patient he encouragingly noted a sudden weight loss of three-quarters of an ounce. The second registered an ounce and a half, and another a half-ounce. Although in the case of the three other patients the readings were less certain, in 1907 MacDougall produced a paper for the *Journal of the American Society for Psychical Research* in which he argued that this weight loss seemed attributable only to the departure of something resembling what religion has called a soul.[10]

However, MacDougall's experiment suffered from two serious drawbacks. The first of these, as we have noted earlier, is that precisely determining the time of death is notoriously difficult. The second is that MacDougall had no way of measuring any water vapour lost from pre-mortem sweating and the cessation of respiration. The relevance of this became all too clear when during the 1930s H. L. Twining of the Los Angeles High School's physics and electrical engineering department tried replicating MacDougall's work using various animals including mice. Twining found that, if an animal was poisoned in open air, a small but perceptible weight loss did seem to occur, as if in corroboration of MacDougall's findings. But when he tried the experiment again using a mouse sealed in a tube, there was no weight loss. As Twining deduced, if whatever the mouse lost at death could not get out of the tube, 'the suspicion is aroused that it is some kind of coarse matter with which we are acquainted that is lost, and not a soul'.[11] Via a series of elimination experiments including the drowning of mice in water, Twining effectively proved his point and destroyed MacDougall's. If there is a soul we can be confident it is weightless, just as the out-of-the-body near-death experiencers have described.

Could there be some other means of determining whether a genuine departure from the body occurs, perhaps using living subjects who claim that they can do this at will? One such has been Alex Tanous, a psychic from the far north-east American state of Maine, who has claimed to be able to do this since the age of five. Tanous agreed to take part in experiments set up by the already mentioned psychical researcher Dr Karlis Osis and his assistant Donna McCormick, during which he was asked to rest in a sound-proofed room, then to allow his disembodied self to pass into a specially constructed double-thickness steel chamber located six doors away. Inside the chamber Osis had set up a randomly changing display of a variety of images which it was the task of Tanous's disembodied self to 'see' and report on.

According to Osis's report of the experiment, Tanous had preliminary difficulties, but then gradually began to score impressive results.[12] In a further development, Osis and McCormick set up a polygraph – the machine used for lie-detection – inside the chamber. This was attached to strain gauges, with the idea that it might be able to register any perceptible vibrations that might be caused by Tanous's disembodied self entering or leaving. According to Osis and McCormick, the polygraph appeared to show signs of greater activation when Tanous's 'self' was theoretically viewing the images inside.

Although this experiment, like MacDougall's, might sound potentially encouraging, British researcher Dr Susan Blackmore, already noted for her criticisms of non-crisis-type out-of-the-body experiences, has been justifiably unconvinced. The randomly changing display set up by Osis and McCormick inside the chamber was one with four possible colours, four quadrants in which a picture could appear, and five line-drawing pictures; a 'hit' was scored if Tanous perceived any one of these aspects correctly. Tanous was told when his information was accurate. So although, according to Osis, Tanous scored a creditable 114 hits in 197 trials, this becomes somewhat less impressive when it is related to what would be obtained by chance. As noted by Dr Blackmore: 'If you work it out yourself, you will see that with so many target aspects there is a .55 probability of a hit on each trial, and so 108 hits would be expected by chance. Now 114 does not sound so good.'[13]

This may prove only the spuriousness of non-crisis-type out-of-the-body experiences, with arguably only those in which the subject is near death having any validity. Very similar criteria apply to the equally inconclusive card-guessing experiments that have been used in an attempt to 'prove' the existence of telepathy. It may be that it needs a real crisis for there to be some form of mental leap from one kind to another, just as it needs a real life-threatening situation for any potentially death-surviving element of us to leave the body. But this is not much help to Dr Morris at Edinburgh in his attempts to find something safe for working with volunteers in a laboratory.

One of Dr Morris's first priorities, as he rightly recognizes, is to think out and set up experiments and lines of enquiry that might produce scientific results. In line with the dying Pope Paul VI's apparent effect on his alarm-clock, one line of approach he plans to follow up is the investigation of living individuals who appear to affect and upset delicate instruments without even touching them – the phenomenon psychical researchers often refer to as 'psychokinesis', or 'PK'. Quite independent from the most likely overblown claims of Uri Geller and his like, there seem to occur instances of company employees who involuntarily and without physical intervention cause technical failures and malfunctions in complex and specialist apparatus without anyone knowing the reason why. Nor is Pope Paul VI the only individual whose passing has been noted to have had a strange effect on a clock. Thomas Edison may not have been able to develop the after death communication machine he dreamed of, but on his death his personal clock is reported to have mysteriously stopped within moments. This also apparently occurred with the deaths of some of Edison's colleagues. Similar strange behaviour was also reported of the clock of the Prussian King Frederick the Great, who died near Postdam on 17 August 1786.

Might there be any other way of setting up some experiment capable of offering proof of survival after death? Several of the early psychical researchers tried to think out something of this kind, most prominent among these being one of the founder members of the British Society for Psychical Research, and its President in 1900, Frederic W. H. Myers. Myers had been told by a medium that he would die in 1902, and so was a little unprepared when, at the age of fifty-seven, he died in Rome on 17 January 1901. None the less, some years beforehand he had left with Sir Oliver Lodge, his successor as President, a message in a sealed envelope with the instruction that this was to be opened only when, after his death, some medium claimed to be receiving messages from him. Close friends of Myers during his lifetime had been the Cambridge scholars Arthur and Margaret Verrall, and it was Margaret who, although very rationalist-minded, decided to try to communicate with her dead friend by automatic writing – that is, by putting her mind into a relaxed state whereby Myers, or any other dead person, might guide her hand and transmit some message from beyond the grave.

At first, perhaps through inexperience, Margaret Verrall's scribblings were garbled and meaningless. Only slightly more promising was a piece of bad Latin with Myers's name appended. But then more fluent material began to come through, including the following cryptic message: 'Myers's sealed envelope left with Lodge. . . . It has in it the words from the *Symposium* about love bridging the chasm.'

Sir Oliver Lodge was immediately contacted, and Myers's sealed envelope was eagerly opened, only to be found to contain the words: 'If I can revisit any earthly scene, I should choose the Valley in the grounds of Hallsteads, Cumberland.'

In fact, although everyone's initial reaction was one of disappointment, further consideration revealed that there was a genuine connection. In 1873, when only thirty, Myers had fallen headlong in love with his cousin's wife Annie Marshall, who lived at Hallsteads in Cumberland. Three years later Annie committed suicide by throwing herself into Ullswater Lake, and in her memory Myers had published privately a book called *Fragments of an Inner Life* in which he specifically referred to the *Symposium*, Plato's great dialogue on love.

Possibly, to a subtle, classically educated mind like Myers's, this might have been both conceived in life and executed in death as a brilliant demonstration of beyond-the-grave communication. In its wake there followed an extraordinary literature of so-called 'cross-correspondences'; Myers and other departed were purported to have transmitted via a variety of living individuals mediumistic and automatic-writing messages which on their own made little sense yet which put together could appear very meaningful. But although those who have explored these complex writings in depth have have often found them very convincing, scientifically they fall a long way short of anything that can be expected to be accepted as outright 'proof'.

Appealing though the 'sealed packet' type of survival demonstration might appear, it does have several disadvantages, not least its non-repeatability. As noted by British psychologist and psychical researcher Dr Robert H. Thouless, if a medium produces an incorrect message, the fact that the packet has been opened means there can be no opportunity for a second try. It also requires the holder of the sealed packet to be trusted that he or she has not surreptitiously found some means of opening it. Accordingly in 1948 Thouless arranged, for his own personal implementation, a carefully considered variant of this, a specially enciphered message of a kind available for anyone to inspect, but impossible to decode except with a verbal 'key' which Thouless intended to tell no one except, if it proved possible, from beyond the grave. In his own words:

I have myself left two such passages in cipher with the intention of trying to communicate their keys after my death. . . . It is to be hoped that, after I have died, a number of people will try to get in touch with me through a medium and to get from me a message giving the keys to both or to one of the enciphered messages. The keys are simple ones which I hoped would be easy to remember: references to an identifiable passage of literature in one case and two words in the other. If anyone thinks he has succeeded in receiving such a message he should communicate the keys to the Society for Psychical Research (1 Adam and Eve Mews, London W8

6UQ). They will check whether the key proposed for each enciphered passage enable that passage to be read. The preliminary part of this experiment, in which attempts have been made by mediums to obtain the keys by ESP [extra-sensory perception] in my lifetime, has already been carried out without success. There is, therefore, no evidence that the task can be accomplished by ESP, so that if the keys come through after my death it will look as if my stream of consciousness is still able to convey information and that it is, therefore, still surviving.

If no such message comes through it will not of course be a proof that I have not survived. The result will obviously be consistent with this possibility, but it might have other explanations. The remembering even of such a simple matter as a key reference or pair of words may be a difficult matter after one has lost the material brain which one has used for remembering during one's lifetime.[14]

As published in his book *From Anecdote to Experiment in Psychical Research*,[15] the coded messages Dr Thouless arranged are as follows:

INXPH  CJKGM  JIRPR  FBCVY  WYWES  NOECN  SCVHE  GYRJQ
TEBJM  TGXAT  YWPNH  CNYBC  FNXPF  LFXRV  QWQL

BTYRR  OOFLH  KCDXK  FWPCZ  KTADR  GFHKA  HTYXO  ALZUP
PYPVF  AYMMF  SDLR  UVUB

Dr Thouless died, at the age of ninety, on 25 September 1984. So far, of eight mediums consulted, none has been able to come forward with the keys to the ciphers. On 8 December 1986 the honorary secretary of the Society for Psychical Research, Mr A. T. Oram, reported to the Society's members:

When Professor Stevenson [of the University of Virginia; see Chapter 3] gave the Society some money to cover the expenses involved in seeing to obtain the keys to the late Dr Thouless's two cipher tests, he made it a condition that one person should be the co-ordinator, should in the main be involved in arranging the sittings, and should prepare a formal report. I offered to do that and I have had about fourteen effective sittings with eight mediums for that pur-pose during the year. It seems to me that I have been able to obtain good contact with Dr Thouless through each of these mediums, but it seems that he cannot remember the keys. One medium reported him saying that it is like trying to remember something from a dream and that he had not expected that. I am keeping Professor Stevenson informed and I am prepared, if necessary, to continue trying for some years in the hope that Dr Thouless might at some stage be able to recall the information he so wanted, during his lifetime, to convey to us after his death. I have asked at a recent sitting whether it could possibly be helpful if he were to try to arrange for a group of friends to help him to recall and transmit the keys, but he says he prefers to handle it himself and expresses confidence that before long he will succeed. [16]

So are we really to believe the mediums that Dr Thouless is genuinely continuing to experience in some after death state, but happens to have forgotten his keys? It is a little suspicious that this is the very excuse that Thouless in his lifetime offered as an advance explanation for failure. It is also somewhat difficult to reconcile with, for instance, the deceased Mr Hugh Talbot's purported communication via Mrs Osborne Leonard of the very page of his notebook on which long ago he had written the extract from *Post Mortem* (see page 166). And surely, if in an afterlife we do not retain memories of our earthly existence (and we have already noted the apparent activation of a memory track at the onset of death), what is it recognizable as 'us' that could survive?

There are a variety of other possible explanations. One is that, when Thouless breathed his last, that really was the end of him, and that nothing of him has survived to be able to communicate. If this is the case, then of course all the intriguing findings by Dr Sabom and Dr Ring have to be accepted as just another red herring among all the other spurious trails in pursuit of an afterlife. Another is that Thouless has survived but that all the mediums who have so far tried to get in touch with him have been either incompetent or impostors. Mediumistic communication might therefore still be practical but in need of a genuine 'white crow' yet to be found. Yet another explanation is that, although Thouless may have survived in an afterlife, something is preventing him from communicating with the living, perhaps the very rules against communication with the living that we noted from the Old Testament.

But perhaps the real reason for the continued failure of all attempts so far to bring evidence for life after death within the confines of accepted science is something different. In line with the anomalies encountered in physics, it may be that what truly constitutes 'us', a complex and evanescent set of memories and emotions, is simply not of an order to be isolated scientifically, or tapped into like some wireless signal, any more than we can isolate or put a measure to those none the less very real emotions of love, fear, and hate. If this is the case, it is likely that the answer will be found not in some impersonal laboratory, nor from the utterances of some medium, but from the dying and from those who have been near to death and survived.

As has been pointed out by physicians such as Dr Sabom, the medical profession has a great deal to answer for in not talking to dying patients sufficiently, and losing interest in them the moment it becomes apparent they are beyond medical help. It is part of doctors' training to pay far more attention to what they are instrumentally able to determine of their patients' symptoms than to anything the patients may say about how they feel. Such an attitude, however commendable scientifically, does not always encourage patients to unburden themselves on matters relating to their mental or emotional state. As one patient told Dr Ring in relation to his near-death experience:

> I find people are very stand-offish when you start talking about it. You know, they'll say, 'Oh really?' and they'll kind of hesitate away from you. I mean, it happened with the doctors at the hospital after the incident did happen to me. . . . They wouldn't listen. For a while I really felt that I was a little crazy, because every time I did broach the subject somebody would change the subject, so I felt the topic probably shouldn't be discussed. [17]

Another patient said: 'I'll be damned if I share my feelings about dying with someone who manages two-minute U-turns at the foot of my bed.'[18]

Ironically, in all our society's diverse social groups, one of the few to provide an atmosphere that supports and encourages people to relate near-death experiences is the Church of Latter-Day Saints, or Mormons. This is because what patients report in near-death experiences matches rather well the Mormon belief in an afterlife, which is much more clearly defined than that in conventional Christianity.[19]

However, in recent years particularly encouraging in this same direction has been the growth of the hospice movement, with its establishment of specialized centres for the dying. Instead of a conventional hospital, in which they represent technological failure and waste of resources and bed-space, if they are lucky the dying find themselves in an environment in which, with their condition fully recognized, every attempt is made to help them meet death with a dignity which modern society otherwise annihilates via drips and drugs. They find attending them staff who, because they are not preoccupied with any struggle to keep people alive, have the time to listen to those in their charge; the patients in their turn have the opportunity to open up their fears and emotions without the slightest need any longer to keep up pretences and appearances. In the all too naked face of impending death the dying can be truly themselves, for perhaps the first time in their lives, and it can be an extraordinarily salutary experience.

As I have personally observed, the shock on visiting a well-run hospice is to find that, instead of the anticipated atmosphere of gloom and despair, the accent is on cheerfulness, love, and sheer joy of living such as would be difficult to find almost anywhere else. Eyes can be bright and quite clearly at peace even in a body obviously in the countdown hours to whatever might lie beyond. If there is experience after death, we see in those eyes the very interface between physical and non-physical worlds; if we could read the eyes properly we might understand this transition a great deal better than at present.

Although this very idea of learning from the dying raises some of this century's most deep-seated taboos, pioneers such as Elisabeth Kübler-Ross have shown the way. In Britain at least one hospice founder, Father Francis O'Leary of the Lancashire-based St Joseph's Hospice Association (whose hospices I have visited), has recognized that his patients should be more scientifically studied and listened to. For Father O'Leary this is not least because of some remarkable instances of individuals who, entering his hospice to die, have found such fresh resources within themselves that it has been their 'terminal' illness that has given up the ghost. At the time of writing he is in the process of founding, as an adjunct to his Thornton, Lancashire, hospice, a special academy for precisely this purpose.

We may perhaps look to a future in which Professor Robert Morris and/or whoever takes charge of Father O'Leary's pioneering academy may succeed where so many 'psychical' researchers have failed.

# 15

# ON NOT BEING AFRAID

So what have we achieved? At least, I hope, some fresh insights and perspectives. Those who may have been mesmerized by the apparent convincingness of 'past lives' of the hypnotic and non-hypnotic variety may perhaps have been persuaded to think again. Those previously seduced by the reincarnationist charms of Shirley MacLaine may perhaps now regard their interests better served by her rather more considerable talents as an actress. Those who have fallen under the spell of grandmotherly Doris Stokes may perhaps now realize, with Hamlet, that one can smile, and smile, and still be not all one seems. On the positive side we may not have proved that there really is some form of after death experience, but perhaps we have at least furnished sufficient for the issue to be taken seriously, and to have some effect on the way we conduct our future lives.

For, as was cogently pointed out by the pioneering United Nations Secretary-General, Dag Hammarskjöld, who himself died so tragically in a plane crash:

> No choice is uninfluenced by the way in which the personal-
> ity regards its destiny, and the body its death. In the last
> analysis, it is our conception of death which decides our
> answers to all the questions that life puts to us. [1]

The need to strike just the right balance in our attitudes is particularly important in the highly polarized world in which we find ourselves. At the very commencement of this book we noted some unhappy instances of those, such as James Jones and his followers, who have too fanatically believed in a life after death. The unctuous Bible Belt preachers who uncritically proclaim plastic paradise for the well-heeled godly and hellfire for the damned are scarcely a whit more palatable than the ayatollahs and imams who promise instant Islamic paradise to those who martyr themselves in the current Gulf War. In Britain, Doris Stokes told her audiences that death is a 'great adventure', while in a popular American book on near-death experiences, *Afterlife: Reports from the*

*Threshold of Death*, author Archie Matson has actually given one chapter the title 'The Thrill of Dying'.[2] In the face of such attitudes I have considerable sympathy with the sceptically minded Californian psycho-pharmacologist Dr Ronald K. Siegel, who comments that Matson has 'made the experience seem as harmless as an amusement-park ride'.[3] Death is death – certain, repellant, and degrading. It is sheer deceit and hypocrisy for anyone to try to present it as otherwise.

But almost equally deplorable is the denial of death that has become almost a keynote of modern society. Fictionalized death in the form of adventure, crime, and war films is all too liberally served up as 'entertainment' on our television screens; yet paradoxically those same screens' newscasts when reporting real-life atrocities shield us from any too explicit sight of these on the grounds that they would offend public taste. The same thanatal prudery causes the dead to be swiftly covered at the scene of any accident, and a sheet to be immediately drawn over the face of those who die in hospital.

This is not to advocate any new fad for 'full-frontal' death, but it is none the less merely a step removed from the extraordinary pantomime of deception that occurs in so many families when a close relative is known or suspected to be approaching death. The dying person, it is reasoned, would of course be 'best' in the hands of professionals. Thus, unless a hospice is chosen, too often that individual, at the very time of most needing family love, comfort, and companionship, finds himself or herself shuffled like a parcel to a hospital ward, and to the doubtful comfort of spending the last hours hooked up to impersonal drips and drains.

At this point the game of deception takes on a new form: non-admission of the inevitable. Not only do more and more doctors shrink from telling patients or their relatives that they will not get better, the relatives who suspect go along with the pretence. As for the person who is dying, while they too may well know in themselves that they have merely a matter of hours, they play along with the same game – all in the name of avoiding distress and an embarrassing display of feelings.

Nor does the pretence end even when the death has occurred. In Britain children who may well have been schooled in every detail of sexual intercourse may be screened from seeing their grandmother in death; they may also be 'spared' attending her funeral, and even perhaps told some euphemism such as that she has 'gone away'. The now ingrained British cost-consciousness tends to regard it as the most terrible waste even to send flowers to a funeral, one growing fashion being for any money for these to be donated to cancer research, as if this will somehow prevent death. And while the joggers and health-food fanatics dream up yet better but ultimately futile ways to keep themselves alive, in London's great suburban cemeteries hundreds of masterpieces of Victorian tomb sculpture lie neglected and vandalized as monuments to a society almost desperately trying to convince itself that death does not or need not exist.[4]

In the United States funerals are far more showy, expensive affairs, and cemeteries much better kept, but the pretence merely takes a different form. The money lavished on plush caskets and elaborate embalming is ultimately so that everyone can persuade themselves that, just as among the ancient Egyptians and Incas, the dead corpse is not really dead at all, but still alive. From the USA comes a story that perhaps epitomizes modern society's concern to brush death under the carpet (in this case almost literally). British business man Peter George relates how, on arrival at a New York hotel, he found the room he had been booked into had a prior occupant: a corpse. Hastily returning to the reception to report this, to George's astonishment the desk clerk did not even look up. He simply swivelled his chair round, handed over a new key, and remarked laconically:

'OK, you're now in room 201.'[5]

Some see nothing to be deplored in such modern attitudes to death and its accompaniments. Paul Robinson has remarked in 'Five Models for Dying':

> The neglect of death – its reduction 'to the insignificance of an ordinary event' – is, I would argue, a measure of our psychic maturity. . . . Death may have been such [a great central fact of life] in the past, but I see nothing lost – and much gained – in its relegation to the periphery of human experience.[6]

But what, and for whom, is the so-called gain? For the dying person fearful and lonely amidst drips and drains? For the bereaved widow socially ostracized if she begins trying to talk about her loss? For the child, puzzled and bewildered about a 'gone-away' grandmother? Is a society a truly healthy one if doctors feel obliged to pretend to their patients that they are not dying? If families are increasingly discouraged from attending a dying person's perhaps precious last moments? If the experiences that dying person may wish to impart with his or her closing breaths are brushed aside by overburdened medical staff as merely the terminal ramblings of someone of no further consequence?

While no one should wish to dwell on death (my own feelings during the writing of much of this book), to contend that it is 'psychic maturity' to sweep everything about it under the carpet is to fly in the face of one of the most remarkable features to emerge from those reporting near-death experiences. This is the consistent claim that nearly dying has paradoxically left them with both an almost total loss of all formerly held fears of death and a renewed zest for life, for treating every extra moment as precious and to be savoured to the fullest extent. This was expressed by one of Dr Sabom's subjects, who said that the near-death experience

> just changed my whole life a flip-flop. . . . I used to worry about life and living it and trying to get ahead, trying to make life easier by working harder to make more money to make life easier. I don't do that no more . . . I just live from day to day . . . but I'm going to live what I've got left, and I'm going to enjoy it. I know where I'm headed to, so that I don't have to worry about dying any more.[7]

One of Dr Ring's patients put it this way:

> I used to be afraid of death. Now, it seems like that, you know, it was a little scary at first, the wandering aspect, but talking to God and the warmth I felt when I was with Him, you know – it was really – Oh! I just get the chills thinking about it, it was so *good*, you know? And I feel that when my time for death comes, that I won't be afraid to go.[8]

In these respects the near-death experience seems to give those who survive it not only the same peace of mind and conviction of an afterlife as those who end their days in hospices, but also an altogether healthier attitude to the real values of life. This aspect was expressed by a British subject, John Hunt, former general secretary of the Institute of Incorporated Photographers, who had a near-death experience as a result of a cardiac arrest:

> My sense of values has altered completely since the whole thing. Materialism to me is an evil thing. I see the evils of the expense account. I'm not the slightest bit impressed by the £40,000 car. Things like Rolls-Royces don't mean a thing. I enjoy the trees and being by the sea – things Nature has to offer which before I had never even noticed.[9]

Another of Dr Ring's subjects said: 'It's given me tolerance. It's made me less judgemental.'[10]

And Dr Sabom was told by an Illinois salesman: 'I feel that we are measured a great deal by what we do for others. That we're all put here to help one another. . . . The greatest law that we have is love.'[11]

What cannot be avoided are the profound implications that arise from any acceptance that there is some form of soul to us, something beyond the mere confines of our physical bodies. However much politicians may profess religion and, as in Britain, be actually responsible for higher clerical appointments, the decisions they make on human affairs are all too often grounded in this-worldly considerations.

For instance, although it may seem at the other end of the spectrum to death as we normally understand it, there is the artificial termination of foetal life in a mother's womb that we euphemistically call an abortion. If there is such an element as a soul within us, the question arises as to what point this joins the foetus, a critical consideration for any religious-minded surgeon asked to carry out an abortion operation.

Genetically it is known that, even at the very moment of conception, features of the future human being such as the colour of the hair and eyes, build, gifts, and talents will already have been determined. By eleven weeks, when the greatest number of abortion operations are performed, the baby-to-be is already unmistakably a miniature human being, breathing, swallowing, digesting, and urinating, and with brain, stomach, liver, and kidneys all functioning. As evident from ultrasound technology, babies at this stage turn somersaults in the womb, and make themselves comfortable to conform with their mother; and by fifteen weeks, according to research psychologist Clifford Olds of Rochford General Hospital, Essex, they can distinguish between their mother's voice and that of any other woman reading the same story.[12] At about the same time they will also react pleasurably to soothing music, or distressfully to harsh external sounds or some threat to the mother. There can be no doubt that they are experiencing. The possibility that some form of soul may already be present is attested by Lyndhurst psychiatrist Dr Kenneth McAll, who has described patients whose psychiatric distress seems to have arisen from their being unconsciously haunted by an aborted baby whose death they have never sacramentally put to rest.[13] Yet according to our law such babies can be allowed to develop for another three months before it is no longer lawful for them to be killed for social convenience.

Also questionable is the equally widespread though more underhand medical practice euphemistically described by doctors as 'easing the passing'. A famous instance of this recently brought to public attention concerns the last hours of King George V, whose physician was Lord Dawson of Penn. On the evening of Monday, 20 January 1936, Dawson scribbled on a menu card as a bulletin for the benefit of the world's press: 'The King's life is moving peacefully towards its close.' What has only subsequently come to light, thanks to a study of Dawson's personal papers made by his biographer Kenneth Rose, has been that rather than George V's life having slipped away passively, Dawson himself was responsible for speeding up the process. According to Dawson's personal notes:

> At about 11 o'clock it was evident that the last stage might endure for many hours unknown to the Patient but little comporting with that dignity and serenity which he so richly merited and which demanded a brief final scene. . . . I therefore decided to determine the end, and injected myself morphia gr. ¾ & shortly afterwards cocaine gr. 1 into the distended jugular vein. . . . Intervals between respirations lengthened and life passed so quietly and gently that it was difficult to determine the actual moment.[14]

However much one might want to brush this action aside as that of a loyal and well-intentioned physician merely making his patient's last hours more comfortable, two facts militate against this. First, on Dawson's own admission George V was already comatose and therefore hardly in pain at the time of the fatal injection. Second, as Dawson also disclosed for posterity, he considered it rather more fitting that the news of the King's death should be carried by responsible morning newspapers such as *The Times* rather than by the evening press, which would otherwise be first with the news if the King died some time during the next day. Like the abortionists, therefore, Dawson's motive was none other than social convenience.

In an odd footnote to this story the notoriously quirky Margot Asquith, widow of George V's first Prime Minister, was intriguingly reported to say some while after the King's death: 'The King told me he would never have died if it had not been for that old fool Dawson of Penn.'[15] Was she suggesting that George V visited her in death? In the light of what we have read on drop-in 'friendly' ghosts, might she have had more percipience than anyone has yet accredited to her?

We can never know how many times other physicians have quietly and on their own initiative acted in the same way as Dawson. Yet at least in this instance its admissibility remains unrecognized in English law, a view reaffirmed only recently by High Court judge Mr Justice Mars-Jones in a ruling against a physician who deliberately administered an overdose of phenobarbitone to a dying cancer patient:

> However gravely ill a man may be, however near death he is, he is entitled in our law to every hour, nay every minute of life that God has granted him. That hour or hours may be the most precious and most important hours of a man's life. There may be business to transact, gifts to give, forgivenesses to be asked, attitudes to be expressed, farewells to be made, one hundred and one bits of unfinished business.[16]

This has a bearing on some of the lesser-known practices relating to transplant surgery, which involves the removal of vital organs from so-called brain-dead patients in order that they can be used for 'brain-alive' patients in need of replacement hearts, kidneys, and suchlike. Undeniably that a life can be saved by such methods is a phenomenon of modern medical pioneering that one would not wish to check. But it does involve certain considerations that have only recently been brought to public attention.

Thus one of the techniques the transplant surgeons have learned is that their success rate improves if the donor's blood is kept circulating. As often happens, after being told that there is no hope for their loved one, relatives are discreetly asked permission for the switching off of the life-support machine, and for the removal of vital organs to help another patient to live. While the automatic assumption on the part of the relatives is that these procedures will be carried out *in that order*, this is by no means what actually happens behind the operating theatre's closed doors.

While unquestionably everything is done in the best interests of the patient receiving the removed organs, such serious ethical issues are involved in respect of the donor that in 1976 the British Conference of the Medical Colleges decided it had to redefine the criteria for determining a patient 'dead'. Theoretically stringent tests were drawn up for determining that, while a patient might be continuing to breathe and his or her heart continuing to beat on a life-support machine, he or she could be defined as 'brain-stem dead'. The tests consist of procedures such as squirting ice-cold water in the ears, shining a light in the eyes, stroking the cornea, and briefly switching off all aids to the patient's breathing, all to stimulate reflexes that might prompt the continuance of life. The question arises of whether, even with negative results from all such tests, the patient might still not be in some real sense as 'alive' as those patients whose returns from clinical death we have studied.

The issues here are illustrated by the concerns of a British medical practitioner who is today a Fellow of the Royal College of Surgeons. Back in 1978 he was a junior surgeon who took part in an operation to remove the kidneys of a female patient who had been involved in a road accident and had been certified 'brain dead'. All the various permissions had been granted; the consultant surgeon in charge duly performed the forty-minute operation of removing the kidneys, and, while he washed these in a preserving solution, it fell to the junior to dissect some of the body's minor tissues prior to sewing up in readiness for removal to the mortuary. Suddenly, to the junior doctor's horror, the 'dead' woman gasped for breath, not merely once, but repeatedly. It was obvious that she was alive, even though she was without life support and now without any kidneys. As the junior told interviewer Neville Hodgkinson of the *Sunday Times*: 'I drew it to the consultant's attention; he did something then of which I very much disapproved.'[17] That something, as he was reluctantly persuaded to reveal, was the removal of the tube routinely used to keep the airways open in a deeply unconscious patient. Deprived of this support to life, within a few minutes the woman really was unequivocally dead.

The experience sufficiently horrified the junior surgeon that he changed his career ambitions away from renal surgery and into a different branch of medicine. For obvious reasons he cannot be identified; but one who certainly represents his views is Dr David Wainwright Evans, one of three cardiologists at Papworth Hospital, near Cambridge, who has refused to carry out transplant surgery since 1980 specifically because of the continuing uncertainties surrounding the criteria for determining death before organs are removed.

Dr Evans argues that brain-stem death, the criterion for removing hearts and lungs, 'does not necessarily equate death in ordinarily understood terms'. For instance, in normal circumstances there will be muscular resistance when a transplant surgeon makes the first cut for the removal of a 'dead' patient's heart and lungs, an occurrence which is routinely countered by a paralysing drug, and can perhaps be dismissed as mere reflex. But, more ominously, it is by no means unusual for the 'dead' donor's heart rate and blood pressure to show a steep rise during the early stages of the operation to remove his or her vital organs. Such rises are difficult to interpret other than as signs of distress indicative of at least some form of continuing life. Dr Wainwright Evans says: 'I personally could not give permission for surgeons to remove the heart of my child while it was still beating and his circulation going, but it and the liver must be removed from the donor in that state for use in transplants.'[18]

As some mitigation, if all that we have learned of near-death patients' reminiscences is any guide, they (whatever 'they' may be) are likely to be 'out-of-their-bodies' and thereby removed from pain in such circumstances. But just how comfortable are Britain's two and a half million holders of organ donor cards (one of those myself), with the thought that they may be truly dead only after, rather than before, the removal of those organs? That they are, in effect, giving the surgeon a licence to kill them? Could it be that surgeons of the future may one day look back on such practices as barbarous as we today consider the surgery of the Middle Ages?

Yet another issue, this time at the individual level of personal choice, is that related to suicides. As we have noted in earlier chapters, historically suicide has been the most execrated of deaths, hence the practice of staking the bodies (to avoid their ghost walking) and not burying them in consecrated ground.

Intriguingly, and as a sombre warning to people tempted at any time to take their own lives, when the near-death experiences of attempted suicides are studied, they would seem to support this idea. One of Dr Moody's patients was a man who fell into a deep depression as a result of his wife's death, shot himself, 'died', but was then successfully brought back to life. According to the account he gave of his near-death experience in these circumstances: 'I didn't go where [my wife] was. I went to an awful place. I immediately saw the mistake I had made. I thought, I wish I hadn't done it.'[19]

As evident from one of Dr Ring's patients, those who attempt suicide, almost alone of near-death experiencers, are the ones who do not lose their fear of death. This is largely a result of the 'place' they sometimes find themselves in having nothing of the blissful qualities otherwise reported, but seeming to be more in the nature of a limbo. To quote another of Dr Ring's patients:

> When I think about dying, it bothers me. . . . For some time
> I haven't had any faith in Christianity, and so that makes
> it even worse, thinking you're going to die, because you
> don't think that you're going to *go* anywhere. Before, I
> thought that there would be a heaven or something. But
> now – I don't know – you go into limbo or something like
> that.[20]

The starkest warning on this theme was volunteered by another of Dr Moody's patients, not himself a suicide attempter:

> [While I was 'over there'] I got the feeling that two things it
> was completely forbidden for me to do would be to kill myself
> or to kill another person. . . . If I were to commit suicide, I

would be throwing God's gift back in his face; killing somebody else would be interfering with God's purpose for that
individual.[21]

David Ayre, the British suicide attempter whom I interviewed, whose
experience may have been ameliorated by his preliminary prayers,
would endorse this same view.

This evidence must affect our attitudes to the idea of some form of
heaven or hell as our after death fate. I have to confess that, despite being
a convert to Christianity (specifically to my own very liberal brand of
Roman Catholicism), I have remained too much of a rationalist to be
able to accept fully the conventional image of realms such as heaven,
hell, and a limbo at face value. Along with many other Christians, I am
sure, I have preferred to keep an open mind. This is easy enough,
because modern clergy, themselves concerned to be far more rational
than their medieval predecesors, rarely include such contentious
matters in their sermons.

Now, while after all the researches conducted for this book I have
been able to offer nothing I would consider proof of life after death, and I
would still balk at the idea of heavenly prefabs in the sky, I have to
acknowledge that my conceptions have inclined much more sympathetically towards the conventional imagery than I could ever previously
have contemplated.

In this connection one illuminating commentary on a near-death
experience has come from a British business man, Deryck Millington,
from Kent. Millington 'died' in the intensive-care unit of Ramsgate
Hospital on 12 June 1980, and afterwards lived on for a further eight-
een months, during which he wrote a moving account of what he
remembered, culminating in the following:

> I did not realize how much I had been affected by my
> experience until a long-standing friend, a car dealer, tele-
> phoned me. Jokingly he asked: 'Did you see the Pearly
> Gates?' Before, I would probably have laughed and retorted:
> 'Yes – and there was a notice outside: "No Car Dealers".'
> Now this question was offensive to me. . . . My wife tells me
> that I have become a more compassionate person. I am still
> not a church-goer, but I can stand up to any man and say,
> 'Yes, I believe in God.'[22]

Perhaps the most pertinent of Jesus Christ's remarkably rare utterances on the question of life after death is his parable of the rich man

outside whose gate a poor man, Lazarus, used to beg every day, covered in sores. When both died, their roles became reversed. While the rich man languished in hell, far aloft in heaven he espied Lazarus with the patriarch Abraham now enjoying all the comforts he had been denied in life. At last realizing the error of his earthly ways, the rich man implored Abraham to send Lazarus back to earth in order to warn his five brothers, who otherwise might find themselves suffering the same fate. He was told:

'They have Moses and the prophets, let them listen to them.'

'Ah, no, father Abraham,' responded the rich man, 'but if someone comes to them from the dead, then they will repent.'

But Abraham shook his head: 'If they will not listen either to Moses or to the prophets, they will not be convinced even if someone should rise from the dead.'[23]

The originator of that parable was the one individual in all history who, if the Christian Gospels are to be believed, *did* rise from the dead in what remains to this day the most spectacular after death experience of all time. What makes Jesus' resurrection appearances so different from anything else before or since, and so astonished the witnesses of the time, is that Jesus seemed to break all the 'rules' of being either a ghost or a flesh-and-blood human being. He was apparently able to pass through closed doors, thus behaving in a manner to be expected of a ghost.[24] But as if to confound this – and to show his total command of dimensions both physical and non-physical – he is also described as being tangible,[25] and as pointedly eating food with his disciples,[26] thus flouting the law traditionally thought to determine the point of no return between the realm of the living and the realm of the dead.[27]

Is it mere fancy that those westerners who have had an encounter of the 'other-worldly' kind as part of their near-death experience have felt that the mysterious 'Being of light' was either Jesus, or God, or both somehow rolled into one? Is it mere coincidence that all the synoptic Gospels report an extraordinary light-associated occurrence during Jesus' normal earthly existence when he appeared transfigured before them – 'his face shone like the sun and his clothes . . . white as the light'?[28] Can it be similar mere chance that the fourth Gospel writer, apparently one of the witnesses of this event, writing nearly two thousand years before Raymond Moody, specifically speaks of Jesus as 'the true light that enlightens all men',[29] emphatically stating: 'We saw his glory, the glory that is his as the only Son of the Father'?[30]

All through this book I have tried to stay dispassionate, balanced, and fair to all points of view. But there is only one ending that I feel appropriate, one that essentially sums up and crystallizes everything that has gone before. This is the real-life story of North Yorkshire physician and family man Dr Colin MacCallum, who towards the end of 1979, at the age of only thirty-nine, was diagnosed as having inoperable cancer. After a false start as a lawyer Colin first trained then for his last twelve years practised as a doctor, and up to this point, according to his widow Marilyn, behaved like 'a human dynamo' who 'never stood still a minute'. With every waking moment preoccupied with his medical practice, keeping up with clinical developments, the renovation of his farm, attention to his children as a father, and to his wife as a husband, Colin still sometimes felt there was something missing in his life; but there never seemed time to try to discover what it was. In Marilyn's words:

> His mind was always open to the possibility of God, but faith was something he could not rationalise. In his two professions his mind was clouded by the necessity for logic and wisdom. There was always a need for absolute proof or explanatory symptoms so he could intelligently reach a correct conclusion or diagnosis. His life was based on facts, indisputable facts. God was only a possibility and not something he could prove.[31]

Then Colin was struck the bombshell that he had but weeks to live, accompanied by intense pain such as he had never experienced before. Suddenly, despite life so rapidly slipping away from him, he had forced on him what he had never allowed himself before: time to think, and thus to discover that something that all along he had been missing. According to Marilyn:

> In spite of intense pain and perhaps a sense of bitterness at the hopelessness of his situation, he was able to write in his diary on 9th January [1980], 'My faith is a great comfort to me, and I rejoice in the love of God.' . . . Colin was a very private man and it was completely out of character for him to try to influence people by the way he felt. Nevertheless his shyness vanished beneath the conviction and exultation of his relationship with God. All who visited him expected a broken, sad, dispirited man. Instead, they found him contented, giving a warmth and inspiration as he had never done before, either as a doctor or as a friend. It is strange that Colin, his body weak and dying, and depending completely on others – nurses, doctors, family and friends – proved at his

weakest more powerful than ever before in his life. That strength came from outside himself. It could only have come from God.

Towards the middle of January Colin became so unwell that the MacCallums' Anglican vicar, the Reverend Stuart Burns, was called to give the Last Rites, and on anointing Colin's body felt, for the first time in his experience, an inexplicable heat accompanied by violent trembling of his own hands and inability to remove these for several minutes. A week later, when Stuart was again present, Colin's consultant gave him final pain-killing drugs and confided that he would probably never regain consciousness, although his physical strength might keep his body going for another two days. Marilyn asked to be alone with her husband, but within a few minutes a nurse came running to summon Stuart. As Marilyn has described what happened next:

> [Colin] came totally and completely out of unconsciousness to speak clearly, convincingly and rationally. His face was radiant, healthy and shining strangely white, his eyes wide open and filled with indescribable joy. We were stunned yet elated by the power of the moment. He had a vision of God calling him? Of paradise? Of eternity? He struggled to articulate what he could see – his face and his eyes told more than his words – and spoke clearly: 'I'm going now – I think I'm going now. It's marvellous . . . marvellous . . . it's marvellous.'
>
> His joy was so infectious that we could only laugh with him as we were caught up in his experience. At that moment I felt a great sense of urgency, and almost gladly I encouraged him to go, so that nothing should hold him back.

Marilyn, with all the burden of the responsibilities Colin left behind, has added an equally moving epitaph to this:

> How could he die so happily, so willingly and with such serenity when he had so much to live for, so many responsibilities and so much that offered him earthly pleasures? He had an insight into an eternity with God. . . . If you knew Colin as a doctor or a friend, don't let his dying count for nothing. While looking forward to death he longed for just one hour of normal living to be given to him. He would have used it to visit his patients and friends – to plead with them to

stop and think. He felt that some, *including himself,* had got life all wrong. He had realised in his suffering and dying that, if the love of God were made the focal point of people's lives, they would be *living well.*

I never met Dr Colin MacCallum, but I think I knew him, if that is the right tense. That Marilyn's testament is founded on something more than widowish sentimentality has been very forcefully confirmed to me by the Reverend Stuart Burns, a vicar not normally given to mystical experiences, but who has unreservedly called Colin's death 'the most wonderful few minutes I have ever spent'.

We have but two choices. We can put it all down to some form of hallucination, and undeniably in his last hours Colin's consultant administered to him some very powerful drugs. Or we can believe, with Marilyn, that Colin, in the moments of his death, really did touch the face of eternity and become caught up in an all-too-genuine experience of the Living God. Which to choose? Only one thing is certain. This very moment is the beginning of the rest of *your* life.

# NOTES AND REFERENCES

1 *The Oldest Belief*
1 Edward O. Wilson, *The Insect Societies*, Cambridge, Belknap, 1971.
2 Sylvia Sikes, *The Natural History of the African Elephant*, London, Weidenfeld & Nicolson, 1970.
3 Iain and Oria Douglas-Hamilton, *Among the Elephants*, New York, Viking, 1975.
4 Ralph S. Solecki, 'Shanidar IV, a Neanderthal Flower Burial in Northern Iraq', *Science*, vol. 190, 28 November 1975, p. 881.
5 Howard Carter and A. C. Mace, *The Tomb of Tut Ankh Amen*, vol. II, London, Cassell, 1927.
6 Jacob Krall, 'Die Etruskischen Mumienbinder des Agramers Nationmuseums', *Akademie er Wissenschaften*, Md. 41, Vienna, F. Tempsky, 1892.
7 Herodotus, *The Histories*, trans. Aubrey de Selincourt, Harmondsworth, Penguin, 1954, book 4, p. 264.
8 Garcilaso de la Vega, *Commentarios reales de los Incas*, part 1, vol. 133 (1609, pt I, bk V, chap. XX), Madrid, Biblioteca de Autores Españoles, 1963.
9 Homer, *The Iliad*, trans. E. V. Rieu, Harmondsworth, Penguin, 1950, Book 23, p. 414.

2 *In Touch with Departed*
1 John W. Hedges, *Tomb of the Eagles: A Window on Stone Age Tribal Britain*, London, John Murray, 1985.
2 E. R. Dodds, *The Greeks and the Irrational*, Berkeley, University of California Press, 1951.
3 James M. Vreeland Jr and Aidan Cockburn, 'Mummies of Peru', in Aidan and Eve Cockburn (eds.), *Mummies, Disease and Ancient Cultures*, Cambridge University Press, 1980, p. 149.
4 Adrian Boshier, 'The Religions of Africa', in Arnold Toynbee, Arthur Koestler, *et al.*, *Life after Death*, London, Weidenfeld & Nicolson, 1976, pp. 62–3.
5 Geoffrey Gorer, *Africa Dances*, London. Faber, 1935, pp. 233, 234. 234.
6 M. S. Seale 'Islamic Society', in Toynbee, Koestler, *et al.*, *Life after Death*, op. cit., p. 123.
7 Bart McDowell, 'The Aztecs', *National Geographic Magazine*, vol. 158, no. 6, December 1980, p. 751.
8 Adrian Boshier, op. cit., p. 64.

9   John D. Ray 'Ancient Egypt' in Michael Loewe and Carmen Blacker
    (eds), *Divination and Oracles*, London, Allen & Unwin, 1981, p. 179.
10  Adrian Boshier, op. cit., p. 64.
11  Homer, *The Odyssey*, book XI.
12  M. Ni Sheaghda, *Tóruigheacht Dhiarmada agus Ghráinne* [The Pursuit
    of Diarmaid and Gráinne], Dublin, 1967; quoted in M. J. O'Kelly,
    *Newgrange*, London, Thames & Hudson, p. 43.
13  Homer, *The Iliad*, trans E. V. Riev, Harmondsworth, Penguin, book 1,
    pp. 197 ff.
14  Ibid., book 4, pp. 437 ff.
15  Ibid., book 3, pp. 164 ff.
16  Ibid, book 2, pp. 56 ff.
17  Julian Jaynes, *The Origin of Consciousness in the Breakdown of the
    Bicameral Mind*, Boston, Houghton Mifflin, 1976, p. 72.
18  J. Perrot, 'Excavations at Eynan, 1959 Season', *Israel Exploration
    Journal*, 1961.
19  John Romer, *Ancient Lives: The Story of the Pharaohs' Tombmakers*,
    London, Weidenfeld & Nicolson, 1984, p. 102.
20  Ibid., p. 102.
21  'Opium Traces in Ancient Poppy Jugs', *The Times*, 3 June 1986.
22  A.W. Brøgger, quoted in Johannes Brønsted, *The Vikings*, trans. Estrid
    Bannister-Good, Harmondsworth, Penguin, 1960.
23  W. Y. Evans-Wentz, foreword to *The Tibetan Book of the Dead*, Oxford
    University Press, 1960, p. lxxv, footnote 2.

3   *Have We Lived Before?*

1   *Sunday Telegraph*, 15 April 1979.
2   George Gallup Jr, with William Proctor, *Adventures in Immortality*: A
    *Look beyond the Threshold of Death*, London, Souvenir, 1983.
3   Dr Ian Stevenson, 'The Evidence for Survival from Claimed Memories of
    Former Incarnations', *Journal of the American Society for Psychical
    Research*, vol. 54, 1958 pp. 51–71, 95–117.
4   Dr Ian Stevenson, 'The Explanatory Value of the Idea of Reincarnation',
    *Journal of Nervous and Mental Disease*, vol. 164, no. 5, 1977, pp. 307–8.
5   Stevenson's main works include: *Twenty Cases Suggestive of Reincar-
    nation*, 1974; *Cases of the Reincarnation Type*, Vol. 1, *Ten Cases in
    India*, 1975; and *Cases of the Reincarnation Type*, Vol. 2, *Ten Cases in Sri
    Lanka*, 1977; all published at Charlottesville by the University Press of
    Virginia.
6   Stevenson, *Twenty Cases*, op. cit., pp. 91–105.
7   Ibid., p. 101.
8   Dr Harold I. Lief, 'Commentary on Dr Ian Stevenson's "The Evidence of
    Man's Survival after Death"', *Journal of Nervous and Mental Disease*,
    vol. 165, no. 3, 1977, p. 171.
9   For a more comprehensive chart and a fuller discussion, see my own *Mind
    Out of Time?*, London, Gollancz, 1981, p. 59.

10  Stevenson, *Ten Cases in India*, op. cit., pp. 107–43.
11  Ibid.
12  Edward Ryall, *Second Time Around*, with an introduction and notes by Dr Ian Stevenson, Sudbury, Neville Spearman, 1974.
13  Letter sent to Dr Ian Stevenson 7 November 1979 by Mr John Dawes, who kindly supplied a copy to the author.
14  In an interview in the September–October 1986 issue of *Venture Inward*, published by the Association for Research and Enlightenment, Stevenson conceded that he does not regard the case as 'enthusiastically' as he did ten years ago, but he neglects even to mention the Michael Green exposure.

4  'You're Going Back Through Time . . .'
 1  Morey Bernstein, *The Search for Bridey Murphy*, London, Hutchinson, 1956, p. 108.
 2  For information on the activities of this and other US newspapers in connection with the Bridey Murphy case, see Professor C. J. Ducasse, 'How the Case of *The Search for Bridey Murphy* Stands Today', *Journal of the American Society for Psychical Research*, vol. 54, 1960, pp. 3—22.
 3  Jeffrey Iverson, *More Lives than One?*, London, Pan Books, 1977.
 4  Ibid., pp. 47–8.
 5  Ibid., p. 54.
 6  Ibid., p. 58.
 7  Ibid., pp. 45–6.
 8  *The Bloxham Tapes*, documentary narrated by Magnus Magnusson and shown on BBC TV, 19 December 1976.
 9  Cover of the Pan paperback edition of Iverson, op. cit.
10  Reima Kampman, 'Hypnotically Induced Multiple Personality', *Acta Universitatis Ouluensis*, Series D Medica No. 6, Psychiatrica No. 3, 1973; 'Hypnotically Induced Multiple Personality: An Experimental Study', *International Journal of Clinical and Experimental Hypnosis*, vol. 24, no. 3, July 1976, pp. 215–27.
11  Louis de Wohl, *The Living Wood*, London, Gollancz, 1947; republished in paperback as *The Empress Helena*, Paul Elek, 1960.
12  Melvin Harris, 'Are "Past Life" Regressions evidence of Reincarnation?', *Free Inquiry*, vol. 6, no. 4, Fall 1986, p. 22.
13  Royal Commission on Historical Monuments, *York*, vol. V (the central area), 1981, p. 31.
14  Dame Joan Evans, *Life in Mediaeval France*, London, Phaidon, 1969.
15  C. B. Costain, *The Moneyman*, London, Staples Press, 1948.
16  Iverson, op. cit. p. 82.
17  Costain, op. cit. p. 8.
18  Dr Ian Stevenson, *Xenoglosy: A Review and Report of a Case*, Charlottesville, University Press of Virginia, 1974.
19  Shirley MacLaine, *Out on a Limb*, London, Elm Tree, 1983.

20  Ibid., p. 237.
21  See for instance Geza Vermes, *Jesus the Jew*, London, Collins, 1973.
22  Some very profound questions are raised concerning how 'past life' personalities are fabricated, embodying such complex sets of memories. For a fuller discussion on this, see the chapters on multiple personality in my own *Mind Out of Time?*, London, Gollancz, 1981.


5 *Raising Spirits*
 1  Homer, *The Odyssey*, trans. E. V. Rieu, Harmondsworth, Penguin, 1946, book XI.
 2  Deuteronomy 18: 10–11.
 3  1 Samuel 28: 3.
 4  1 Samuel 28: 7.
 5  1 Samuel 28: 8.
 6  Euripides, *Helen*, quoted in J. S. Morrison 'The Classical World', in Michael Loewe and Carmen Blacker (eds), *Divination and Oracles*, London, Allen & Unwin, 1981, p. 106.
 7  1 Corinthians 12: 7–10.
 8  Signe Toksvig, *Emanuel Swedenborg: Scientist and Mystic*, London, Faber, 1949, p. 9.
 9  Swedenborg, Dream Diary [*Swedenborgs Drömmar*], pp. 10 ff.; quoted in Toksvig, op. cit., p. 143.
10  Swedenborg, Spiritual Diary, para. 2542; quoted in David Lorimer, *Survival, Body, Mind and Death in the Light of Psychic Experience*, London, Routledge, p. 198.
11  Toksvig, op. cit., p. 297.
12  Swedenborg, *Compendium of the Theological and Spiritual Writings of Emanuel Swedenborg*, Boston, Crosby & Nichols, 1853, pp. 160–197.
13  R. L. Tafel, *Documents Concerning the Life and Character of Emanuel Swedenborg*, London, Swedenborg Society, 1875–7, 3 vols, document 274 B.
14  Ibid., doc. 275 P.
15  See Toksvig, op. cit., p. 190.
17  Swedenborg, *Arcana Celestia*, para. 68.
18  E. E. Lewis, *A Report of the Mysterious Noises Heard in the House of Mr. John D. Fox*, Canandaigua, E. E. Lewis, 1848, quoted Colin Wilson, *Afterlife*, London, Harrap, 1985.
19  Eric J. Dingwall, *The Critics' Dilemma*, Battle, Sussex, private publication, 1966.
20  Renée Haynes, *The Society for Psychical Research, 1882–1982: A History*, London, Macdonald, 1982, p. 23.
21  Mrs H. Salter, 'Impressions of some early workers in the SPR', *Journal of Parapsychology*, vol. 14 (1950), pp. 24–36.
22  Quoted in Haynes, op. cit., p. 83.

## 6 *In Search of White Crows*

1 Richard Hodgson, 'A Further Record of Observations of Certain Phenomena of Trance', *Proceedings of the Society for Psychical Research*, vol. 13, 1897–8, pp. 485–6.

2 William James 'What Psychical Research Has Achieved' Presidential Address, *Proceedings of the Society for Psychical Research*, 1896–7.

3 Renée Haynes, *The Society for Psychical Research 1882–1982: A History*, London, Macdonald, 1982, p. 85.

4 C. Drayton Thomas, 'A Proxy Experiment of Significant Success', *Proceedings of the Society for Psychical Research*, vol. 45, 1938–9, pp. 265–9.

5 Doris Stokes (with Linda Dearsley), *Voices in my Ear: The Autobiography of a Medium*, London, Macdonald, Futura, 1980.

6 Doris Stokes, op. cit., Futura paperback edn, pp. 174–6.

7 That the Palladium show was not a mere one-off aberration has been corroborated by London journalist Joanna Moorhead. While working as a reporter for the *Halifax Courier* she happened to cover a performance Doris Stokes put on the evening of 23 November 1984, at the Halifax Civic Theatre. Meeting up afterwards with one subject for whom Doris had produced particularly detailed information she remarked how impressive this seemed. The woman herself, however, was much more dismissive, explaining that she had been specially invited to the show by Doris as a result of a letter written by her daughter, and that Doris had twice talked to her on the telephone prior to the show. In other words, another set up.

8 Doris Stokes, op. cit. p. 75.

9 Renée Haynes, op. cit., p. 145.


## 7 *Spontaneous Transmissions*

1 Pliny the Younger, *Letters*, trans. William Melmoth, Loeb Classical Library, Heinemann, London, 1915, Book 7, Letter 27, pp. 70–3.

2 Society for Psychical Research, *Newsletter Supplement*, December 1985, pp. 1–2.

3 Celia Green and Charles McCreery, *Apparitions*, London, Hamish Hamilton, 1975, p. 80.

4 Paul Bannister, *Strange Happenings*, New York, Grosset & Dunlap, 1978.

5 Society for Psychical Research, *Newsletter Supplement*, October 1986, p. 8. Macrory does not identify the doctor by name; this information is provided in Andrew Mackenzie, *Hauntings and Apparitions*, London, Granada, 1983, p. 203; Mackenzie also quotes corroboration from Lady Carson.

6 Quoted in Clare Gittings, *Death, Burial and the Individual in Early Modern England*, London, Croom Helm, 1984, pp. 72–3.

7 Dr Alan Gauld, 'The Haunting of Abbey House, Cambridge', *Journal of the Society for Psychical Research*, vol. 46, 1972, pp. 109–23.

Notes and References 215

8 Quoted in Andrew Mackenzie, op. cit., p. 220.
9 W. Dewi Rees, 'The Hallucinations of Widowhood', *British Medical Journal*, vol. 4, 2 October 1971, pp. 37–41.
10 Barbara Bunce and Beryl Statham, *About Bereavement*, London, Churches' Fellowship for Psychical and Spiritual Studies, 1983, p. 16.
11 Celia Green and Charles McCreery, op. cit., p. 190.
12 J. B. Phillips, quoted in *Into the Unknown*, Pleasantville, NY, Reader's Digest, 1981, p. 167.
13 John Bailey, *Somerset and Avon Ghosts, Witches and Legends*, Bristol, Redcliffe Press, 1985.
14 Dr Morton Schatzman, *The Story of Ruth: One Woman's Haunting Psychiatric Odyssey*, London, Duckworth, 1980.
15 'Case of the Will of James L. Chaffin', *Proceedings of the Society for Psychical Research*, vol. 36, 1928, pp. 517–24.
16 Beryl Statham, letter in *Christian Parapsychologist*, Churches' Fellowship for Psychical and Spiritual Studies, September 1986.

8 *Learning from the Dying*

1 Ronald Rose, *Living Magic: The Realities Underlying the Psychical Practices and Beliefs of Australian Aborigines*, London, Chatto & Windus, 1957.
2 Henry Brougham, *The Life and Times of Henry, Lord Brougham, Written by Himself*, 3 vols, 1871, vol. 1, pp. 146–8.
3 Personal communication.
4 Philippe Ariès, *The Hour of our Death*, trans. Helen Weaver, London, Allen Lane, 1981.
5 Musée des Augustins, Toulouse, no. 835.
6 Mme Dunoyer, *Lettres et Histoires Galantes*, Amsterdam, 1780, vol. 1, p. 300; quoted in Ariès, op. cit., p. 9.
7 A. N. Exton-Smith and M. D. Cantaub, 'Terminal Illness in the Aged', *The Lancet*, vol. 2, 1961, p. 305.
8 J. H. Phillips, *Caring for the Dying Patient and his Family*, New York, Health Sciences Publishing Corporation, 1973, panel presentations on p. 45; I owe both this and the previous quotation to Dr Michael Sabom, *Recollections of Death*, New York, Harper & Row, 1982.
9 Sir William Barrett, *Death-Bed Visions*, London, Psychic Press, 1926.
10 Dr Karlis Osis, *Deathbed Observations by Physicians and Nurses*, New York, Parapsychology Foundation, 1961.
11 Dr Elisabeth Kübler-Ross, 'Life, Death and Life after Death', tape-recorded lecture distributed by Friends of Shanti Nilaya, London.
12 Osis, op. cit., p. 23.
13 J. H. Hyslop, *Psychical Research and the Resurrection*, London, Fisher Unwin, 1908, p. 97.
14 Quoted in George Gallup Jr (with William Proctor), *Adventures in Immortality*, London, Souvenir, 1983, p. 14.
15 Ian Watson, *Sunday Telegraph*, 30 November 1986, p. 8.

16   Barrett, op. cit., pp. 10–15.
17   Kübler-Ross, op. cit.
18   Ibid.
19   Personal interview with Mrs Janet T.
20   Gordon Thomas, *Issels: The Biography of a Doctor*, London, Hodder & Stoughton, 1975, pp. 161–2.


9 *Tales from the Resuscitated*
 1   Rob Hughes, 'Life after Drowning', *Sunday Times* magazine, 16 June 1985, pp. 44 ff.
 2   Philippe Ariès, *The Hour of our Death*, op. cit., p. 399.
 3   Quoted in Robert Kastenbaum and Ruth Aisenberg, *The Psychology of Death*, New York, Springer, 1976.
 4   Plato, *The Republic*, trans. A. D. Lindsay, London, Dent, 1925, book X.
 5   Bede, *A History of the English Church and People*, trans. Leo Sherley-Price, Harmondsworth, Penguin, 1955, pp. 284 ff.
 6   Bryant S. Hinckley, *The Faith of our Pioneering Fathers*, Salt Lake City, Deseret, 1959, p. 183.
 7   *St Louis Medical and Surgical Journal*, February 1890.
 8   Dr Michael Sabom, *Recollections of Death: A Medical Investigation*, New York, Harper & Row, 1982, pp. 81–2; Although Dr Sabon does not identify Bayne by name, Bayne seems independently identified from a story in *Newsweek*, 13 November 1967.
 9   Margot Grey, *Return from Death: An Exploration of the Near-Death Experience*, London, Arkana, 1985.
10   Dr Raymond Moody, *Life after Life*, Covington, Ga., Mockingbird Books, 1975.
11   Introduction to Dr Kenneth Ring, *Life at Death: A Scientific Investigation of the Near-Death Experience*, New York, Coward, McCann & Geoghegan, 1980, p. 13.
12   Sabom, op. cit., p. 3.
13   Ibid., p. 4.
14   Dr Maurice Rawlings, *Beyond Death's Door*, London, Sheldon Press, 1978.
15   Ring, op. cit.
16   Grey, op. cit.
17   Ring, op. cit., pp. 39, 40.
18   Ibid., p. 41.
19   Sabom, op. cit., p. 19.
20   Ibid., p. 17.
21   Ring, op. cit., p. 90.
22   Sabom, op. cit., p. 116.
23   Anonymous contribution to BBC Radio 2, September 1986; quoted in *IANDS News Bulletin*, International Association for Near-Death Studies (UK), Winter/Spring 1986–7, p. 2.
24   Sabom, op. cit., pp. 69–70.

25    Dr Kenneth Ring, *Heading toward Omega: In Search of the Meaning of the Near-Death Experience*, New York, Morrow, 1984, p. 43.

26    Ring, *Life at Death*, op. cit., p. 45.

27    Ibid.

28    Ibid., p. 97.

29    Sabom, op. cit., p. 73.

30    Ibid., p. 32.

31    Sir Alexander Ogston, *Reminiscences of Three Campaigns: Part II, South African War*, London, Hodder, 1919, ch. xvi, pp. 222–3.

32    Sir Auckland Campbell Geddes, 'A Voice from the Grandstand', address to the Royal Medical Society, 26 February 1927; quoted in G. N. M. Tyrrell, *The Personality of Man*, Harmondsworth, Penguin, 1947.

33    Sabom, op. cit., p. 34.

34    Ring, *Life at Death*, op. cit., p. 51.

## 10   Truly Out of the Body?

1    Sabom, *Recollections of Death*, op. cit., p. 157.

2    Dr A. Lukianowicz, Autoscopic Phenomena', *Archives of Neurology and Psychiatry*, vol. 80, (August 1958, p. 199; quoted in Sabom, op. cit., pp. 164–5.

3    'Woman Awake for Surgery', *Guardian*, 7 June 1985.

4    Sabom, op. cit., pp. 155–6.

5    Ibid., p. 16.

6    Ibid.

7    Dr Richard S. Blacher, 'To Sleep, Perchance to Dream', *Journal of the American Medical Association*, vol. 242, 1979, p. 2291.

8    Dr R. A. McFarland, 'The Psychological Effects of Oxygen Deprivation (Anoxaemia) on Human Behaviour', quoted in Sabom, op. cit., p. 176.

9    Dr Susan J. Blackmore, *Beyond the Body: An Investigation of Out-of-the-Body Experiences*, London, Heinemann, 1982.

10    Kübler-Ross, 'Life, Death and Life after Death', op. cit.

11    Ring, *Heading towards Omega*, op. cit., pp. 42–3.

12    Rawlings, *Beyond Death's Door*, op. cit., pp. 74–5.

13    Kimberly Clark, 'Clinical Interventions with Near-Death Experiencers', in Bruce Greyson and Charles P. Flynn (eds), *The Near-Death Experience: Problems, Prospects, Perspectives*, Springfield, Ill, Charles C. Thomas, 1984.

14    Sabom, op. cit., pp. 64–9.

15    Ibid., pp. 65–6.

16    Ibid., pp. 66–7.

17    Ibid., pp. 100–1.

18    Ibid., p. 104.

19    Ibid., pp. 111–12.

20    Ibid., pp. 112–13.

**11 Into the Light**
1    For an English translation of Jan van Ruysbroeck, see *Adornment of the Spiritual Marriage*, etc., trans. P. Wynschenk Dom, London, 1916.
2    Rawlings, *Beyond Death's Door*, op. cit., pp. 80–1.
3    Ring, *Life at Death*, op. cit., p. 54.
4    Moody, *Life after Life*, op. cit., Bantam edn, 1976, p. 33.
5    Ring, *Life at Death*, op. cit., p. 57.
6    Sabom, *Recollections of Death*, op. cit., p. 453.
7    Ibid., p. 44.
8    Ring, *Life at Death*, op. cit., p. 59.
9    Sabom, op. cit., p. 209.
10   Rawlings, op. cit., pp. 98–9.
11   Ring, *Life at Death*, op. cit., p. 63.
12   Ibid., pp. 63, 64.
13   Sabom, op. cit., p. 48.
14   Ibid., p. 49.
15   Rawlings, op. cit., p. 99.
16   Moody, op. cit., p. 56.
17   Sabom, op. cit., p. 47.
18   Ring, *Life at Death*, p. 76.
19   Rawlings, op. cit., p. 88.
20   Moody, op. cit., pp. 56, 66.
21   Ring, *Life at Death*, op. cit., p. 71.
22   Ibid., pp. 71–2.
23   Ibid., p. 81.
24   Moody, op. cit., pp. 95–6.
25   Ring, *Life at Death*, op. cit., p. 169.
26   Ring, *Heading towards Omega*, op. cit., pp. 39, 40.
27   Bede, *History*, op. cit., p. 288.

**12 Truly Out of This World?**
1    Margot Grey, *Return from Death*, op. cit., pp. 54–5.
2    Ronald Rose, *Living Magic*, op. cit., p. 130.
3    Sabom, *Recollections of Death*, op. cit., p. 22.
4    Osis, *Deathbed Observations*, op. cit., p. 24.
5    Sabom, op. cit., p. 136.
6    Father Louis Tucker, *Clerical Errors*, New York, Harper, 1943, pp. 221–5.
7    Sabom, op. cit., p. 47.
8    Evans-Wentz (ed.), *The Tibetan Book of the Dead*, op. cit., p. 32.
9    Ibid., pp. 33–4.
10   G. N. N. Tyrrell, 'Apparitions', Myers Memorial Lecture, Society for Psychical Research, 1943.
11   Sir J. G. Frazer, *The Belief in Immortality and the Worship of the Dead*, Gifford Lectures, London, Macmillan, 1913, vol. I, p. 361.

12   John R. Goody, *Death, Property and the Ancestors: A Study of the Mortuary Customs of the Lodagaa of West Africa*, London, Tavistock, 1962.
13   Ring, *Life at Death*, op. cit., p. 47.
14   Moody, *Life after Life*, op. cit., p. 41.
15   Evans-Wentz, op. cit., p. 38.
16   Swedenborg, *Arcana Celestia*, op. cit., para. 320.
17   Sabom, op. cit., p. 95.
18   R. O. Faulkner (ed.), *The Ancient Egyptian Book of the Dead*, London, British Museum, revised edn, 1985, pp. 29–31.
19   Quoted in Johannes Brønsted, *The Vikings*, op. cit., p. 282.
20   I. Hallowell, 'Spirits of the Dead in Salteaux Life and Thought', *Journal of the Royal Anthropological Institute*, vol. 70, 1940, p. 29.
21   Robert Codrington, *The Melanesians. Studies in their Anthropology and Folklore*, Oxford, Clarendon, 1891.
22   Edward Shortland, *Traditions and Superstitions of the New Zealanders*, London, 1854, p. 150.
23   Mary H. Eastman, *Dahcotah: or Life and Legends of the Sioux around Fort Snelling*, New York, 1849, p. 177. This and the previous quotation are from Edward B. Tylor, *Primitive Culture*, 2 vols, London, John Murray, vol. 2. p. 52 n.
24   Grey, op. cit., pp. 54–5.
25   Rawlings, *Beyond Death's Door*, op. cit., p. 19.
26   Osis, op. cit., p. 30.
27   Dr Melvin Morse, Doug Conner and Dr Donald Tyler 'Near Death Experiences in a Pediatric Population', *American Journal of Diseases of Children*, June 1985, pp. 595–600.
28   Siegel, in Greyson and Flynn, *The Near-Death Experience*, op. cit., p. 110.
29   Margot Grey, 'The Psychic Implications of Near-Death Experiences', lecture to the Society for Psychical Research, 17 July 1986.
30   Ring, *Life at Death*, op. cit., pp. 207, 208.
31   Mrs Henry Sidgwick 'An Examination of Book Tests', *Proceedings of the Society for Psychical Research*, vol. 31, pp. 253–260.
32   Anonymous author, *Post Mortem*, Blackwood, 1881.
33   *Proceedings of the Society for Psychical Research*, loc. cit., p. 253.
34   Osis, op. cit., p. 48.
35   Ibid.
36   Sabom, op. cit., pp. 160–5.

13  *What Might Survive?*

 1   Doris Stokes, *Voices in my Ear*, op. cit., p. 167.
 2   See discussion in Ring, *Life at Death*, op. cit., pp. 225 ff.
 3   Ring, *Life at Death*, op. cit., p. 45.
 4   Moody, *Life after Life*, op. cit., p. 42.

5  Sabom, *Recollections of Death*, op. cit., p. 21.
6  Celia Green, *Out of the Body Experiences*, New York, Ballantine, 1968.
7  Sabom, op. cit., pp. 116–17.
8  Dr Wilder Penfield, *The Mystery of the Mind*, Princeton University Press, 1975, pp. 39, 45; quoted in Sabom, op. cit., pp. 182–3.
9  Professor Karl Lashley, quoted in Penfield, 'Engrams in the Human Brain', Gold Medal Lecture, *Proceedings of the Royal Society of Medicine*, vol. 61, August 1968, p. 831.
10  In Penfield's papers she is referred to as M.M. The account of her operation, recorded by Penfield's stenographer, has been built up from Penfield and Lamar Roberts, *Speech and Brain Mechanisms*, Princeton University Press, 1959; and Penfield and Phanor Perot, 'The Brain's Record of Auditory and Visual Experience: A Final Summary and Discussion', *Brain*, vol. 86, no. IV, 1963, pp. 595–696.
11  R. Noyes and R. Kletti, 'The Experience of Dying from Falls', *Omega*, vol. 3, 1972, pp. 45–52.
12  Ring, *Life at Death*, op. cit., p. 116.
13  Dr Henry Freeborn, 'Temporary Reminiscence of a Long Forgotten Language during the Delirium of Broncho-Pneumonia', *The Lancet*, 14 June 1902, pp. 1685–6.
14  Revd Peter Rinaldi SDB, *In Verdant Pastures: From a Pastor's Diary*, New York, Don Bosco Publications, 1985.
15  Alison Miller, 'Ladi Di', *Sunday Times* magazine, 12 July 1981, p. 40.
16  Marjorie Wallace, 'The Genius of Christopher Nolan', *Sunday Times* magazine, December 1979.
17  Osis, *Deathbed Observations*, op. cit., p. 24.
18  Hornell Hart, *The Enigma of Survival*, London, Rider, 1959, p. 15.
19  Eugène Marais, *The Soul of the White Ant*, London, Methuen, 1937, last chapter.
20  Phyllis Battelle, 'Triplets – and They didn't Know It', *Reader's Digest*, UK edn, June 1981, pp. 51–5.
21  Ibid., p. 53.
22  See Peter Watson, *Twins*, London, Hutchinson, 1981.
23  Ibid., p. 46.
24  Ibid., p. 51.
25  Penfield, *The Mystery of the Mind*, op. cit., p. 88.
26  W. Y. Evans-Wentz, *The Fairy-Faith in Celtic Countries*, London, Henry Frowde, 1911.
27  Ring, *Heading Towards Omega*, op. cit., p. 176.
28  Quoted in personal communication from Ken Watson. For further examples, and additional bibliography, see Carlos S. Alvarado 'Observations of Luminous Phenomena around the Human Body', *Journal of the Society for Psychical Research*, vol. 54, no. 806, Jan. 1987, pp. 38–60.
29  Penfield, *The Mystery of the Mind*, op. cit., pp. 88–89.

14  *Physics of the Non-Physical*
1   Gordon Thomas and Max Morgan-Witts, *Pontiff*, New York, Doubleday, 1983, pp. 77–78.
2   Thomas Edison, interview reported in *Scientific American*, October 1920.
3   Dr Donald West, Presidential Address to the Society for Psychical Research, 1984.
4   Dr Hans Driesch, *Science and Philosophy of the Organism*, London. A & C Black, 1908.
5   Dr Hans Driesch, presidential address to the Society for Psychical Research, 1926; quoted in Renée Haynes, *The Society for Psychical Research, 1882–1982: A History*, London, Macdonald, 1982, p. 203.
6   Sir Alister Hardy, *Journal of the Society for Psychical Research*, May–June 1950.
7   Rupert Sheldrake, *A New Science of Life: The Hypothesis of Formative Causation*, London, Blond & Briggs, 1981.
8   Danah Zohar, 'Why Einstein Was Wrong about Light', *Sunday Times*, 20 February 1983.
9   Arthur Koestler, *Dialogue with Death*, trans. Trevor and Phyllis Blewitt, published as part of *Spanish Testament*, London, Gollancz, 1937.
10  D. MacDougall, 'Hypothesis Concerning Soul Substance Together with Experimental Evidence of the Existence of Such Substance', *Journal of the American Society for Psychical Research*, vol. 1, 1907, pp. 237–44.
11  W. Carington, *Laboratory Investigations into Psychic Phenomena*, London, Rider, 1939.
12  Karlis Osis, 'Perceptual Experiments on Out-of-Body Experiences', in W. G. Roll, R. L. Morris, and J. D. Morris (eds), *Research in Parapsychology 1974*, Metuchen, NJ, Scarecrow Press, 1975, pp. 53–5.
13  Dr Susan Blackmore, *Beyond the Body*, op. cit., p. 195.
14  Robert H. Thouless, 'Do We Survive Bodily Death?', *Proceedings of the Society for Psychical Research*, vol. 57, no. 213, October 1984, p. 24.
15  Robert H. Thouless, *From Anecdote to Experiment in Psychical Research*, London, Routledge & Kegan Paul, 1972.
16  A. T. Oram, letter to members of the Society for Psychical Research, 8 December 1986.
17  Ring, *Life at Death*, op. cit., p. 86.
18  C. A. Garfield, 'Elements of Psychosocial Ontology: Doctor–Patient Relationships in Terminal Illness', in *Psychosocial Care of the Dying Patient*, New York, McGraw-Hill, 1978, p. 103; quoted in Sabom, op. cit., p. 141.
19  Craig R. Lundahl, 'Near-Death Experiences of Mormons', in *A Collection of Near-Death Research Readings*, Chicago, Nelson-Hall, 1982, pp. 165–79.

15  *On Not Being Afraid*
1   Dag Hammarskjöld, *Markings*, trans, W. H. Auden and Leif Sjoberg, Faber and Faber, 1966, p. 136.

2   Archie Matson, *Afterlife: Reports from the Threshold of Death*, New York, Harper & Row, 1975.
3   Ronald K. Siegel, 'The Psychology of Life after Death', in Greyson and Flynn (eds), *The Near-Death Experience*, op. cit., p. 111.
4   Geoffrey Munn, 'Where Great Art Lies Dying', *The Times*, 26 July 1986.
5   Robin Young, 'A Room with a View . . . and a Corpse', *The Times*, 25 April 1986; quoted in *Executive Travel* magazine.
6   Paul Robinson, 'Five Models for Dying', 1981.
7   Sabom, *Recollections of Death*, op. cit., p. 126.
8   Ring, *Life at Death*, op. cit., p. 178.
9   Paul Pickering, 'Back from the Dead', *Observer* magazine, 12 December 1976, p. 31.
10  Ring, *Life at Death*, op. cit., p. 156.
11  Sabom, op. cit., p. 132.
12  Quoted in leaflet of the Society for the Protection of Unborn Children.
13  Dr Kenneth McAll, *Healing the Family Tree*, London, Sheldon Press, 1982, ch. 5.
14  Kenneth Rose, 'The Shocking Dr Dawson', *Sunday Telegraph*, 30 November 1986.
15  Ibid.
16  Neville Hodgkinson, 'Euthanasia: A Judge Warns Doctors Must Not Play God', *Sunday Times*, 30 November 1986.
17  Neville Hodgkinson, 'Dead or Alive?', *Sunday Times*, 21 December 1986.
18  Ibid.
19  Moody, *Life after Life*, op. cit., p. 143.
20  Ring, *Life at Death*, op. cit., p. 179.
21  Moody, op. cit., p. 144.
22  Deryck Millington, 'Visions from Life after Death', *Reader's Digest*, August 1982.
23  Luke 16: 19–31.
24  John 20: 19.
25  John 20: 27.
26  Luke 24: 43.
27  See page 160.
28  Matthew 17: 1–13; Mark 9: 2–13; Luke 9: 28–36.
29  John 1: 9.
30  John 1: 14.
31  This and subsequent quotations derive from a privately circulated memorandum by Mrs Marilyn MacCallum and the Reverend Stuart Burns.

# SELECT BIBLIOGRAPHY

Ariès, Philippe, *The Hour of our Death*, trans. Helen Weaver, London, Allen Lane, 1981.

Ariès, Philippe, *Images of Man and Death*, trans. Janet Lloyd, Cambridge, Mass., Harvard University Press, 1985.

Badham, Paul, *Christian Beliefs about Life after Death*, London, Macmillan, 1976.

Badham, Paul and Linda, *Immortality or Extinction?*, London, Macmillan, 1982.

Baines, John and Málek, Jaromir, *Atlas of Ancient Egypt*, Oxford, Phaidon, 1980.

Barrett, Sir William, *Death-Bed Visions: The Psychical Experiences of the Dying*, London, Psychic Press, 1926.

Bede, *A History of the English Church and People*, trans. Leo Sherley-Price, Harmondsworth, Penguin, 1955, book V, ch. 12.

Blacher, R. S., 'On Awakening Paralyzed During Surgery – a Syndrome of Traumatic Neurosis', *Journal of the American Medical Association*, vol. 234, 1975, p. 67.

Blackmore, Susan J., *Beyond the Body: An Investigation of Out-of-the-Body Experiences*, London, Heinemann, 1982.

Brougham, H., *The Life and Times of Henry, Lord Brougham, Written by Himself*, 3 vols, 1871.

Campbell, Joseph, *The Way of the Animal Powers: Historical Atlas of World Mythology*, vol. I, London, Times Books, 1983.

Clifford, Terry, *Tibetan Buddhist Medicine and Psychiatry*, Wellingborough, Aquarian Press, 1984.

Cockburn, Aidan and Eve, *Mummies, Disease and Ancient Cultures*, Cambridge University Press, 1980.

Crabtree, Adam, *Multiple Man: Explorations in Possession and Multiple Personality*, London, Holt, Rinehart & Winston, 1985.

Cummins, Geraldine, *Swan on a Black Sea*, London, Routledge & Kegan Paul, 1965.

Cummins, Geraldine, *The Road to Immortality*, London, Psychic Press, 1967.

Enright, D. J., *The Oxford Book of Death*, Oxford University Press, 1983.

Evans-Wentz, W. Y., *The Fairy-Faith in Celtic Countries*, London, Henry Frowde, 1911.

Evans-Wentz, W. Y. (ed.), *The Tibetan Book of the Dead*, Oxford University Press, 1960.

Exton-Smith, A. N. and Cantaub, M. D., 'Terminal Illness in the Aged', *The Lancet*, vol. 2, 1961, p. 305.

Faulkner, R. O. (ed.), *The Ancient Egyptian Book of the Dead*, London, British Museum, revised edn, 1985.

Gallup, George, Jr (with William Proctor), *Adventures in Immortality: A Look beyond the Threshold of Death*, London, Souvenir, 1983.

Gardiner, A. H. and Sethe, K., *Egyptian Letters to the Dead*, London, 1928.

Gauld, Alan, *Mediumship and Survival: A Century of Investigations*, London, Heinemann, 1982.

Gittings, Clare, *Death, Burial and the Individual in Early Modern England*, London, Croom Helm, 1984.

Gorer, Geoffrey, *Death, Grief and Mourning*, New York, Doubleday, 1965.

Green, Celia and McCreery, Charles, *Apparitions*, London, Hamish Hamilton, 1975.

Grey, Margot, *Return from Death: An Exploration of the Near-Death Experience*, London, Arkana, 1985.

Greyson, Bruce and Flynn, Charles P. (eds), *The Near-Death Experience: Problems, Prospects, Perspectives*, Springfield, Ill., Charles C. Thomas, 1984.

Hallowell, Irving, 'Spirits of the Dead in Salteaux Life and Thought', *Journal of the Royal Anthropological Institute*, vol. 70, 1940, pp. 29–51.

Hampe, J. C., *To Die Is Gain*, London, Darton, Longman & Todd, 1979.

Haynes, Renée, *The Hidden Springs: An Enquiry into Extra-Sensory Perception*, London, Hutchinson, 1973.

Haynes, Renée, *The Society for Psychical Research, 1882–1982: A History*, London, Macdonald, 1982.

Hedges, John W., *Tomb of the Eagles: A Window on Stone Age Tribal Britain*, London, John Murray, 1985.

Heim, Albert, 'Remarks on Fatal Falls', *Swiss Alpine Club Yearbook*, 27, pp. 327–37.

Hick, John, *Death and Eternal Life*, New York, Harper & Row, 1976.

Homer, *The Iliad*, trans. E. V. Rieu, Harmondsworth, Penguin, 1950.

Idowu, E. Bolaji, *African Traditional Religion*, London, SCM Press, 1973.

Iverson, Jeffrey, *More Lives than One?*, London, Pan Books 1977.

Jaynes, Julian, *The Origin of Consciousness in the Breakdown of the Bicameral Mind*, Boston, Houghton Mifflin, 1976.

Kübler-Ross, Elisabeth, *On Death and Dying*, London, Tavistock, 1973.

Loewe, Michael and Blacker, Carmen (eds), *Divination and Oracles*, London, Allen & Unwin, 1981.

Lorimer, David, *Survival? Body, Mind and Death in the Light of Psychic Experience*, London, Routledge & Kegan Paul, 1984.

Lukianowicz, A., 'Autoscopic Phenomena', *Archives of Neurology and Psychiatry* (American Medical Association), vol. 80, August 1958, p. 199.

Lundahl, Craig R. (ed.), *A Collection of Near-Death Research Readings*, Chicago, Nelson-Hall, 1982.

Mackenzie, Andrew, *Hauntings and Apparitions*, London, Granada, 1983.

MacLaine, Shirley, *Out on a Limb*, London, Elm Tree, 1983.

Marais, Eugène, *The Soul of the White Ant*, London, Methuen, 1937.

McAdams, Elizabeth E. and Bayless, Raymond. *The Case for Life after Death: Parapsychologists Look at the Evidence*, Chicago, Nelson-Hall, 1981.

McAll, Kenneth, *Healing the Family Tree*, London, Sheldon Press, 1982.

Mitford, Jessica, *The American Way of Death*, New York, Simon & Schuster, 1963.

Moody, Raymond, *Life after Life*, Covington, Ga., Mockingbird Books, 1975; London, Corgi, 1977.

Myers, F. W. H., *Human Personality and its Survival of Bodily Death*, 2 vols, London, Longmans Green, 1903.

Neil-Smith, Christopher, *The Exorcist and the Possessed*, St Ives, James Pike, 1974.

Noyes, Russell, Jr and Kletti, Roy, 'Depersonalisation in the Face of Life-Threatening Danger: An Interpretation', *Omega*, 1976, pp. 103–14.

Osis, Karlis, *Deathbed Observations by Physicians and Nurses*, New York, Parapsychology Foundation, 1961.

Osis, Karlis and Haraldsson, Erlendu, *At the Hour of Death*, New York, Avon, 1977.

Penfield, Wilder, *The Mystery of the Mind*, Princeton University Press, 1975.

Plato, *The Republic*, trans. A. D. Lindsay, London, Dent, 1925, book X, sections 614–21.

Pliny the Younger, *Letters*, trans. William Mclmoth, Loeb Classical Library Heinemann, London 1915 book 7, letter 27.

Rawlings, Dr Maurice, *Beyond Death's Door*, London, Sheldon Press, 1978.

Raynes, S. H., 'Post-Humous Experience' (account of the after death experience of Raynes's patient Dr A. S. Wiltse), *St Louis Medical and Surgical Journal*. November 1889.

Rees, W. D., 'The Hallucinations of Widows', *British Medical Journal*, vol. 4, 1971, pp. 37–41.

Ring, Kenneth, *Life at Death: A Scientific Investigation of the Near-Death Experience*, New York, Coward, McCann & Geoghegan, 1980.

Ring, Kenneth, *Heading toward Omega: In Search of the Meaning of the Near-Death Experience*, New York, Morrow, 1984.

Ritchie, George, MD, with Sherrill, Elisabeth, *Return from Tomorrow*, Chosen Books, Lincoln, Virginia 1978.

Romer, John, *Ancient Lives: The Story of the Pharaohs' Tombmakers*, London, Weidenfeld & Nicolson, 1984.

Rose, Ronald, *Living Magic: The Realities Underlying the Psychical Practices and Beliefs of Australian Aborigines*, London, Chatto & Windus, 1957.

Sabom, Michael B., *Recollections of Death: A Medical Investigation*, New York, Harper & Row, 1982.

Schatzman, Morton, *The Story of Ruth: One Woman's Haunting Psychiatric Odyssey*, London, Duckworth, 1980.

Sheldrake, Rupert, *A New Science of Life: The Hypothesis of Formative Causation*, London, Blond & Briggs, 1981.

Solecki, Ralph S., 'Shanidar IV, A Neanderthal Flower Burial in Northern Iraq', *Science*, vol. 190, 28 November 1975, pp. 880–1.

Stannard, David E. (ed.), *Death in America*, Philadelphia, University of Pennsylvania Press, 1975.

Stevenson, Ian, *Twenty Cases Suggestive of Reincarnation*, Charlottesville, University Press of Virginia, 2nd ed 1974.

Stevenson, Ian, *Xenoglossy: A Review and Report of a Case*, Charlottesville, University Press of Virginia, 1974.

Stevenson, Ian, *Cases of the Reincarnation Type, Vol. 1, Ten Cases in India*, Charlottesville, University Press of Virginia, 1975.

Stevenson, Ian, *Cases of the Reincarnation Type: Vol. 2, Ten Cases in Sri Lanka*, Charlottesville, University Press of Virginia, 1977.

Stevenson, Ian, 'Research into the Evidence of Man's Survival after Death', *Journal of Nervous and Mental Disease*, vol. 165, no. 3, September 1977, pp. 152–70.

Stokes, Doris (with Linda Dearsley), *Voices in my Ear: The Autobiography of a Medium*, London, Macdonald/Futura, 1980.

Stokes, Doris, *More Voices in my Ear*, London, Macdonald/Futura, 1981.

Story, Francis, *Rebirth as Doctrine and Experience*, Buddhist Publication Society, 1975.

Swedenborg, Emanuel, *Compendium of the Theological Writings of Emanuel Swedenborg*, selected by Samuel M. Warren, London, Swedenborg Society, 1954.

Swedenborg, Emanuel, *Heaven and Hell*, London, Swedenborg Society, 1958.

Tambiah, S. J., *Buddhism and the Spirit Cults of N. E. Thailand*, Cambridge University Press, 1970.

Thomas, Reverend Charles Drayton, *Life beyond Death with Evidence*, London, Collins, 1928.

Thomas, Gordon, *Issels: The Biography of a Doctor*, London, Hodder & Stoughton, 1975.

Thouless, Robert H., 'Do We Survive Bodily Death?', *Proceedings of the Society for Psychical Research*, vol. 57, no. 213, October 1984.

Toksvig, Signe, *Emanuel Swedenborg: Scientist and Mystic*, London, Faber, 1949.

Toynbee, Arnold, Koestler, Arthur, *et al. Life after Death*, London, Weidenfeld & Nicolson, 1976.

Tucker, Louis, *Clerical Errors*, New York, Harper, 1943.

Tylor, Edward B., *Primitive Culture*, 2 vols., London, John Murray, 1903.

Tyrrell, G. N. M., *The Personality of Man*, Harmondsworth, Penguin, 1947.

Tyrrell, G. N. M., *Apparitions*, London, Duckworth, 1953.

Underhill, Evelyn, *Mysticism*, London, Methuen, 1930.

Wallis-Budge, Sir E. A. (ed.), *The Egyptian Book of the Dead*, London, Routledge & Kegan Paul, 1969.

Watson, Peter, *Twins: An Investigation into the Strange Coincidences in the Lives of Separated Twins*, London, Hutchinson, 1981.

Weisman, A. D. and Hackett, T. P., 'Predilection to Death', *Psychosomatic Medicine*, vol. 23, 1961, p. 247.

Wilson, Colin, *Afterlife*, London, Harrap, 1985.
Wilson, Ian, *Mind Out of Time?*, London, Gollancz, 1981.
Wolf, Arthur S. (ed.), *Religion and Ritual in Chinese Society*, Stanford University Press, 1974.
Woolley, Sir Leonard, *Ur of the Chaldees*, London, 1929.

# INDEX